Criminal Justice Act 1993

with annotations by

Rudi F. Fortson
LL.B.(Lond.) of the Middle Temple, Barrister

LONDON
SWEET & MAXWELL
1993

Published in 1993 by
Sweet & Maxwell Limited of
South Quay Plaza,
183 Marsh Wall, London
Typeset by MFK Typesetting Ltd.,
Hitchin, Herts.
Printed and bound in Great Britain by
Butler & Tanner Ltd., Frome and London

A CIP catalogue record for this book is available
from the British Library

ISBN 0–421–49840–4

Criminal Justice Act 1993

This

(

AUSTRALIA
The Law Book Company
Brisbane : Sydney : Melbourne : Perth

CANADA
Carswell
Ottawa : Toronto : Calgary : Montreal : Vancouver

Agents:
Steimatzky's Agency Ltd., Tel Aviv;
N. M. Tripathi (Private) Ltd., Bombay;
Eastern Law House (Private) Ltd., Calcutta;
M.P.P. House, Bangalore;
Universal Book Traders, Delhi;
Aditya Books, Delhi;
MacMillan Shuppan KK, Tokyo;
Pakistan Law House, Karachi

CONTENTS

Criminal Justice Act 1993

References are to page numbers

CONTENTS

TABLE OF CASES

References are to section and Schedule number

Where a section number appears followed by N, this refers to the notes for that particular section or subsection.

e.g.   s.33N refers to the General Note following s.33
          s.33(5)N refers to the notes for subs. (5) of s.33

TABLE OF CASES

TABLE OF STATUTES

References are to section and Schedule number

Where a section number appears followed by N, this refers to the notes for that particular section or subsection.

e.g. s.33N refers to the General Note following s.33
s.33(5)N refers to the notes for subs. (5) of s.33

TABLE OF FOREIGN STATUTES

References are to section and Schedule number

Where a section number appears followed by N, this refers to the notes for that particular section or subsection.

e.g. s.33N refers to the General Note following s.33
s.33(5)N refers to the notes for subs. (5) of s.33

CRIMINAL JUSTICE ACT 1993*

(1993 c. 36)

ARRANGEMENT OF SECTIONS

PART I

JURISDICTION

PART II

DRUG TRAFFICKING OFFENCES

Confiscation orders

Death or absence of defendant

Offences

Enforcement

Miscellaneous

PART III

PROCEEDS OF CRIMINAL CONDUCT

Confiscation orders

Money laundering and other offences

---

* Annotations by Rudi F. Fortson, LL.B.(Lond.) of the Middle Temple, Barrister.

Part IV

Financing etc. of Terrorism

Amendments of the 1991 Act

Amendments of the 1989 Act

Part V

Insider Dealing

The offence of insider dealing

Interpretation

Miscellaneous

Part VI

Miscellaneous

An Act to make provision about the jurisdiction of courts in England and Wales in relation to certain offences of dishonesty and blackmail; to amend the law about drug trafficking offences and to implement provisions of the Community Council Directive No. 91/308/EEC; to amend Part VI of the Criminal Justice Act 1988; to make provision with respect to the financing of terrorism, the proceeds of terrorist-related activities and the investigation of terrorist activities; to amend Part I of the Criminal Justice Act 1991; to implement provisions of the Community Council Directive No. 89/592/EEC and to amend and restate the law about insider dealing in securities; to provide for certain offences created by the Banking Coordination (Second Council Directive) Regulations 1992 to be punishable in the same way as offences under sections 39, 40 and 41 of the Banking Act 1987 and to enable regulations implementing Article 15 of the Community Council Directive No. 89/646/EEC and articles 3, 6 and 7 of the Community Council Directive No. 92/30/EEC to create offences punishable in that way; to make provision with respect to the penalty for causing death by dangerous driving or causing death by careless driving while under the influence of drink or drugs; to make it an offence to assist in or induce certain conduct which for the purposes of, or in connection with, the provisions of Community law is unlawful in another member State; to provide for the introduction of safeguards in connection with the return of persons under backing of warrants arrangements; to amend the Criminal Procedure (Scotland) Act 1975 and Part I of the Prisoners and Criminal Proceedings (Scotland) Act 1993; and for connected purposes.

[27th July 1993]

PARLIAMENTARY DEBATES
Hansard, H.L. Vol. 539, col. 1347; Vol. 540, cols. 90, 721, 1255, 1469, 1483; Vol. 541, col. 317; Vol. 548, col. 1022; H.C. Vol. 222, col. 859; Vol. 227, col. 837.
The Bill was discussed in Standing Committee B between May 25 and June 22, 1993.

INTRODUCTION AND GENERAL NOTE
On October 22, 1992, the Criminal Justice Bill came before Parliament. It then consisted of six Parts and a total of 48 clauses. By the date of Royal Assent (July 27, 1993) the Bill had

expanded to seven Parts but with a total of 79 clauses. The storm of judicial and public complaints concerning the criminal justice system, and the unsatisfactory operation of certain areas of the Criminal Justice Act 1991, partly explain that expansion but, at a late stage in the Bill's development, Parliament introduced substantial amendments to both the Northern Ireland (Emergency Provisions) Act 1991 and the Prevention of Terrorism (Temporary Provisions) Act 1989 as well as substantially overhauling or amending clauses which had originally formed part of the Bill in relation to insider dealing. Sections 68, 69, 75, 76 (Scotland) and 79 (extent) came into force on July 27, 1993. Section 66 (which amends, *inter alia*, ss. 1 and 29 of the Criminal Justice Act 1991) and s.67 (penalties for causing death by dangerous driving, etc.) came into force on August 16, 1993. Section 65 and Sched. 3 (abolition of the unit fine system) came into force on September 20, 1993. The Criminal Justice Act 1993 (Commencement No. 1) Order 1993 (S.I. No. 1968) was made on August 1, 1993, and brought the following sections into force for England and Wales only:

  s.66 (powers of courts to deal with offenders), August 16, 1993;
  s.67 (penalties for causing death by dangerous driving, etc.), August 16, 1993;
  s.65 and Sched. 3 (the abolition of the unit fine system) and consequential repeals to
  Criminal Justice Act 1991 and the Magistrates' Courts Act 1980, September 20, 1993.

   The Criminal Justice Act 1993 (Commencement No. 2 Transitional Provisions and Savings) (Scotland) Order 1993 (S.I. 1993 No. 2035) was made on August 11, 1993, and relates to Scotland only.

   The rest of the Act will be brought into force by commencement order as soon as possible, with likely commencement dates later in 1993.

   The reforms introduced by every Part of the Act are substantial. What they have in common is an international perspective. The purpose of Pt. I is to extend the jurisdiction of courts in England and Wales to try a range of substantive and inchoate offences contrary to the Theft Acts of 1968 and 1978 (including blackmail) and offences contrary to the Forgery and Counterfeiting Act 1981, where there is a significant foreign element in their commission. At common law, jurisdiction is determined by reference to the place where the last act or event took place or was intended to take place and, as a general rule, this proposition is good whether the offence is either a so-called "conduct crime" (*e.g.* theft) or a "result-crime" (*e.g.* obtaining property by deception). For the purposes of Pt. I of the Act this test no longer applies. All that is required (for the full offence) is proof that one of the ingredients of the offence occurred in England and Wales. The Criminal Law Act 1977 and the Criminal Attempts Act 1981 are also amended so that a conspiracy (or an attempt) to commit a Group A offence abroad, is now triable here (providing certain conditions are fulfilled, including a test of 'double criminality').

   When looking at Pt. I, it is as well to have in mind s.71, which is designed to enable the U.K. to take action against fraud which is perpetrated against a Member State of the E.C. The section bears a superficial resemblance to the type of offence to be found in s.20 of the Misuse of Drugs Act 1971 which creates a substantive offence, triable in this country, if a person assists in (or induces) the commission of an offence which contravenes a "corresponding law" abroad. Accordingly, s.71 of the 1993 Act makes it an offence to assist in or induce any conduct outside the U.K. which involves the commission of a "serious offence" against the law of another Member State (s.71(1)). A "serious offence" is one which (by the laws of the foreign state) carries a maximum sentence of at least 12 months imprisonment (s.71(3)). The serious offence which is relevant here must relate to conduct specified in s.71(2) (*i.e.* taxation, payment of duties, agricultural spending, and—significantly—prohibitions and restrictions provided for by or under a Community instrument or Regulation). "Conduct" includes acts, omissions and statements (s.71(9)).

   In certain cases the prosecution will also be required to prove that the conduct complained of was "calculated to have an effect in that Member State in relation to any of [the matters specified in s.71(2)]". Statutory defences are provided by s.71(4) and, once again, the burden of proving any of these defences falls upon the accused.

   Part II will be of particular importance to most practitioners. In short, the Drug Trafficking Offences Act 1986 is radically overhauled. A court will no longer be obliged to embark on a DTOA enquiry in every case where a defendant appears to be sentenced for a drug trafficking offence. DTOA enquiries may be heard after sentence. Controversially, *R.* v. *Dickens* [1990] 2 Q.B. 102 and *R.* v. *Enwezor* (1991) 93 Cr.App.R. 233 are overruled insofar as they held that the criminal standard of proof applies to determine whether a person has benefited from drug trafficking (or the amount to be recovered). In practice, the civil standard of proof will apply throughout the proceedings (s.7(2)). Assumptions are no longer discretionary but mandatory. They may be rebutted by the defendant. A receiver may apply to the High Court for a confiscation order to be varied. Within a period of six years after the date of conviction, the court may revise its assessment of the amount of the defendant's proceeds of drug trafficking, or the amount which might be realised under an order, or, if no confiscation order was either sought or made, make one (s.12).

   Previously, where a defendant was ordered to serve a term of imprisonment in default of payment of all, or part, of a confiscation order the effect was that proceedings were concluded against him and therefore the court was not empowered to continue to enforce the amount due. This will change once s.13 of the 1993 Act is brought into force. Serving a sentence in default of payment will not, under s.13, extinguish the amount to be paid by the defendant.

The High Court has power to confiscate the proceeds of drug trafficking if the defendant dies or absconds after conviction. The High Court may confiscate such proceeds even if there has been no conviction where a defendant has absconded for a period of two years. He may be compensated if he returns and is acquitted. New money laundering offences are created. A failure to disclose knowledge or suspicion of drug-money laundering is an offence (see s.18). The Northern Ireland (Emergency Provisions) Act 1991 (insofar as that relates to the financing of terrorism) is amended in a similar fashion (Pt. IV). Less draconian measures have been added to the Criminal Justice Act 1988 (confiscation orders) but, again, the civil standard of proof is applicable; proceedings may be postponed and money laundering offences are created (Pt. III).

The Company Securities (Insider Dealing) Act 1985 has been repealed (and so has the Companies (Northern Ireland) Order 1989). Part V of the 1993 Act implements the provisions of the European Directive on Insider Dealing (89/592/EEC). The three offences of (i) acquiring and disposing of securities; (ii) encouraging another to do likewise; and (iii) disclosing inside information to another, are grouped together (s.52) followed by a string of defences (s.53 and Sched. 3). It is no longer necessary to show a connection between the insider and the company. Information must be "specific or precise" and thus excludes rumour. It is debatable to what extent it was necessary or desirable to include the word "specific"—Art. 1 of the Directive only refers to "precise" which is narrower.

Section 70 implements two major European Council Directives concerning the operation, regulation and administration of "credit institutions". The Second Banking Co-ordination Directive (the "SBCD") (89/646/EEC) will permit credit institutions such as banks to offer services and to establish branches throughout the European Community on the basis of one licence ("authorisation") and to be supervised on a consolidated basis by the regulator of at least one Member State: see the Supervision of Credit Institutions Directive (European Council Directive (92/30/EEC)) which is also known as the "second consolidated supervision directive" (the "Supervision Directive"). Both of these Directives will be implemented by secondary legislation under the European Communities Act 1972. These Directives (plus those dealing with "own funding" and "solvency ratios") are important in preventing difficulties which have manifested themselves in the collapse of BCCI.

Under Art. 15 of the SBCD, the U.K. is required to make provision to enable "supervisory authorities" abroad to have access to information, and to have powers of inspection, in respect of branches of credit institutions which are operating in the U.K. under a licence granted abroad. These powers are obviously important to ensure effective supervision of credit institutions and thus similar powers are required by the "Supervision Directive" (see Art. 3, para. 4, Art. 6 and Art. 7, para. 1).

Section 70 of the 1993 Act makes it lawful for the Regulations which implement Directives 89/646/EEC and 92/30/EEC to provide a maximum term of six months imprisonment.

Both Directives play a crucial part in liberalising movement of services (including financial services) within the internal market while permitting competition from countries outside the European Community. The SBCD seeks to abolish the "minimum endowment capital requirement", which many countries insisted upon, and which applied to each branch operating abroad. This was a major disincentive to credit institutions which wished to open branches overseas. By contrast, the U.K. has operated an open banking system and imposed fewer restrictions on institutions operating here.

The proper and adequate funding of credit institutions is obviously important and, to this end, two other Directives are relevant, namely, the Council Directive (86/635/EEC) and the Council Directive on Solvency Ratios for Credit Institutions (89/647/EEC).

STATUTORY INTERPRETATION

Both the Criminal Justice Act 1991 and the Drug Trafficking Offences Act 1986 (DTOA) have given rise to difficult problems of construction and nowhere has this been more marked than in respect of the incidence and standard of proof to be applied at various stages of confiscation proceedings under the 1986 Act. 'Draconian' though the DTOA is, the courts have been reluctant to hold that only a civil standard of proof is required in respect of a finding that the defendant has benefited from drug trafficking: see *R.* v. *Dickens* [1990] 2 Q.B. 102. However, this was clearly the intention of Parliament when the DTOA was then being debated as a Bill (see *Hansard*, H.L. Vol. 471, col. 727).

The reforms and amendments made in the 1993 Act are extensive and often complex. Together with the introduction of many novel concepts, these provisions will inevitably attract much judicial attention.

Certain aspects of the 1993 Act can be clarified by reference to Parliamentary material (*e.g.* the effect of Pt. I and the application of the civil standard of proof in Pt. II) but such an exercise is likely to prove less effective when construing provisions of a highly technical nature such as those found in Pt. V (insider dealing). In short there is much in the Parliamentary material that sheds light on various mischiefs which the 1993 Act is intended to avoid but it is likely to prove a great deal less helpful for the purpose of discovering the meaning of words and phrases used by Parliament to cure any of the mischiefs in question. In *Pepper (Inspector of Taxes)* v. *Hart* [1992] 3 W.L.R. 1032, the House of Lords relaxed the rule prohibiting the courts from referring to Parliamentary material where (a) the legislation was obscure or ambiguous or the literal meaning of a provision led to an absurdity and (b) the material was relevant consisted of statements made by a Minister which led to the enactment of the provision in question (*per* Lord Browne-Wilkinson at p. 1061). Lord Denning was clearly concerned that the provisions of s.31 of the DTOA (then cl. 30) might be misunderstood and seen to be in conflict because the courts would have to resolve ambiguities without reference to *Hansard* (*Hansard*, H.L. Vol. 476, col. 454). Under the principles enunciated in *Pepper* v. *Hart, supra,* this difficulty has been removed.

For the general rule that references to Parliamentary material as an aid to construction is not permissible, see: *Davis* v. *Johnson* [1979] A.C. 264, *Hadmor Productions* v. *Hamilton* [1983] 1 A.C. 191 and *Beswick* v. *Beswick* [1968] A.C. 58. For cases where exceptions were made to the general rule, see: *Eastman Photographic Materials Co.* v. *Comptroller-General of Patents and Designs and Trade-Marks* [1898] A.C. 571, *R.* v. *Secretary of State for Transport,* ex p. *Factortame* [1990] 2 A.C. 85 and *Pickstone* v. *Freemans plc.* [1989] A.C. 66, but contrast *Black-Clawson International* v. *Papierwerke Waldhof-Aschaftenburg Aktiengesellschaft* [1975] A.C. 591.

For the reasons given above it is therefore appropriate to provide a more detailed reference to Parliamentary material in these annotations than would otherwise be the case.

PART I

JURISDICTION

GENERAL NOTE

Part I of the 1993 Act applies only to England and Wales; Scotland and Northern Ireland having their own legal systems: s.79(9). The Secretary of State for the Home Department described Pt. I as being a "largely technical adjustment of existing rules" but, in fact, the reforms are both significant and substantial (*Hansard*, H.C. Vol. 222, col. 862).

In the House of Commons, the Secretary of State suggested that the Act is intended to provide that the Courts in England and Wales will have jurisdiction in cases where ". . . fraud has a significant connection with this country . . . whether or not the final element of the crime occurred here" (*ibid.*, col. 863). In fact, Pt. I of the Act goes very much further than that. The purpose of Pt. I is to extend the jurisdiction of courts in England and Wales to try a range of substantive and inchoate offences contrary to the Theft Acts of 1968 and 1978 (including blackmail) and offences contrary to the Forgery and Counterfeiting Act 1981, where there is a significant foreign element in the commission. At common law, jurisdiction is determined by reference to the place where the last act or event took place or was intended to take place and, as a general rule, this proposition is good whether the offence is either a so-called "conduct crime" (*e.g.* theft) or a "result crime" (*e.g.* obtaining property by deception). For the purposes of Pt. I of the Act this test no longer applies. All that is required (for the full offence) is proof that one of the ingredients of the offence occurred in England and Wales. The Criminal Law Act 1977 and the Criminal Attempts Act 1981 are also amended so that a conspiracy (or an attempt) to commit a Group A offence abroad, is now triable here (providing certain conditions are fulfilled, including a test of "double criminality" in respect of conspiracies and attempts to commit an offence, of a Group A type, wholly abroad). Furthermore, ss.5 and 6 are intended to give our courts jurisdiction over incitements, conspiracies and attempts which are performed in England and Wales, but which are aimed at the commission abroad of an equivalent substantive offence to those listed in "Group A" in s.1 of the Act, so that persons who conspire to defraud victims in Singapore will commit an offence contrary to English law and they will now be triable here (see *Hansard*, H.C. Vol. 222, col. 863).

Reform of the rules relating to jurisdiction have been under active consideration for some 23 years: see *Territorial and Extraterritorial Extent of the Criminal Law* (Law Com. Working Paper No. 29, 1970); *Report on the Territorial and Extraterritorial Extent of the Criminal Law* (Law Com. Rep. No. 91, 1978); *Attempt and Impossibility in relation to Attempt, Conspiracy and Incitement* (Law Com. Rep. No. 102, 1980); *Report on Offences Against the Person* (Criminal Law Revision Committee, Cmnd. 7844, 1980, paras. 295–304), Lord Roskill's *Report of the Fraud Trials Committee* (1986, para. 3.17) and most recently, the Law Commission's Report *Jurisdiction Over Offences of Fraud and Dishonesty with a Foreign Element* as well as the draft Bill annexed to it (Law Com. Rep. No. 180, 1989).

A number of sections of Pt. I of the 1993 Act either mirror, or give effect to, various provisions in that draft Bill. The brief overview of the law set out in the Report, was given before the decisions of the Privy Council, and the Court of Appeal, in *Liangsiriprasert (Somchai)* v. *Government of the United States of America* [1991] 1 A.C. 225, and *R.* v. *Sansom; R.* v. *Williams; R.* v. *Smith; R.* v. *Wilkins* [1991] 2 Q.B. 130, C.A., respectively.

The Philosophy Behind Pt. I of the Act

The problems, giving rise to Pt. I of the 1993 Act, were summarised by the Law Commission as stemming from the nature of "modern crimes of dishonesty" being crimes which:

"often involve complex operations designed to conceal the dishonest conduct and to make detection and conviction as difficult as possible, and the planning, preparation and execution of the many operations which are involved in a complicated swindle frequently take place in several different countries. Under the present law none of the participants can be prosecuted here unless the *last* event which makes up the underlying crime occurs in England and Wales. Moreover, in cases in which those concerned are detected before they have completed their purpose, it is likely that they will be prosecuted in the country where they plan to reap the benefit, and because the underlying crime was not completed here they cannot be tried in England and Wales. In the result, they will in all probability not be convicted anywhere" (Law Com. Rep. No. 180, 1989, para. 1.2).

Four issues emerge from this statement which warrant careful attention; these are considered below.

(1) *The Nature of Crime and Major Offences*

The first issue concerns the nature of modern criminal enterprises of which many do have an international dimension, not merely due to more cross-border travel, but also because technological advances make the transfer of information and money around the globe "an easy and ... every-minute activity" (Secretary of State for the Home Department, *Hansard*, H.C. Vol. 222, col. 863). The Law Commission regarded it as particularly important that this country, as a leading international finance centre, should have (and be seen to have) an effective and straightforward way of tackling fraudulent conduct connected with this country:

"We also have in mind, in considering questions of policy, that London is one of the world's principal financial centres, and that it is in the national interest for it to remain so. Should it be thought that large-scale frauds could be carried out here with impunity, confidence in London as a major international centre would rapidly be undermined. These considerations would appear to lend added force to the need for this country to be seen as vigilant in proceeding against international fraudsters. The traditional approach, it seems to us, fails to take into account these significant considerations" (Law Com. Rep. No. 180, 1989, para. 2.24).

The Law Commission also noted that the existing law as to jurisdiction of offences had become "increasingly difficult, complicated and controversial to apply" resulting in a loss of court time dealing with technical legal arguments (see Law Com. Rep. No. 180, 1989, para. 1.4).

However, the same problems also exist in respect of other types of criminal activity and which (for the moment) fall outside Pt. I of the 1993 Act—notably drug trafficking and international terrorism. The categories of offences set out in Pt. I are not closed and may be extended or reduced by way of Statutory Instrument laid before Parliament (s.1(4), (5) and (6)).

In theory (and subject to any argument that the Secretary of State acted *ultra vires*) it would seem possible to add offences which are not generally regarded as offences of "fraud" but are offences of dishonesty (*e.g.* burglary and robbery and fraudulent evasion under s.170 of the Customs and Excise Management Act 1979). However, such a development would not reflect the intention of Parliament and would run counter to the wishes of the Law Commission in its Report (Law Com. Rep. No. 180, 1989).

The Legislature's intention appears to be that any amendments made to the categories of offences listed in s.1 of the 1993 Act, should relate to offences created under the Theft Acts of 1968 and 1978, and under the Forgery and Counterfeiting Act 1981, but new offences could be added under, for example, the Companies Acts (if necessary) following Parliamentary debate (Standing Committee B, col. 29, May 25, 1993). It has been suggested by one contributor to the Law Commission, that *all* indictable offences should be covered but this was rejected on the basis that "no commentator suggested that the present jurisdictional rules had been found to be defective in practice or to give rise to difficulty" (Law Com. Rep. No. 180, 1989, para. 3.4).

There were, however, two pragmatic reasons given by the Law Commission for not widening the category of Group A offences. The first is that a detailed examination of the issues would delay the reforms which the Law Commission proposed in their Report and which now substantially appear in Pt. I of the Act. Under s.1(2)(a) of the 1993 Act, blackmail is included as a "Group A" offence. The Law Commission acknowledge that blackmail is not included in the category of offences described under the 1993 Act as "Group A offences" but included it because "... it has given rise to difficulties relating to jurisdiction which are similar to those arising in relation to fraud offences, and the present exercise affords a convenient opportunity of resolving them" (Law Com. Rep. No. 180, 1989, footnote No. 29). The second reason relates to drug trafficking offences, and enforcement, which involve provisions created by statute in order to give effect to a variety of multilateral treaties and bilateral agreements. Given that drug trafficking and money laundering operate on an international scale, many of the provisions of the DTOA (and subsequent legislation) are the product of diplomatic efforts and rooted in several treaties, conventions, bilateral agreements and (now) European Directives: see, for example, the European Convention on Mutual Assistance 1957 (which the U.K. was not able to ratify until the enactment of the Criminal Justice (International Co-operation) Act 1990); the United Nations Convention Against Illicit Traffic in Narcotic Drugs and Psychotropic Substances 1988 (the "Vienna Convention"), ratified by the U.K. in 1991; the Council of Europe Convention on Laundering, Search, Seizure and Confiscation of the Proceeds of Crime 1990 (yet to be ratified by the U.K.). See also the European Council Directive (91/308/EEC).

Note also s.26 of the DTOA (as amended) and the Drug Trafficking Offences Act 1986 (Designated Countries and Territories) Order 1990 (S.I. 1990 No. 1199) (as amended by S.I. 1991 No. 1465). Orders made in Scotland under the Criminal Justice (Scotland) Act 1987 may now be enforced in England and Wales: see the Drug Trafficking Offences (Enforcement in England and Wales) Order 1988 (S.I. 1988 No. 593). See generally the Drug Trafficking Offences Act 1986, Pt. II of the 1993 Act and the Criminal Justice (International Co-operation) Act 1990.

Under s.20 of the Misuse of Drugs Act 1971 it is an offence to assist in, or induce, in the U.K., the commission elsewhere of an offence punishable under the provisions of a "corresponding law" in the place where it is committed (see *R.* v. *Vickers* [1975] 2 Q.B. 664; *R.* v. *Johnston* (unreported) March 22, 1974; *R.* v. *Evans (Ian)* (1977) 64 Cr.App.R. 237, *R.* v. *Panayi*; *R.* v. *Karte* (1986) 86 Cr.App.R. 261; and *R.* v. *Murtaq Ali* [1990] Crim.L.R. 648).

(2) *The Scope of The Previous Law—The "Last Act" Rule*

The second issue which arises under the Law Commission's reasoning in their Report (Law Com. Rep. No. 180, 1989), concerns the scope of the previous law. Historically, the jurisdiction to try criminal cases was summarised by Lord Halsbury L.C. in *McLeod* v. *Att.-Gen. for New South Wales* [1891] A.C. 455, 458 when he said: "all crime is local" and that "jurisdiction over the crime belongs to the country where the crime is *committed* [emphasis added]". These observations remain relevant in respect of those full offences which are not covered by Pt. I of the 1993 Act, but they have long been less relevant in respect of attempts made abroad to commit an offence in this country (see *R.* v. *Baxter* [1972] 1 Q.B. 1; *D.P.P.* v. *Stonehouse* [1978] A.C. 55). In cases of conspiracy, it has recently been clarified that acts performed abroad which are intended to result in the commission of criminal offences in England are justiciable in England notwithstanding that no overt act can be proved as having been performed in that country in furtherance of the conspiracy (*Liangsiriprasert (Somchai)* v. *Government of the United States of America* [1991] 1 A.C. 225, and *R.* v. *Sansom*; *R.* v. *Williams*; *R.* v. *Smith*; *R.* v. *Wilkins* [1991] 2 Q.B. 130, C.A.).

Lord Griffiths stated, as the rationale of the territorial principle of jurisdiction, that "... the criminal law is developed to protect English society and not that of other nations which must be left to make and enforce such laws as they see fit to protect their own societies ... It was for this reason that the law of extradition was introduced between civilised nations so that fugitive offenders might be returned for trial in the country against whose laws they had offended" (*Liangsiriprasert (Somchai)* v. *Government of the United States of America* (ante, p. 244 c/d).

This general principle is subject to a number of exceptions, including murder and manslaughter committed by a British subject abroad (see s.9 of the Offences Against the Person Act 1861); torture (s.134 of the Criminal Justice Act 1988); and proceedings on indictment for offences committed within the jurisdiction of the Admiralty of England (s.46(2) of the Supreme Court Act 1981, and the Territorial Waters Jurisdiction Act 1878). See also *R.* v. *Anderson* (1868) L.R. 1; C.C.R. 161. See also ss.18–21 of the Criminal Justice (International Co-operation) Act 1990.

Following from the above principles, the position at common law is that unless a contrary intention appears, offences created by Statute are presumed to be triable only if they are committed in England and Wales (see *Liangsiriprasert (Somchai)* v. *Government of the United States of America, ante,* and *Air India* v. *Wiggins* [1980] 1 W.L.R. 815; but, *cf. Cox* v. *Army Council* [1963] A.C. 48 and *Black-Clawson International* v. *Papierwerke Waldhof-Aschaftenburg Aktiengesellschaft* [1975] A.C. 591).

As the Minister of State for the Home Office (Earl Ferrers) observed (*Hansard*, H.L. Vol. 539, col. 1348), the main problem, which has given rise to Pt. I, is the narrow way in which the law decides whether an offence has been committed in this country and which may therefore be tried here. The general rule is (subject to the decisions in *Liangsiriprasert (Somchai)* v. *Government of the United States of America* [1991] 1 A.C. 225, and *R.* v. *Sansom*; *R.* v. *Williams*; *R.* v. *Smith*; *R.* v. *Wilkins* [1991] 2 Q.B. 130, C.A.) that jurisdiction will be assumed by the courts in England and Wales where the *last* act or event (which is required to be performed to complete the offence) took place in England or Wales. This is because a crime (amounting to the full offence) is clearly not committed until all relevant acts or events, which make up that offence, have been performed. Accordingly, the moment of "commission" of the offence is the moment when the last act or event is performed and (for the purposes of jurisdiction) it follows that the last act or event must take place here before it can be said that the offence was committed here (Law Com. Rep. No. 180, 1989, para. 2).

This principle applies at common law whether the full offence is either a so-called "conduct" crime (being of a defined type, *e.g.* theft) or a "result crime" (*e.g.* where a particular result must flow from the actor's conduct—*e.g.* obtaining property by deception). In the latter, the obtaining had to occur in England or Wales and it was not sufficient to prove that the deception took place there (*R.* v. *Harden* [1963] 1 Q.B. 8, *R.* v. *Thompson (Michael)* [1984] 1 W.L.R. 962; and see *Treacy* v. *D.P.P.* [1971] A.C. 537, *per* Lord Diplock at p. 560g). However, where part of the result was performed in this country, such conduct would be sufficient to found jurisdiction (*Secretary of State for Trade* v. *Markus* [1976] A.C. 35; and see *D.P.P.* v. *Stonehouse* [1978] A.C. 55).

"Conduct crimes" are not without difficulty in terms of determining whether the courts of England and Wales have the jurisdiction to try them. In *R.* v. *Governor of Pentonville Prison*, ex p. *Osman* [1990] 1 W.L.R. 277, the Divisional Court had to examine whether an act of appropriation (for the purposes of the law of theft in Hong Kong) took place in Hong Kong. If (as the court held) the appropriation took place in that territory, then the offence was justiciable there.

It was these kinds of technical arguments which prompted the enactment of Pt. I of the 1993 Act.

In *Osman*, *ante*, the defendant sent telexes from Hong Kong to an overseas bank debiting one account and crediting another. Those acts amounted to a usurpation of the rights of an owner and was thus an appropriation. Presumably there would have been no appropriation (and thus no jurisdiction) if Osman had simply withdrawn the money abroad and imported it into Hong Kong.

Similarly, Earl Ferrers (Minister of State for the Home Office) gave as a practical example, the case of a criminal in Birmingham who places an advertisement in a local newspaper which invites people to invest monies in a non-existent farm in France by paying money into a French bank account. Where a victim then responds to the advertisement and transfers money to that French account which is then withdrawn by the criminal in France and brought back to England, no offence was previously committed under English law because the last act (the obtaining) took place abroad (*Hansard*, H.L. Vol. 539, col. 1348). The courts will now have jurisdiction to try such cases under Pt. I of this Act.

The principal recommendation of the Law Commission was that the courts should have jurisdiction to try "... one of the listed offences if any event that is required to be proved in order to obtain a conviction of that offence takes place in England and Wales. That would, in particular, mean that where the definition of the offence forbids conduct producing a certain result our courts would have jurisdiction if any part of that conduct, or any part of the defined specified result, took place here. Similarly, our courts would have jurisdiction over crimes the definition of which relates only to the accused's conduct (as has been suggested to be the case with theft) if any part of the conduct forbidden by the definition of the offence took place here" (Law Com. Rep. No. 180, 1989, para. 2.27). The Law Commission's proposed new rules were intended to be "along the lines" of s.7 of the New Zealand Crimes Act 1961 which provides that: "For the purpose of jurisdiction, where any act or omission forming part of any offence, or any event necessary to the completion of any offence, occurs in New Zealand, the offence shall be deemed to be committed in New Zealand, whether the person charged with the offence was in New Zealand or not at the time of the act, omission, or event".

Sections 2 and 3(1) of the 1993 Act, are broadly in accordance with that model.

(3) *Inchoate Offences*

In its 1989 Report (Law Com. Rep. No. 180), the Law Commission remarked that the above principles also apply both to the statutory offence of conspiracy (Criminal Law Act 1977, s.1(1) and (2) as amended) and, to the common law offence of conspiracy to defraud. Accordingly, the court had to consider (a) whether the offence that the conspirators had in view, is triable in this country and (b) whether the conspiracy itself is to be "regarded as connected with England and Wales so as to be triable here" (para. 4.2). However, the definition of a conspiracy, for the purposes of the Criminal Law Act 1977, is that the agreed course of conduct must "necessarily amount to or involve the commission of any offence" and the offence must be one triable in England and Wales (s.1(4)); see *Board of Trade* v. *Owen* [1957] A.C. 602 and *Att.-Gen.'s Reference (No. 1 of 1982)* [1983] Q.B. 751. In other words, the offence must be committed in England and therefore the last act would have been performed here. It is submitted that a conspiracy to contravene s.20 of the Misuse of Drugs Act 1971 is a conspiracy to commit a *substantive* offence (*i.e.* that s.20 creates such an offence) which is then triable in this country, even though the *result* is to be performed or achieved abroad.

Given that the rules relating to jurisdiction for offences listed under Pt. I have now been extended (so that the court may look to the performance of any "relevant event" in this country) it follows that the court's jurisdiction over conspiracies to commit an offence is similarly extended. Thus, it no longer matters for the purposes of Pt. I that the *obtaining* (contrary to s.15 of the Theft Act 1968) is planned to occur abroad if the agreement is to perform acts of deception in this country.

At the time of writing their Report (1989), the Law Commission did not have the benefit of the decisions of the Privy Council in *Liangsiriprasert*, *supra*, which was applied by the Court of Appeal in *Sansom*, *supra*. In 1989 the generally held view was that a conspiracy formed abroad which was intended to result in the commission of a crime in England, was not justiciable in that country without proof that some overt act pursuant to the conspiracy takes place in England or (at the very least) that the impact of the conspiracy is "felt" in England (see para. 95 of *Territorial and Extraterritorial Extent of the Criminal Law* (Law Com. Working Paper No. 29, 1970)).

There is some support for the view that the development of conspiracy is allied to the law of attempts (see *Poulterers' Case* (1611) Co. Rep. 50b, 55b; *Holdsworth, History of English Law*). Lord Tucker in *Board of Trade* v. *Owen* [1957] A.C. 602, 626 suggested that "the whole object of making such agreements punishable is to prevent the commission of [a] substantive offence before it has even reached the stage of an attempt". Lord Tucker therefore felt unable to accept the view that "the locality of the acts to be done and of the object to be attained are matters irrelevant to the criminality of the agreement" (and see *Att.-Gen. Reference (No. 1 of 1982)* [1983] Q.B. 751).

Even before the passing of the Criminal Attempts Act 1981 (which does not affect the common law position in respect of jurisdiction) there was authority for the proposition that the courts have jurisdiction in relation to a charge of attempt which is intended to have, and has, "an effect" in England and Wales (*R.* v. *Baxter* [1972] 1 Q.B. 1).

However, in *D.P.P.* v. *Stonehouse* [1978] A.C. 55, this proposition was called into question. On the one hand Lord Keith of Kinkel held that ". . . there would appear to be nothing contrary to international comity in holding that an act done abroad intended to result in damage in England, but which for some reason independent of the actor's volition had no effect there, was justiciable in England. But if that were to be the law, I consider that it would require to be enacted by Parliament". On the other hand, Lord Diplock took the view that "once it is appreciated that territorial jurisdiction over a "result crime" does not depend upon acts done by the offender in England but on consequences which he causes to occur in England, I see no ground for holding that an attempt to commit a crime which, if the attempt succeeded would be justiciable in England, does not also fall within the jurisdiction of the English courts notwithstanding that the physical acts intended to produce the proscribed consequences in England were all of them done abroad". (In the event, on the facts in *Stonehouse* an "effect" was felt in this country and therefore the point did not call for a final determination).

As the law of attempts developed, the law of conspiracy also seemed to require something "to be done" or felt in this country. Thus, in *R.* v. *Doot* [1973] A.C. 807, Lord Pearson (at p. 827) said "on principle, apart from authority, I think (and it would seem that the Court of Appeal also thought) that a conspiracy to commit in England an offence against English law ought to be triable in England if it has been wholly or partly performed in England".

Similarly, the Law Commission in their Working Paper, *Territorial and Extraterritorial Extent of the Criminal Law* (Working Paper No. 29, 1970, para. 96) took the view that conspiracies abroad to commit offences in England, should not constitute offences in English law unless overt acts pursuant to that conspiracy took place in England.

However, in *Liangsiriprasert (Somchai)* v. *Government of the United States of America* [1991] 1 A.C. 225, 251, Lord Griffiths questioned why proof of any overt act should be necessary to found jurisdiction other than to establish a link between the conspiracy and this country.

Proof of overt acts may prove that link but they also serve to act as evidence as to the existence of the alleged conspiracy.

The Law Commission modified its position in their 1989 Report and recommended that the courts should have jurisdiction to try an attempt to commit a "listed offence" whether or not the attempt was made here and "whether or not it had an effect here" (Law Com. Rep. No. 180, 1989, para. 4.11). The Law Commission's draft Bill (annexed to the Report (cl. 3)), provided that the questions whether any act or omission or other event occurred in England and Wales (for a conspiracy), or whether it had an effect in England and Wales (for an attempt) should be disregarded as being immaterial to guilt. Consistent with this approach, Lord Griffiths in *Liangsiriprasert, supra* said "their Lordships can find nothing in precedent, comity or good sense that should inhibit the common law from regarding as justiciable in England inchoate crimes committed abroad which are intended to result in the commission of criminal offences in England" (and see *R.* v. *Sansom*; *R.* v. *Williams*; *R.* v. *Smith*; *R.* v. *Wilkins* [1991] 2 Q.B. 130).

It will be seen that s.3(2)(b) and s.3(3)(b) now give statutory effect to the Law Commission's draft Bill, cl. 3. The present legislation confines the description of the development of juris-diction in England expressed by La Forest J. in *Libman* v. *The Queen*, 21 C.C.C. (3d) 206 when he said:

"the English courts have decisively begun to move away from definitional obsessions and technical formulations aimed at finding a single situs of a crime by locating where the gist of the crime occurred or where it was completed. Rather, they now appear to seek by an examination of relevant policies to apply the English criminal law where a substantial measure of the activities constituting a crime take place in England, and restrict its appli-cation in such circumstances solely in cases where it can seriously be argued on a reasonable view that these activities should, on the basis of international comity, be dealt with by another country".

(4) *Extraterritorial jurisdiction and double criminality*
In *Board of Trade* v. *Owen* [1957] A.C. 602, 634, the House of Lords expressly reserved the question whether a conspiracy in this country which is wholly to be carried out abroad may not be indictable here unless there was proof that its performance would produce a public mischief in this country or injure a person resident here by causing him damage abroad.

It was a point only loosely touched upon in *Liangsiriprasert (Somchai)* v. *United States of America* [1991] 1 A.C. 225. In *R.* v. *Cox (Peter Stanley)* [1968] 1 W.L.R. 88, the conviction was quashed where the defendant conspired in England to obtain goods by deception in France with the intention of selling them in England. In that case Winn L.J. remarked "it is the law of this country as it now stands ... that there cannot be an indictment laid in this country for the commission of criminal offences abroad with the exception of murder and, I think, probably treason". There are, in fact, a number of other exceptions. With reference to the decision of the House of Lords in *Board of Trade* v. *Owen* [1957] A.C. 602, Winn L.J. said (at 93) "There is no doubt ... at all ... that even as the law stands it might be possible to indict persons here for conspiracy if the conspiracy consisted of committing crimes abroad provided it could be shown that the performance of the conspiracy would cause a public mischief in this country or injure a person here by causing him damage abroad. Neither of the possibilities referred to in the speech of Lord Tucker comprises the situation with which this court has to deal today. Improvement, let us hope there will soon be. Let us hope that this loophole will be stopped up before [others] see fit to risk using it".

In 1970, the provisional view of the Law Commission was that the law should follow the lines laid down in *Board of Trade* v. *Owen, supra* and thus a conspiracy here to commit a crime abroad should not be indictable here unless that crime, although committed abroad, is one for which an indictment would lie in that country (Law Com. Working Paper No. 29, 1970, para. 96, but see by contrast, para. 302 of the Criminal Law Revision Committee's 14th Report; 1980; Cmnd. 7844).

A similarly narrow approach was taken in respect of attempts and incitements so that attempts (or incitements) in England to commit an offence abroad should not be triable in England "unless the law has made a specific provision to that effect" (para. 98) and that such a provision should be on the grounds that the crime attempted or incited "has so close a connection with English institutions or policy as to justify this treatment" (para. 99(b)).

Although, in 1978, the Law Commission published their *Report on the Territorial and Extraterritorial Extent of the Criminal Law* (Law Com. Rep. No. 91, 1978), that document was confined to an examination of the delimitation of the territory of England and Wales for the purposes of the criminal law (para. 8).

The view of the Law Commission altered little by 1985 (Law Com. Rep. No. 143, 1985); and see Law Com. Rep. No. 177, 1989 and the Code Bills annexed thereto. The Law Commission was clearly influenced by what it described as the "assumption" that to be an offence against English law, conduct must in some degree be connected with the territory of England and Wales. A connection by reference to "harmful effects or results" felt in this country was likely to be problematic from an international perspective (Law Com. Rep. No. 91, 1978, paras. 7 and 8). In its 14th Report, the Criminal Law Revision Committee were concerned with offences against the person but concluded that the courts in this country should be able to control the activities of persons here who threaten the safety of persons abroad and thus it should be an offence to incite, conspire or attempt in this country to commit an act abroad which if committed here would amount to one of a limited range of offences (*Report on Offences Against the Person* (Criminal Law Revision Committee, Cmnd. 7844, 1980)). The Criminal Law Revision Committee did not discuss to what extent such offences would require proof of the performance of particular acts or events in this country.

By 1989 the Law Commission's stated aim in respect of inchoate offences was to combat the use of this country by those who plan dishonest activities here and which damage the financial interests of other countries: "This country's important reputation as an international financial centre could in our view be seriously affected if it came to be perceived as a haven from which international fraud can be directed with impunity. Our recommendations aim to remove that possibility". In so recommending, the Law Commission made two reservations: (a) that our law should only concern itself with conduct abroad that would be punishable by the laws of England and Wales if that conduct had been performed in this country and (b) that we should not seek to take action in relation to such conduct if, when committed, it would not be criminal by the law of the country where it occurred (Law Com. Rep. No. 180, 1989, para. 5.4). The latter principle is said to rest upon respect for the laws of other countries and thus the requirement of proof of "double criminality", *i.e.* that the intended course of conduct would be an offence both under the laws of this country and under the legal system where the conduct is to be carried out (para. 5.23). The Law Commission acknowledged that proof of a foreign law before a jury would be "a novelty" (para. 5.23; but see s.20 of the Misuse of Drugs Act 1971). An exception appears to be considered appropriate in respect of the full offences of murder and manslaughter committed abroad; in that instance, the Law Commission considered that a person should not be able to plead foreign law in defence (14th Report of the Criminal Law Revision Committee, Cmnd. 7844, 1980, para. 302). The principle of "double criminality" is given statutory force under s.6(1) or (2).

An interesting provision is s.6(3) of the 1993 Act which provides that "conduct punishable under the law in force in any place is an offence under that law for the purposes of this section, however it is described in that law". In some countries conduct which would constitute a criminal offence here, is "punishable" abroad even though liability is derived from the civil code. Is forfeiture or confiscation of assets punishment for the purposes of s.6(3)? By s.6(7) questions of foreign law should be determined by the judge alone. This is in accordance with the views of the Law Commission (Law Com. Rep. No. 180, 1989, para. 5.29) and therefore s.6(7) displaces the ordinary rules at common law (*Nelson* v. *Bridport* (1845) 8 Beav. 527; 50 E.R. 207; and *R.* v. *Ditta, Hussain and Kora* [1988] Crim.L.R. 43, C.A.).

Offences to which this Part applies

1.—(1) This Part applies to two groups of offences—
  (a) any offence mentioned in subsection (2) (a "Group A offence"); and
  (b) any offence mentioned in subsection (3) (a "Group B offence").
  (2) The Group A offences are—
  (a) an offence under any of the following provisions of the Theft Act 1968—
          section 1 (theft);
          section 15 (obtaining property by deception);
          section 16 (obtaining pecuniary advantage by deception);
          section 17 (false accounting);
          section 19 (false statements by company directors, etc.);
          section 20(2) (procuring execution of valuable security by deception);
          section 21 (blackmail);
          section 22 (handling stolen goods);
  (b) an offence under either of the following provisions of the Theft Act 1978—
          section 1 (obtaining services by deception);
          section 2 (avoiding liability by deception);
  (c) an offence under any of the following provisions of the Forgery and Counterfeiting Act 1981—
          section 1 (forgery);
          section 2 (copying a false instrument);
          section 3 (using a false instrument);
          section 4 (using a copy of a false instrument);
          section 5 (offences which relate to money orders, share certificates, passports, etc.);
  (d) the common law offence of cheating in relation to the public revenue.
  (3) The Group B offences are—
  (a) conspiracy to commit a Group A offence;
  (b) conspiracy to defraud;
  (c) attempting to commit a Group A offence;
  (d) incitement to commit a Group A offence.
  (4) The Secretary of State may by order amend subsection (2) or (3) by adding or removing any offence.
  (5) The power to make such an order shall be exercisable by statutory instrument.
  (6) No order shall be made under subsection (4) unless a draft of it has been laid before and approved by a resolution of each House of Parliament.

DEFINITIONS
  "Group A Offence": s.1(2).
  "Group B Offence": s.1(3).

GENERAL NOTE
   Part I of the 1993 Act follows the recommendations of the Law Commission in their Report on *Jurisdiction Over Offences of Fraud and Dishonesty With a Foreign Element* (Law Com. Rep. No. 180, 1989): see the General Note to Pt. I.
   Reform of the rules relating to jurisdiction have been under active consideration for some 23 years: see *Territorial and Extraterritorial Extent of the Criminal Law* (Law Com. Working Paper No. 29, 1970); *Law Commission Report,* (Law Com. Rep. No. 91, 1978); *Attempt and Impossibility in Relation to Attempt, Conspiracy and Incitement* (Law Com. Rep. No. 102, 1980); *Report on Offences Against the Person* (Criminal Law Revision Committee, Cmnd. 7844, 1980, paras. 295–304); and Lord Roskill's *Report of the Fraud Trials Committee* (1986, para. 3.17).
   A number of sections in Pt. I of the 1993 Act either mirror, or give effect to, various provisions in the draft Bill annexed to Law Com. Rep. No. 180, 1989. The brief overview of the law, set out in the report was given before the decisions of the Privy Council, and the Court of Appeal, in *Liangsiriprasert (Somchai)* v. *Government of the United States of America* [1991] 1 A.C. 225, and *R.* v. *Sansom; R.* v. *Williams; R.* v. *Smith; R.* v. *Wilkins* [1991] 2 Q.B. 130, C.A., respectively and see the General Note to Pt. I.

Subss. (1)–(3)
   The purpose of s.1 is to particularise those offences to which the new provisions in respect of jurisdiction apply and to empower the Secretary of State to modify the list by way of Statutory Instrument laid before Parliament. This is an important safeguard to enable both Houses of Parliament to scrutinise the purpose in modifying the list of offences and to keep the list within the preamble to the Act and to remove from the Secretary of State the unfettered power to modify the list without the scrutiny of Parliament (which would have been the effect of the Act had the Bill not been amended at a fairly early stage).
   Group A lists substantive offences to which Pt. I of the 1993 Act applies. Group B relates to inchoate offences.
   It was necessary to provide two separate lists because the rules applicable to determine jurisdiction in respect of either a Group A or B offence differ. For the commission of a Group A offence there must be proof that a "relevant event" took place in this country even if the result occurred abroad.
   At common law, the general rule is that jurisdiction will be assumed by the courts in England and Wales where the *last* act or event (which is required to be performed to complete the offence) took place in England or Wales. This is because a crime (amounting to the full offence) is clearly not committed until all relevant acts or events, which make up that offence, have been performed. Accordingly, the moment of "commission" is the moment when the last act or event is performed and (for the purposes of jurisdiction) it follows that the last act or event must take place here before it can be said that the offence was committed here (and see Law Com. Rep. No. 180, 1989, para. 21). See also *R.* v. *Harden* [1963] 1 Q.B. 8; *R.* v. *Thompson (Michael)* [1984] 1 W.L.R. 962; *Treacy* v. *D.P.P.* [1971] A.C. 537, *per* Lord Diplock at p. 560G; *Secretary of State for Trade* v. *Markus* [1976] A.C. 35; *D.P.P.* v. *Stonehouse* [1978] A.C. 55.
   In *R.* v. *Governor of Pentonville Prison, ex p. Osman* [1990] 1 W.L.R. 277, the defendant sent telexes from Hong Kong to an overseas bank debiting one account and crediting another. Those acts amounted to a usurpation of the rights of an owner and were thus held to be an "appropriation" for the purposes of the theft laws in Hong Kong and the offence was therefore justiciable there. Presumably there would have been no appropriation (and thus no jurisdiction) if Osman had simply withdrawn the money abroad and imported it into Hong Kong.
   The principal recommendation of the Law Commission was that the courts should have jurisdiction to try "... one of the listed offences if any event that is required to be proved in order to obtain a conviction of that offence takes place in England and Wales. That would, in particular, mean that where the definition of the offence forbids conduct producing a certain result our courts would have jurisdiction if any part of that conduct, or any part of the defined specified result, took place here. Similarly, our courts would have jurisdiction over crimes the definition of which relates only to the accused's conduct (as has been suggested to be the case with theft) if any part of the conduct forbidden by the definition of the offence took place here" (Law Com. Rep. No. 180, 1989, para. 2.27).
   In respect of Group B offences, different rules apply depending on whether the inchoate offence is a conspiracy or an attempt, and whether the inchoate offence relates to an offence to be committed in this country (s.3) or abroad (s.5).
   All the offences listed in Group A, s.1(2)(a) to (c), were recommended by the Law Commission (Law Com. Rep. No. 180, 1989) which they termed "listed offences". This list was itself based upon comments received by the Law Commission in response to their consultation paper published in 1987 (*Jurisdiction over Fraud Offences with a Foreign Element*) and which originally limited the list of offences to theft, obtaining by deception, false accounting, and

blackmail under the Theft Acts 1968 and 1978 and offences of forgery set out in Pt. I of the Forgery and Counterfeiting Act 1981.

As a result of representations made by the Law Commission, a number of other offences were considered of which three Theft Act offences were recommended by the Law Commission to be added to the list, namely: (i) false statements by company directors (s.19); (ii) dishonestly procuring by deception the execution of a valuable security (s.20(2)); and (iii) handling stolen goods (s.22). These three offences are included as Group A offences in s.1 of the 1993 Act. Offences under s.19 of the Theft Act were added on the basis that it would be undesirable for various fraud offences to be governed by different rules as to jurisdiction (Law Com. Rep. No. 180, 1989, para. 3.25). Given the close relationship between theft and handling, the Commission decided that it would be anomalous to attach new rules to only theft and thus s.22 offences were added (para. 3.30). Again, given the impact and social implications of offences under s.20(2) of the Theft Act 1968 it was considered desirable to add this offence (para. 3.22; and see *R.* v. *Nanayakkara*; *R.* v. *Knor*; *R.* v. *Tan* [1987] W.L.R. 265, *R.* v. *Beck (Brian)* [1985] 1 W.L.R. 22 and *R.* v. *Young* [1988] Crim.L.R. 372).

It will be seen by s.1(2)(d), of the 1993 Act, that the common law offence of cheating in relation to the public revenue is also a Group A offence. This appears to be contrary to the recommendations made by the Law Commission which regarded this offence as falling outside the core offences involving fraud and dishonesty (para. 3.16).

Other offences considered, but not recommended for inclusion, were insider dealing, fraudulent trading, bribery and corruption offences, drug trafficking, and offences under s.47 of the Financial Services Act 1986 and s.35 of the Banking Act 1987.

Subss. (4), (5) *and* (6)

During the debates on the Bill in Committee (Standing Committee B, col. 23, May 25, 1993) an amendment was moved to restrict the Secretary of State's power to add offences beyond the provisions of the Theft Acts 1968 and 1978 and the Forgery and Counterfeiting Acts 1981 or the common law offence of cheating the Revenue. This was to ensure that Parliament does not inadvertently give powers to the Home Secretary that are much wider than was intended by either the House of Lords or the House of Commons. To this end Mr Alun Michael asked whether it was the Government's intention that the clause would only be used in relation to offences which were covered by the amendment. In answering the question affirmatively, the Minister of State for the Home Office, indicated that new offences may be added, *e.g.* under the Companies Act, but that ". . . the power exists purely to give Parliament the flexibility to act in the light of possible future events. There is no hidden agenda whereby a raft of other offences could be added" (Standing Committee B, col. 30, May 25, 1993). It was not the intention of the legislature to use s.1(4) of the 1993 Act in order to create a new offence and to add that offence to the list of Group A or B offences (Standing Committee B, col. 30, May 25, 1993).

Jurisdiction in respect of Group A offences

2.—(1) For the purposes of this Part, "relevant event", in relation to any Group A offence, means any act or omission or other event (including any result of one or more acts or omissions) proof of which is required for conviction of the offence.

(2) For the purpose of determining whether or not a particular event is a relevant event in relation to a Group A offence, any question as to where it occurred is to be disregarded.

(3) A person may be guilty of a Group A offence if any of the events which are relevant events in relation to the offence occurred in England and Wales.

DEFINITIONS
  "Group A Offence": s.1(2).
  "Group B Offence": s.1(3).
  "relevant event": s.2(1).

GENERAL NOTE

The meaning of a "Relevant Event"
  Section 7 of the New Zealand Crimes Act 1961 provides that:
  "For the purpose of jurisdiction, where any act or omission forming part of any offence, or any event necessary to the completion of any offence, occurs in New Zealand, the offence shall be deemed to be committed in New Zealand, whether the person charged with the offence was in New Zealand or not at the time of the act, omission, or event".

Although s.7 of the New Zealand Crimes Act 1961 was employed as a model, there are important differences. In s.7 of the New Zealand Crimes Act 1961 the provision distinguishes between acts or omissions which form "part of any offence" and events which are "necessary to the completion of an offence". Such terminology may have been considered necessary to reflect a distinction drawn between so-called "conduct crimes" and "result crimes". By contrast, s.2(1) of the 1993 Act rolls up both types of offences so that any act or commission, "or other event", which must be proved for conviction of the offence, will be a "relevant event" for jurisdictional purposes. Thus, by s.15 of the Theft Act 1968 the *obtaining* of property is a "result" which flows from acts of *deception* (*i.e.* conduct). It is submitted that such a result would constitute some "other event" but the matter is put beyond doubt by the words in parenthesis "including any result . . .".

Secondly, s.7 of the New Zealand Crimes Act 1961 is essentially a "deeming" provision for jurisdictional purposes. Section 2 of the 1993 Act does not go as far as that. It merely provides that a person "may be guilty" of a Group A offence in any of the events which are relevant events in relation to the offence occurred in England and Wales.

The continued effect of subs. (2) and s.3(1) are similar to s.7 of the New Zealand Crimes Act 1961 in that neither provision regards the presence of the actor in the relevant country as being material to jurisdiction for the purposes of an offence listed in Group A or B.

Subss. (2) *and* (3)

Subsections (2) and (3) of s.2 of the 1993 Act follow the model of the Law Commission's clauses in their draft Bill (Law Com. Rep. No. 180, 1989, cl. 1(2) and 2, respectively).

At first sight subss. (2) and (3) of s.2 of the 1993 Act appear to be in conflict—if not in total contradiction—particularly if subs. (3) is read before subs. (2). The New Zealand model has no equivalent provision so why has subs. (2) been included? The reasoning appears to be as follows. Given that the common law, for jurisdictional purposes, looks to the *last* act or event to determine whether an offence was committed in this country, some formula is required to indicate that the common law rules no longer apply in respect of Pt. I of the Act. Accordingly the first step is to look at subs. (3) (not subs. (1)) because it is subs. (3) which provides the crucial test to be applied to determine jurisdiction. Thus, subs. (3) does not say that a person "will" be guilty of an offence nor (unlike the New Zealand model) does it "deem" an offence to be committed here for jurisdictional purposes. Furthermore, subs. (3) recognises that, in any given case, the facts may reveal a large number of events all of which are in themselves "relevant events" within the meaning of s.2(1). The court need do no more than to look to see whether any one of those events occurred here. Accordingly, on one interpretation, Parliament did not need to enact more than subss. (1) and (3). The Law Commission regarded it as important that jurisdiction should be assumed by the courts of this country only if an element required to be proved for conviction takes place here (Law Com. Rep. No. 180, 1989, para. 2.28). Incidental acts, or acts forming part of the "narrative" were not considered to be sufficient, *e.g.* the mere preparation of documents (para. 2.28). It is for those reasons that subss. (1) and (3) are drafted in their present form.

It appears to have been feared that, without subs. (2), it could be argued that if the bulk of "relevant events" take place abroad and only a relatively minor event (albeit "relevant") takes place here, the court might hold that a "relevant event", for the purposes of subss. (1) and (3) did not occur here (Standing Committee B, col. 43, May 27, 1993). This is not a very convincing reason for including s.2(2). A stronger argument would be that, if it was not clearly established that the rules of the common law have no application, then a court may conclude that the common law rules shall apply so that a "relevant event" is only "relevant" for jurisdictional purposes if (a) it was performed in this country and (b) that it was the *last* act or event "proof of which is required . . . [at common law] . . . for conviction of the offence": adopting the language of s.2. Such a construction of s.2 would obviously defeat the purpose of Pt. I of the Act. Accordingly, the reasoning would seem to be that subs. (2) merely clarifies the meaning of the phrase "relevant event" so that an event may be "relevant" even if it occurred abroad. The relevance of the event is therefore directed to the essential ingredients of the offence and not directly, to the question of jurisdiction. It may be said logically, that subs. (3) should have appeared first, then subs. (1) and lastly subs. (2). Ironically, this is how the clauses were originally arranged in the Bill even (as late as June 22, 1993) but the provisions in s.2 were rearranged by the time the Act received Royal Assent.

Relevance of s.3(1) to s.2

It is important to have regard to s.3(1) of the Act. It is irrelevant whether the accused is a British subject or not. This provision reflects the views expressed by Lord Diplock in *Treacy* v. *D.P.P.* [1971] A.C. 537, 561b where he said:

"Nor ... can I see any reason in comity to prevent Parliament from rendering liable to punishment, if they subsequently come to England, persons who have done outside the United Kingdom physical acts which have had harmful consequences upon victims in England ... Comity gives no right to a state to insist that any person may with impunity do physical acts in its own territory which have harmful consequences to persons within the territory of another state. It may be under no obligation in comity to punish those acts itself, but it has no ground for complaint in international law if the state in which the harmful consequences had their effect punishes, when they do enter its territories, persons who did such acts."

Section 3(1)(b) is relevant both from the point of view of endorsing the decisions in *Liangsiriprasert (Somchai)* v. *Government of the United States of America* [1991] 1 A.C. 225, and *R.* v. *Sansom*; *R.* v. *Williams*; *R.* v. *Smith*; *R.* v. *Wilkins* [1991] 2 Q.B. 130, C.A.

This provision also meets the rule that statutes are not to be interpreted as applying to persons who are not British subjects in respect of acts performed abroad: *Air India* v. *Wiggins* [1980] 1 W.L.R. 815; *R.* v. *Jameson* [1896] 2 Q.B. 425.

Relevance of s.4 to s.2

It will be seen that s.2(1) includes the "result" of one or more acts of omissions. Obtaining property by deception is a "result crime" in the sense that the "obtaining" is the result of the deception. Formerly, jurisdiction (for the full offence) required proof that the result occurred here: *R.* v. *Harden* [1963] 1 Q.B. 8. If the deception occurred abroad but property was despatched from England to a victim in France then (without s.4(a)) it could be argued that the "obtaining" of the property also occurred abroad: and see *R.* v. *Tirado* (1974) 59 Cr.App.R. 80, C.A. Section 4(a) resolves that issue.

Similarly, the transmission of information, and the other activities referred to in s.4(b), are now to be read as occurring both in the place where the information originated and the place where it was received (and see Law Com. Rep. 180, 1989, para. 2.31).

Questions immaterial to jurisdiction in the case of certain offences

3.—(1) A person may be guilty of a Group A or Group B offence whether or not—
   (a) he was a British citizen at any material time;
   (b) he was in England and Wales at any such time.
   (2) On a charge of conspiracy to commit a Group A offence, or on a charge of conspiracy to defraud in England and Wales, the defendant may be guilty of the offence whether or not—
   (a) he became a party to the conspiracy in England and Wales;
   (b) any act or omission or other event in relation to the conspiracy occurred in England and Wales.
   (3) On a charge of attempting to commit a Group A offence, the defendant may be guilty of the offence whether or not—
   (a) the attempt was made in England and Wales;
   (b) it had an effect in England and Wales.
   (4) Subsection (1)(a) does not apply where jurisdiction is given to try the offence in question by an enactment which makes provision by reference to the nationality of the person charged.
   (5) Subsection (2) does not apply in relation to any charge under the Criminal Law Act 1977 brought by virtue of section 1A of that Act.
   (6) Subsection (3) does not apply in relation to any charge under the Criminal Attempts Act 1981 brought by virtue of section 1A of that Act.

DEFINITIONS
   "Group A Offence": s.1(2).
   "Group B Offence": s.1(3).

Subs. (1)
   It is irrelevant whether the accused is a British subject or not. This provision reflects the views expressed by Lord Diplock in *Treacy* v. *D.P.P.* [1971] A.C. 537, 561b. Note, also, the effect of s.3(4).

Subss. (2) *and* (3)
   See the General Note to Pt. I of the Act (above).

Note also that subs. (2) is excluded if subss. (5) or (6) apply.

Subs. (4)
Examples are to be found in s.4 of the Offences Against the Person Act 1861 and s.1 of the War Crimes Act 1991.

Subss. (5) *and* (6)
Section 3 is concerned with conspiracies or attempts which are either performed in this country or abroad but where the parties have in view the commission of a Group A offence (or to defraud) in England and Wales. Section 3 is not concerned with conspiracies, attempts or incitements to commit an offence abroad which would be an offence by the laws of this country and in the country where the result occurred.

Rules for determining certain jurisdictional questions relating to the location of events

4. In relation to a Group A or Group B offence—
(a) there is an obtaining of property in England and Wales if the property is either despatched from or received at a place in England and Wales; and
(b) there is a communication in England and Wales of any information, instruction, request, demand or other matter if it is sent by any means—
  (i) from a place in England and Wales to a place elsewhere; or
  (ii) from a place elsewhere to a place in England and Wales.

DEFINITIONS
"Group A Offence": s.1(2).
"Group B Offence": s.1(3).

GENERAL NOTE
See the commentary to s.2 above.

Conspiracy, attempt and incitement

5.—(1) The following section shall be inserted in the Criminal Law Act 1977, after section 1—

"**Extended jurisdiction over certain conspiracies**
1A.—(1) This Part of this Act has effect in relation to an agreement which falls within this section as it has effect in relation to one which falls within section 1(1) above.
(2) An agreement falls within this section if—
(a) a party to it, or a party's agent, did anything in England and Wales in relation to it before its formation, or
(b) a party to it became a party in England and Wales (by joining it either in person or through an agent), or
(c) a party to it, or a party's agent, did or omitted anything in England and Wales in pursuance of it,
and the agreement would fall within section 1(1) above as an agreement relating to the commission of a Group A offence but for that offence, if committed in accordance with the parties' intentions, not being an offence triable in England and Wales.
(3) In subsection (2) above "Group A offence" has the same meaning as in Part I of the Criminal Justice Act 1993.
(4) Subsection (1) above is subject to the provisions of section 6 of the Act of 1993 (relevance of external law).
(5) An offence which is an offence of conspiracy, by virtue of this section, shall be treated for all purposes as an offence of conspiracy to commit the relevant Group A offence.".
(2) The following section shall be inserted in the Criminal Attempts Act 1981, after section 1—

"Extended jurisdiction in relation to certain attempts

1A.—(1) If this section applies to an act, what the person doing the act had in view shall be treated as an offence to which section 1(1) above applies.

(2) This section applies to an act if—

(a) it is done in England and Wales, and

(b) it would fall within section 1(1) above as more than merely preparatory to the commission of a Group A offence but for the fact that that offence, if completed, would not be an offence triable in England and Wales.

(3) In this section "Group A offence" has the same meaning as in Part I of the Criminal Justice Act 1993.

(4) Subsection (1) above is subject to the provisions of section 6 of the Act of 1993 (relevance of external law).

(5) Where a person does any act to which this section applies, the offence which he commits shall for all purposes be treated as the offence of attempting to commit the relevant Group A offence.".

(3) A person may be guilty of conspiracy to defraud if—

(a) a party to the agreement constituting the conspiracy, or a party's agent, did anything in England and Wales in relation to the agreement before its formation, or

(b) a party to it became a party in England and Wales (by joining it either in person or through an agent), or

(c) a party to it, or a party's agent, did or omitted anything in England and Wales in pursuance of it,

and the conspiracy would be triable in England and Wales but for the fraud which the parties to it had in view not being intended to take place in England and Wales.

(4) A person may be guilty of incitement to commit a Group A offence if the incitement—

(a) takes place in England and Wales; and

(b) would be triable in England and Wales but for what the person charged had in view not being an offence triable in England and Wales.

(5) Subsections (3) and (4) are subject to section 6.

DEFINITIONS

"Group A Offence": s.1(2).

GENERAL NOTE

As the Law Commission observed in their Report (Law Com. Rep. No. 180, 1989) the courts in England and Wales have no jurisdiction at common law to try a charge of conspiracy under s.1 of the Criminal Law Act 1977 where the parties entered into an agreement in this country to commit a Group A type of offence but where the agreement was to be wholly performed abroad. Again, the courts have no jurisdiction to try a common law conspiracy to defraud where the fraud contemplated is to be perpetrated abroad (para. 5.5): see *R.* v. *Cox* (*Peter Stanley*) [1968] 1 W.L.R. 88 and *Att.-Gen.'s Reference* (*No. 1 of 1982*) [1983] Q.B. 751.

One solution would be to create an offence, triable in this country, of contravening a "corresponding law" and would thus require proof that the conduct or result performed (or intended to be carried out) abroad, is an offence by the laws of the foreign state: the offence under s.20 of the Misuse of Drugs Act 1971 is one such example. Such an option would mean identifying those offences abroad (or a particular type) which are considered to be relevant. It is also important that there should be no infringement of the rules of international comity if the courts in this country exercised jurisdiction over dishonest conduct which is performed either in this country or is connected with this country. The Law Commission regarded it as "detrimental to this country, and in particular to its reputation as an international financial centre, if those who, when in this country, conspire, incite others or attempt to commit criminal fraud abroad may do so without being punishable in our courts" (Law Com. Rep. No. 180, 1989, para. 1.5).

Accordingly, what was required was a formula which would involve an appropriate connection with this country as a prerequisite of jurisdiction but that (in the interests of international comity) there should be no jurisdiction to try conduct which if committed, would not be criminal by the laws of the country where the conduct did or was to occur. The Law Commission therefore favoured a principle of "double criminality".

Accordingly, the amendment to the Criminal Law Act 1977 (introduced by subs. (1)), deems that a Group A type of offence will be justiciable in this country (and thus tried as such by virtue of subs. (5)) even though that offence cannot be tried directly under s.1(1) of the Criminal Law Act 1977 because the agreement relates to conduct to be performed abroad and which would not therefore (strictly speaking) "necessarily amount to or involve the commission of any offence" in this country (s.1(1), and s.1(4) of the Criminal Law Act 1977).

In the House of Lords, the Minister of State for the Home Office, suggested that conspiracies and attempts "which are formulated in this country but which are intended to take effect overseas will be treated as though their objective had been in this country" (*Hansard*, H.L. Vol. 540, col. 1469). In fact, subs. (1) of this section is not limited to giving jurisdiction solely on the grounds that the conspiracy was formed in this country. It will be seen from the wording of the new s.1A(2) of the Criminal Law Act 1977 (inserted by subs. (1) of the above Act), that an agreement falls within the relevant section if one of three conditions are fulfilled (see s.1A(2) (a), (b) and (c)). In none of the three situations mentioned in s.1A(2) is it required that the agreement be formed in this country at all. The reason for that is to be gleaned from the observations of Lord Wilberforce in *D.P.P.* v. *Doot* [1973] A.C. 807, 818c which, although not directly comparable, are illustrative of the difficulties:

"A legal principle which would enable concerting law breakers to escape a conspiracy charge by crossing the Channel before making their agreements or, conversely, which would encourage the prosecution into allegation or fiction of a renewed agreement in this country, all this with no compensating merit, is not one which I would endorse".

If A recruits B in England, but A and B recruit C in France, then it would be illogical if only A and B could be tried here. Even if the agreed course of conduct would be an offence by English law, it must also be an offence under the laws in force in the country where the conduct was intended to take place (s.6(2)) and the courts will look to see whether the conduct is "punishable" in that foreign country whether or not that country calls it an "offence" or not (s.6(6)).

The question whether s.6 is fulfilled is to be determined by judge alone (s.6(7)).

Similar considerations apply to the provisions in relation to attempts and incitement.

Relevance of external law

6.—(1) A person is guilty of an offence triable by virtue of section 1A of the Criminal Law Act 1977, or by virtue of section 5(3), only if the pursuit of the agreed course of conduct would at some stage involve—

(a) an act or omission by one or more of the parties, or

(b) the happening of some other event,

constituting an offence under the law in force where the act, omission or other event was intended to take place.

(2) A person is guilty of an offence triable by virtue of section 1A of the Criminal Attempts Act 1981, or by virtue of section 5(4), only if what he had in view would involve the commission of an offence under the law in force where the whole or any part of it was intended to take place.

(3) Conduct punishable under the law in force in any place is an offence under that law for the purposes of this section, however it is described in that law.

(4) Subject to subsection (6), a condition specified in subsection (1) or (2) shall be taken to be satisfied unless, not later than rules of court may provide, the defence serve on the prosecution a notice—

(a) stating that, on the facts as alleged with respect to the relevant conduct, the condition is not in their opinion satisfied;

(b) showing their grounds for that opinion; and

(c) requiring the prosecution to show that it is satisfied.

(5) In subsection (4) "the relevant conduct" means—

(a) where the condition in subsection (1) is in question, the agreed course of conduct; and

(b) where the condition in subsection (2) is in question, what the defendant had in view.

(6) The court, if it thinks fit, may permit the defence to require the prosecution to show that the condition is satisfied without the prior service of a notice under subsection (4).

(7) In the Crown Court, the question whether the condition is satisfied shall be decided by the judge alone.

(8) The following paragraph shall be inserted in section 9(3) of the Criminal Justice Act 1987 (preparatory hearing in a case of serious fraud), before paragraph (b)—

"(aa) a question arising under section 6 of the Criminal Justice Act 1993 (relevance of external law to certain charges of conspiracy, attempt and incitement);".

DEFINITIONS
"relevant conduct": s.6(5).

GENERAL NOTE
As indicated above, if A recruits B in England, but A and B recruit C in France, then it would be illogical if only A and B could be tried here. Even if the agreed course of conduct would be an offence by English law, it must also be an offence under the laws in force in the country where the conduct was intended to take place (subs. (2)) and the courts will look to see whether the conduct is "punishable" in that foreign country whether or not that country terms it an "offence" or not (subs. (6)).

The question whether s.6 is fulfilled is to be determined by judge alone (subs. (7)).

PART II

DRUG TRAFFICKING OFFENCES

GENERAL NOTE
On July 8, 1986, by virtue of the Drug Trafficking Offences Act 1986 (the DTOA), Parliament introduced sweeping and radical changes to the law to enable the courts to recover the proceeds of drug trafficking. Sections 1(3), 2(1), 24, 34, 38 and 40 came into force on September 30, 1986 (see the Drug Trafficking Offences Act 1986 (Commencement No. 1) Order 1986 (S.I. 1986 No. 1488)), followed by ss.27 to 29, 31 and 33 (in force on December 30, 1986 by virtue of the same Order) and the remainder on January 12, 1987 (see the Drug Trafficking Offences Act 1986 (Commencement No. 3) Order 1986 (S.I. 1986 No. 2145)).

The Act has since been amended by the Criminal Justice (Scotland) Act 1987; the Land Registration Act 1988; the Criminal Justice Act 1988; the Criminal Justice (International) Co-operation Act 1990; and now by Pt. II of the Criminal Justice Act 1993.

The Home Office Working Group in their *Report on the Drug Trafficking Offences Act 1986* (May 1991) found that the 1986 Act had worked "reasonably well" (para. 1) but they made a number of recommendations which have, in part, been given statutory force by ss. 7 to 15 (inclusive).

By the end of 1992 some £35 m. had been ordered to be confiscated under the 1986 Act and by May 1992 £15 m. had actually been realised or was subject to receivership (see *Hansard*, H.L. Vol. 539, col. 1383).

It is important to realise that Pt. II does not merely tinker with existing law but radically overhauls the way in which drug trafficking confiscation proceedings are to be investigated and conducted, and strengthens powers of enforcement in respect of the gathering and furnishing of information (relevant to confiscation proceedings) as well as ensuring the satisfaction (in full) of amounts payable under a confiscation order.

Previously, the courts were equipped only with the statutory powers of forfeiture, the making of "deprivation" orders or "criminal bankruptcy" orders, and/or the imposition of fines. Save for criminal bankruptcy orders these powers continue to exist, but they are very limited in scope. Thus, by s.27 of the MDA 1971, only those assets which directly relate to an offence committed by the accused, under that Act, may be forfeited: see *R.* v. *Morgan* [1977] Crim.L.R. 488, C.A. Choses in action and intangibles are not usually capable of being forfeited: see *R.* v. *Khan*; *R.* v. *Crawley* [1982] 1 W.L.R. 1405, C.A. Drug profits, originally received by the accused but which were then transferred to a third party, could not be seized. It was to meet such weaknesses in the law that the DTOA 1986 was enacted following recommendations contained in the Home Affairs Committee Fifth Report "Misuse of Hard Drugs Interim Report" (H.C. 399 (1985)) which had approved the American policy of giving the court "draconian powers" to strip drug dealers of assets acquired during the course of their drug dealing even where their connection with drug trafficking offences is merely "probable".

This seemingly straightforward but important statement of policy conceals the extent of the power required to enforce it. The following points should thus be noted: (1) the policy stems from the scale and nature of the illicit drug trade, often involving more than one jurisdiction and the laundering of substantial sums of money at home and abroad affecting a number of institutions or corporate bodies, many of which may be totally innocent parties; (2) the policy is intended to "remove the profit motive by allowing the confiscation of all the trafficker's proceeds from drug trafficking, following conviction" (*per* Secretary of State for the Home Office, *Hansard*, H.C. Vol. 222, col. 866); (3) the policy is also intended to ensure that drug trafficking profits cannot be recycled to fund further drug trafficking (*ibid.*); (4) the thinking behind the policy would seem to be that in order to achieve the last mentioned objective, the confiscation of assets in circumstances where their connection with drug-trafficking is merely probable is justified; (5) a connection that need only be "probable" suggests the application of a civil standard of proof in confiscation proceedings (see Art. 7 of the Vienna Convention 1988); (6) the stripping of drug assets accrued during the course of the dealer's drug dealing involves tracing assets throughout his career; (7) the gleaning of information and "intelligence" is an essential prerequisite of enforcement.

Some of these afore-mentioned points either "cut across" or challenge traditional principles, and rules of procedure in the context of criminal proceedings. Nowhere has this been more apparent in respect of the DTOA (as originally drafted) than in relation to the application of the burden and standard of proof (see *R.* v. *Dickens* [1990] 2 Q.B. 102); *R.* v. *Redbourne* [1992] 1 W.L.R. 1182 and *R.* v. *Rose* [1993] Crim.L.R. 407; and see "Making Statutory Assumptions Under the Drug Trafficking Offences Act", *Archbold News*, Issue No. 5, May 28, 1993. See now s.1(7A) of the DTOA inserted by s.7(2) of the 1993 Act.

It has been argued that the jurisprudential justification for the approach adopted in the DTOA is that confiscation proceedings are not penal in nature but essentially civil or "reparative" consequent upon a conviction of a "drug trafficking offence" in accordance with traditional principles. This is examined more fully below (and see the speech of Lord Ackner, *Hansard*, H.L. Vol. 540, cols. 744 and 749). Note that the existing legislation has to be viewed alongside an international campaign to tackle international crime of which fraud (hence Pt. I), drug trafficking and terrorism are of the greatest concern.

Originally only Pts. II and III were included in the Bill following the Home Office Working Group's recommendations (see the Reports of the Drug Trafficking Offences Act 1986 (May 1991) and the Criminal Justice Act 1988 (November 1992)). However, Parliament took the opportunity (albeit at a late stage of the Bill's passage through both Houses of Parliament) to widen the scope of the legislation by including new offences in relation to money laundering. These include failing to disclose to a constable, knowledge or suspicion of drug money laundering activities (s.18 of the 1993 Act) and "tipping off" another about a current or proposed drug money laundering investigation (s.19). The provisions of Pt. II are also mirrored in Pts. III and IV (*i.e.* amendments to the Criminal Justice Act 1988 and the Northern Ireland (Emergency Provisions) Act 1991 in respect of the financing of terrorism.

Note also the Community Council Directive 91/308/EEC following the Council of Europe Convention on Laundering, Tracing, Seizure and Confiscation of Proceeds of Crime. Note also s.26 of the DTOA (as amended) and the Drug Trafficking Offences Act (Designated Countries and Territories) Order 1990 (S.I. 1993 No. 1199) (as amended by S.I. 1991 No. 1465). Orders made in Scotland under the Criminal Justice (Scotland) Act 1987 may now be enforced in England and Wales: see the Drug Trafficking Offences (Enforcement in England and Wales) Order 1988 (S.I. 1993 No. 593).

In contrast with American law, the British model remains less draconian (notwithstanding representations made by American law enforcement agencies to the British Government) but the trend is clearly in favour of the American approach. The United States of America has been developing powerful anti-money laundering laws over the last 20 years. The Bank Secrecy Act 1970 (U.S.) applies to financial institutions and businesses which accept large sums of cash. A "financial institution" is very broadly defined: *U.S.* v. *Rigdon* (1989) 874 F.2d 774; *U.S.* v. *Clines* (1992) 958 F.2d 578. The BSA requires businesses and individuals to submit Currency Transaction Reports (CTRs) as well as various reports of currency instruments, foreign bank accounts, and cash payments over 10,000 US$ in a trade or business. Businesses and their employees may be required to lodge Criminal Referral Forms (CRFs) in respect of any "known or suspected criminal violation . . . committed against [or through] a bank" used to facilitate a criminal transaction. Failure to file a CRF may result in so-called civil penalties being assessed against the institution, its officers or employees. Data and intelligence gleaned from these records are collated on a database utilised by FINCEN (Financial Crimes Enforcement Network). The Anti-Abuse Act 1988 includes a requirement upon the Secretary to the Treasury to negotiate with other countries to ensure that they have adequate records on international currency transactions, which might be taken as a requirement for mandatory reporting along

United States lines. The question as to what happens to all this information is a matter of growing concern and debate. The Money Laundering Control Act (1986) (U.S.), creates a number of offences in respect of the knowing participation by any person in transactions with persons who derive their money from specified unlawful activities *e.g.* drug trafficking. Forfeiture, under United States legislation, is permitted under the BSA, the MLCA, the Comprehensive Drug Abuse Prevention and Control Act, the Controlled Substances Act, the Racketeer-Influenced and Corrupt Organisations (RICO) and the Continuing Criminal Enterprise statutes.

Of particular interest are two concepts in American law. First, some statutory provisions enjoy a reduced standard of proof requiring the government to prove only a "probable" cause to believe "that a substantial connection exists between the property to be forfeited" and the act which contravenes the statute: *US* v. *Four Million Dollars* (1985) 762 F.2d 895. Secondly, there is the "Relation-Back Doctrine" which is based on the fiction that illegally obtained property vests in the government at the time of the offence.

Notwithstanding the above, the DTOA has been appropriately described as a "draconian" piece of legislation and was intended to be so (see *Dickens* [1990] 2 Q.B. 102, *per* Lord Lane C.J. at 105), *Comiskey* (1990) 12 Cr.App.R.(S.) 562, *per* Tucker J. at 568; *R.* v. *Smith* (*Ian*) (1989) 89 Cr.App.R. 253, C.A., *per* Lord Lane C.J. at 238; and *R.* v. *Robson* (*Steven Kenneth*) (1991) 92 Cr.App.R. 1). This is particularly apparent in respect of the sweeping assumptions which the court must make—all adverse to the defendant—except in two statutorily defined circumstances. There are also a number of evidential stages at which the defendant shoulders the burden of proof.

Confiscation—is it "penal" or "reparation"?

The answer to this question is not of mere academic interest: it explains how the legislation has developed and explains some of the difficulties of construction which have arisen. On one view the DTOA is *punitive* in nature and should be construed as a penal statute. The alternative view is that the Act is merely *reparative* or *compensatory* in nature (society being the victim) and that the DTOA should therefore be construed and applied according to civil law rules and traditions. Those competing views have been voiced, most notably, in connection with the standard of proof applicable to those matters which the prosecution are required to prove under the DTOA: see *R.* v. *Dickens* [1990] 2 Q.B. 102; *Enwezor* (1991) 93 Cr.App.R. 233, C.A., and *R.* v. *Redbourne* [1992] 1 W.L.R. 1182, C.A.

However, if the DTOA is truly only reparative (being civil in nature) and not penal, then several consequences arguably follow: (i) the appropriate standard of proof is the civil standard; (ii) evidence may be adduced and received in accordance with civil law principles. This is particularly relevant in respect of the admission of hearsay evidence and documentation (are transcripts admissible?); (iii) the appropriate court is a court of civil jurisdiction; (iv) the making of a confiscation order is not a penal order and therefore should not be regarded as a "sentence" for the purposes of an appeal to the Court of Appeal (Criminal Division): by contrast, see *R.* v. *Johnson* [1991] 2 Q.B. 249; and see *R.* v. *Hayden* [1975] 1 W.L.R. 852 at p. 854G; (v) legal aid should be granted under a Civil Legal Aid Order; and (vi) if the DTOA is not penal then a court is not constrained to resolve an ambiguity in favour "of the defendant": see *R.* v. *Chapman*, *The Times*, November 18, 1991.

The view that the DTOA is *reparative* appears to be gaining ground—at least within law enforcement circles. It is strongly advocated by the Home Office, the Central Confiscation Unit and, indeed, by the Government: see the debates in *Hansard* (H.L. Vol. 539, col. 1347 and Vol. 540, cols. 1469, 1483).

On the other hand, although the making of a confiscation order follows a conviction for a "drug trafficking offence" (s.1(1) of the DTOA), nevertheless the amount assessed to represent (and to be recovered) as his proceeds of drug trafficking need not derive from the offence for which he was convicted at all. This is because the defendant's benefit may include proceeds received as a result of drug trafficking carried on by him or "by another"—anywhere in the world: ss.1(2), (3), 2(1), 4(1) of the DTOA. The court may include payments received or made by the defendant which have no connection with the offence before the court but, if any of the assumptions are made within the terms of s.2(2) and (3) of the DTOA then they will be assumed to be in connection with drug trafficking carried on by the defendant himself. Unlike civil judgments, unpaid confiscation orders carrying severe terms of imprisonment in default (depending on the sum outstanding). Lord Lane C.J. in *R.* v. *Dickens* [1990] 2 Q.B. 102 seems to have regarded the DTOA as being penal at least insofar as proving the fact that the defendant has benefited from drug trafficking and the amount of such benefit (*cf.* the *obiter* of Leggatt L.J. in *Thomas, Re* [1992] 4 All E.R. 814, 819).

By contrast, confiscation under the Criminal Justice Act 1988 depends on the prosecution proving that the benefit received by the defendant derived from an offence proved (or admitted) to have been committed by him (s.71 and see s.71(4) of the 1988 Act). The burden of proving the fact that a benefit had been received, and the amount, is on the prosecution— without the assistance of statutory assumptions such as those to be found in s.2 of the DTOA.

When the 1993 Act was being debated as a Bill, both Houses were divided as to whether confiscation proceedings were "civil" in nature. The Minister of State for the Home Office emphasised that the application of a civil standard of proof was always the Government's intention but that the 1986 Act did not make that intention sufficiently clear resulting in the courts applying a criminal standard of proof to be applied at certain stages of the proceedings (see *R.* v. *Dickens* [1990] 2 Q.B. 102; see also *Hansard*, H.L. Vol. 539, cols. 1350, 1383). Lord Ackner and Lord Brightman supported the view that the civil standard should apply (*Hansard*, H.L. Vol. 520, cols. 1471, 1472) while Lord Williams of Mostyn (*Hansard*, H.L. Vol. 540, col. 741) pointed out that confiscation of assets involved a finding that the defendant had benefited from drug trafficking—a criminal activity. This issue is further developed (below) in respect of s.7(2) of the 1993 Act.

(1) THE BROAD APPROACH IN ENGLAND AND WALES
Three points should be borne in mind whenever the court embarks upon a drug trafficking enquiry.

First, what is to be confiscated are the proceeds of drug trafficking and not merely drug profits. A trafficker who receives £1,000 for the sale of a drug cannot seek to deduct the expenses he incurred in buying and transporting it (*R.* v. *Smith* (*Ian*) [1989] 1 W.L.R. 765, C.A.). Broadly speaking his gross receipts are his proceeds. Secondly, the value of a confiscation order will not always signify the extent to which the defendant himself has been engaged in drug trafficking because the Act catches all drug proceeds received by the defendant whether as a result of his drug trafficking or another's (see *R.* v. *Smith* [1990] 1 W.L.R. 765, C.A.; and see also *R.* v. *Comiskey* (1991) 93 Cr.App.R. 227, C.A.). (See also ss.1(3) and 2(1)(a) of the DTOA). Thirdly, it is irrelevant whether the drug trafficking in question took place within the jurisdiction of the courts of the U.K., or abroad subject to a "corresponding law": see s.38(1) and (3) of the DTOA.

The method by which a court may assess the value of the proceeds of drug trafficking is one of the most controversial features of the Act and more so in the light of Pt. II of the 1993 Act. There will often be cases where an accused can be shown to have received property over a period of years but there exists little or no evidence to prove that the property represents the proceeds of drug trafficking. Accordingly, the Act creates a number of far-reaching assumptions which the court is now obliged to make unless the statutory exceptions apply. Inevitably, in complicated and hotly contested confiscation proceedings, much court time will be spent tracing funds and ascertaining their origin.

The Previous and Present Position
Whenever a defendant appeared before the Crown Court to be sentenced in respect of one or more drug trafficking offences, the court was obliged to embark upon a drug trafficking enquiry in every case. This has now changed by virtue of s.7(1) of the 1993 Act.

The relevant steps to be followed (both under the previous and the current law) are, broadly speaking, as follows:

(1) Formerly the court was obliged to ask in every case whether the defendant has benefited from drug trafficking (s.1(2) of the DTOA). This is no longer the case (s.7(1) of the 1993 Act). The court will only embark upon an enquiry under the DTOA if the prosecutor asks it to do so, or (even if the prosecutor has not asked it to do so) it is appropriate for the court to proceed under s.1 of the DTOA. If the prosecutor asks the court to proceed under s.1 of the DTOA then the court must do so. The implications of this are discussed below. When the court does embark on confiscation proceedings it must first decide whether there is a benefit received by the defendant:
   (a) Formerly, the persuasive burden was on the prosecution to prove this issue to the criminal law standard of proof (see *R.* v. *Dickens* [1990] 2 Q.B. 102, C.A. and *R.* v. *Enwezor* (1991) 93 Cr.App.R. 233, C.A.). The persuasive burden remains on the prosecution but to the civil standard (s.7(2) of the 1993 Act). Accordingly, *Dickens* and *Enwezor, supra* are over-ruled on this point.
   (b) The court was empowered (but not obliged) to make any of the statutory assumptions contained in s.2(2) and (3) of the DTOA. The burden of rebuttal was on the defendant (*Dickens* and *Enwezor, supra* and see *R.* v. *Redbourne* [1992] 1 W.L.R. 1182). The court must now make the "required assumption" unless the statutory exceptions apply (s.9 of the 1993 Act).

(2) If question (1) was answered affirmatively, then the court proceeded to assess the value of the proceeds of drug trafficking received by the defendant (ss.1(4) and 4 of the DTOA). This remains the law but note that s.4 has been amended by the 1993 Act (see s.7(3)).
   (a) The value of the defendant's proceeds represents prima facie the "amount to be recovered" under a confiscation order (s.4(1) of the DTOA). This remains the law.
   (b) The persuasive burden was again on the prosecution to the criminal standard of proof

(*Dickens* and *Enwezor, supra.* The persuasive burden remains on the prosecution but now only to the civil standard of proof (s.7(2) of the 1993 Act).

(c) The court could apply the statutory assumptions in appropriate cases (ss.2(2) and (3) of the DTOA). Under Pt. II of the 1993 Act the "required assumptions" must be made unless the statutory exceptions apply (s.9).

(3) The court can be asked (or decide of its volition) to assess the "amount that may be realised" under s.4(3) of the DTOA as defined by s.5(3) of the DTOA, being the total value of realisable property held by the defendant plus the total value of gifts made by him and caught by the Act (ss.4(3), 5(3) and 5(9) of the DTOA). This remains the law but note the amendments to s.4(3) of the DTOA by virtue of s.7(3) of the 1993 Act; see also the amendments made by s.12 (in respect of s.4(3) of the DTOA) and s.10 (in respect of s.5(3) of the DTOA).

(4) If the defendant satisfies the court on a balance of probabilities that the "amount that might be realised" was less than the "amount to be recovered" then the court confiscated the lesser amount (s.4(3) of the DTOA). See *R.* v. *Ilsemann (Horst Reiner)* (1990) 12 Cr.App.R. (S.) 398, C.A.; *R.* v. *Comiskey* (1991) 93 Cr.App.R. 227, C.A.; and *R.* v. *Carroll (Thomas Anthony)* (1992) 13 Cr.App.R.(S.) 99, C.A. The judge issued a certificate recording that finding of fact (s.4(2)). This remains the position. The 1993 Act says nothing about the incidence, or standard of proof, relevant to this issue.

(5) If the defendant fails to discharge the burden on him, or fails to raise the issue at all, then the court may make a confiscation order for the full amount determined under steps (1) and (2) above (but see *Comiskey (supra)* and *R.* v. *Keston* (1990) 12 Cr.App.R.(S.) 93). The law remains unchanged.

(6) The court treats the confiscation order as a fine and imposes a sentence of imprisonment in default (s.6 of the DTOA). This remains the law but even if the defendant serves a sentence of imprisonment in default the court under Pt. II of the 1993 Act may still proceed to enforce payment of the confiscation order (see s.13 of Criminal Justice Act 1993, amending s.6 of the DTOA).

(7) In a proper case, the court may vary or discharge the confiscation order (s.14 of the DTOA (and note s.16 of the Criminal Justice (International Cooperation) Act 1990)). The powers of the court in this regard have been substantially widened and strengthened, thus:

  (a) formerly only a defendant could vary an order under s.14 of the DTOA, but now a receiver appointed under s.8 or 11 of the DTOA may also apply under s.14

  (b) third parties may now make representations (s.11(4) of the Criminal Justice Act 1993)

  (c) a court now has power to:

    (i) make a confiscation order where the evidence did not, originally, justify the making of such an order (s.12 of the Criminal Justice Act 1993);

    (ii) reassess whether the defendant has benefited from drug trafficking (s.12 of the Criminal Justice Act 1993);

    (iii) revise its assessment of the value of the defendant's proceeds of drug trafficking (s.12 of the Criminal Justice Act 1993).

The Court of Appeal has advised judges to state the relevant findings at each stage of the proceedings, *per* Neill L.J. in *R.* v. *Johnson* [1991] 2 Q.B. 249, 260.

Additionally, the court may now proceed to sentence the defendant before embarking upon a DTOA enquiry (s.1A(7) of the DTOA) and to postpone a determination of the confiscation enquiry within the terms of s.1A of the DTOA as inserted by s.8 of the Criminal Justice Act 1993.

Previously, when the court made a confiscation order, it had to determine the amount to be recovered from the defendant before sentencing him (s.1(4) of the DTOA). This is no longer the case and the court may in certain circumstances postpone determinations under the DTOA but proceed to sentence the defendant (s.1A(7) of the DTOA, inserted by s.8 of the 1993 Act). Furthermore, the court was obliged to take account of the order before imposing a fine (s.1(5)(b)(i) of the DTOA), or before making an order under s.27 of the MDA 1971 (forfeiture orders) or s.43 of the Powers of the Criminal Courts Act 1973 (as amended) (deprivation orders) (see DTOA, s.1(5)(b)(ii) and (iii)).

By s.1(5)(c) of the DTOA, the court is obliged to leave the confiscation order out of account in deciding the appropriate sentence to be passed on the defendant (but see *R.* v. *Bragason* [1988] Crim.L.R. 778; *R.* v. *Harper (Terence)* [1989] 11 Cr.App.R.(S.) 240, C.A.; and *R.* v. *Saunders (Raymond)* (1990) 12 Cr.App.R.(S.) 344, C.A.).

Upon the making of a confiscation order, the prosecution may ask the High Court to appoint a receiver to realise assets that are held either by the defendant, or by persons to whom the defendant has directly or indirectly made a "gift" for the purposes of the Act (see ss.5 and 11 of the DTOA). Property realised by the receiver may then be applied towards satisfying the order (see ss.12 and 13 of the DTOA). Special rules will apply in the case of any person (not just the defendant) who is adjudged to be bankrupt but who nevertheless holds "realisable property" (see ss.15 and 16 of the DTOA). Special rules also apply to companies which are in the process of being wound up but which possess realisable property (s.17 of the DTOA).

In order to avoid the risk that a defendant may be tempted to dispose of his assets before a court can confiscate them, the High Court is empowered, upon the application of the prosecutor, to grant a restraint order prohibiting any person from dealing with "realisable property" except as directed by the court (ss.7 and 8 of the DTOA). Furthermore, a receiver may be appointed to take possession of any realisable property and to manage or to otherwise deal with that property (s.8(6) of the DTOA) and note s.24(1) of the 1993 Act which gives the county court for the purposes of s.8(6) of the DTOA.

It is desirable, in cases where a confiscation order has not yet been made, to register a charge on the property to secure the payment of moneys to the Crown. The DTOA provides the necessary machinery for doing so by virtue of s.9. Accordingly, the High Court may, upon the application of the prosecutor, grant a charging order (*ex parte* if necessary) and may appoint a Receiver to take possession of the property (s.11 of the DTOA).

Where a defendant is aggrieved that the prosecution has detrimentally meddled in his financial affairs, and proceedings do not result in a conviction for a drug trafficking offence, he may apply to the High Court for an order of compensation to be paid to him (s.19 of the DTOA (as amended)). There must be "serious default" on the part of a person concerned in the investigation or prosecution of the offence in question resulting in the loss but "the court shall not order compensation to be paid in any case where it appears to the court that the proceedings would have been instituted or continued if the serious default had not occurred (Sched. 5 to the Criminal Justice Act 1988). It is no longer necessary to show that the loss is "substantial". The "amount of compensation . . . shall be such as the High Court thinks just in all the circumstances of the case" (s.19(3) of the DTOA; see the amendments made to that section by s.15 of the 1993 Act).

Is a confiscation order a sentence?

Nothing in the 1993 Act alters the existing law in this regard. Section 9 of the Criminal Appeal Act 1968 states that a person "may appeal to the Court of Appeal against any sentence . . . passed on him for the offence". At first sight, a confiscation order is not passed on the defendant in respect of the offence, or offences, for which he appeared before the court. It is not a penalty but an order of deprivation. By s.50(1) of the Criminal Appeal Act 1968 a sentence includes "any order made by a court when dealing with an offender". In *Johnson* (*supra*), the Court of Appeal held that despite the wording of s.1(4) and (5) of the DTOA a confiscation order does form part of the sentence because the powers of the High Court in relation to a confiscation order can only be exercised where the order is not subject to appeal (see ss.11(1)(b) and 39(13) of the DTOA). Confiscation orders can be made by the Criminal Division of the Court of Appeal (see DTOA, s.6(6)). Finally, the court found support in the words of Lord Widgery C.J. in *R. v. Hayden* [1975] 1 W.L.R. 852, 854G, when he said that an order for costs comes within the definition of "sentence" in s.50(1) of the Criminal Appeal Act 1968 because "it is an order which is contingent upon there having been a conviction and it is contingent on the person by whom the payment is to be made, having been convicted in that way".

In Scotland the matter is put beyond doubt by s.1(4) of the Criminal Justice (Scotland) Act 1987.

However s.1(5)(c) of the DTOA states that the court should "leave the order out of account in determining the appropriate sentence or other manner of dealing with the defendant". The sentiments expressed in s.1(5)(c) are consistent with the general principles of sentencing that an accused is entitled to be sentenced on the basis of what is proved or admitted (to the criminal standard of proof) in respect of the offences for which he falls to be sentenced (see *R. v. Ayensu and Ayensu* (1982) 4 Cr.App.R.(S.) 248; *R. v. Ralf* (1989) 11 Cr.App.R.(S.) 121, C.A.; *R. v. Reeves (R. J.)* (1983) 5 Cr.App.R.(S.) 292, C.A.; *R. v. Bragason* [1988] Crim.L.R. 778; and see the provisions of the Criminal Justice Act 1991 which tend to support that approach).

In *R. v. Harper (Terence)* (1989) 11 Cr.App.R.(S.) 240, the Court of Appeal seems to have encroached on this principle in holding that the sentencer may pay some regard to the evidence placed before him under the DTOA if it rebuts an assertion made in mitigation, *e.g.* that the offence represented an isolated incident. In *R. v. Saunders (Raymond)* (1991) 92 Cr.App.R. 6, Hutchinson J. said (at p. 10):

". . . it would be absurd to say that if in the course of the Drug Trafficking Offences Act investigation the defendant, for example, admitted extensive drug trafficking, the sentencing judge should entirely disregard that in determining the appropriate sentence. He could and should take it into account in the manner indicated a moment ago".

The Court of Appeal in *Saunders* made two other important observations. The first is that the sentencer should be careful not to take into account factual matters of which the sentencer had not been satisfied beyond reasonable doubt, and this presumably remains the law notwithstanding s.1(7A) of the DTOA inserted by s.7 of the 1993 Act. The second point is that the sentencer should not use the assumptions, made under s.2(3) of the DTOA, to make a finding "adverse to the defendant in the realm of sentencing which he would not have made applying the ordinary burden of proof" (*ibid., per* Hutchinson J. at p. 10).

In Scotland, under the Criminal Justice (Scotland) Act 1987, the court is not obliged to sentence at the conclusion of the inquiry. Instead, the court may sentence the offender without delay and deal with the matter of confiscation at an adjourned date exceeding no more than six months after the date of conviction (s.2(1) of the Criminal Justice (Scotland) Act 1987).

Delaying Sentencing

Since a court was debarred from proceeding to sentence until the court had gone through the procedural steps under the DTOA, this often meant that sentence was adjourned for a considerable period of time in order to enable the parties to prepare and to present evidence and arguments in pursuance of the DTOA inquiry. Occasionally the DTOA inquiry is so complicated and protracted that the proceedings take longer to hear than the contested criminal trial itself. In *R.* v. *Smith (Ian)* [1989] 1 W.L.R. 765, the appellant was convicted on January 26, 1988 but sentence, and the making of a confiscation order in the sum of £14,000, was not imposed until May 6, after a three day hearing. In *R.* v. *Robson (Kenneth Steven)* (1991) 92 Cr.App.R. 1, there was a delay of some four months between conviction and sentence. It was difficult to see what justification there was for the mandatory position which then existed under the DTOA. One explanation was that the legislature considered that the court should not be in a position to sentence until all factual matters have been resolved, but this supposes that the sentencer would be entitled to have regard to the evidence placed before him under the DTOA. Under s.1A(7) of the DTOA (inserted by s.8 of the 1993 Act) the court may postpone a determination under s.1 but proceed to sentence the defendant.

Persons to whom s.1 of the DTOA applies

Confiscation orders may only be made against persons who appear before the Crown Court to be sentenced in respect of one or more "drug trafficking offences", a classification which, by s.38(1) of the DTOA (as amended) includes:

   (a) an offence under s.4(2) or (3) or 5(3) of the Misuse of Drugs Act 1971 (production, supply and possession for supply of controlled drugs);
   (b) an offence under s.20 of that Act (assisting in or inducing commission outside U.K. of offence punishable under a corresponding law);
   (c) an offence under:
       (i) s.50(2) or (3) of the Customs and Excise Management Act 1979 (improper importation);
       (ii) s.68(2) of that Act (exportation); or
       (iii) s.170 of that Act (fraudulent evasion), in connection with a prohibition or restriction on importation or exportation having effect by virtue of s.3 of the Misuse of Drugs Act 1971;
   (d) an offence under s.34 of this Act;
   (dd) an offence under ss.12, 14 or 19 of the Criminal Justice (International Co-operation) Act 1990;
   (e) an offence under s.1 of the Criminal Law Act 1977 or conspiracy to commit any of the offences in paragraphs (a) to (dd) above;
   (f) an offence under s.1 of the Criminal Attempts Act 1981 of attempting to commit any of those offences;
   (g) an offence of inciting another to commit any of those offences, whether under section 19 of the Misuse of Drugs Act 1971 or at common law; and
   (h) aiding, abetting, counselling or procuring the commission of any of those offences.

Only the Crown Court is empowered to make a confiscation order under s.1 of the DTOA. Although the section applies in cases where the defendant is committed by the magistrates' court to the Crown Court for sentence pursuant to s.38 of the Magistrates' Courts Act 1980, it does not apply to juveniles who are committed to the Crown Court with a view to being sentenced to youth custody under s.37 of the Magistrates' Courts Act 1980 (as amended by the Criminal Justice Act 1991) or where the powers of the court are limited to dealing with the defendant in a way in which a magistrates' court might have dealt with him in connection with the offence charged (DTOA, s.1(7)(b)). Accordingly, s.1 of the DTOA does not apply to defendants who appeal to the Crown Court against their conviction and/or sentence in the magistrates' court. Furthermore, s.1 has no application where a defendant has been "previously ... sentenced or otherwise dealt with in respect of his conviction for the offence or ... any of the offences concerned" (s.1(1)). Section 1 therefore does not apply to persons who are in breach of a community service order or a suspended sentence of imprisonment.

Making a Confiscation Order

If the court decides to embark upon an enquiry under s.1 of the DTOA it must first determine whether the defendant has benefited from drug trafficking (s.1(2) of the DTOA), and if he has, to determine the amount to be recovered (see ss.1(4) and 4 of the DTOA). Realistically, each element must be examined in the context of the other, since an amount can only be recovered if it represents a benefit of drug trafficking, and vice versa (and see *R.* v. *Simmons* [1993] Crim.L.R. 719).

Accordingly, one cannot divorce the method by which the court must determine whether the defendant has benefited from drug trafficking, from the procedure laid down in the Act for assessing the value of the defendant's proceeds of that trade. Section 1(4) of the DTOA provides (as amended by the 1993 Act) that:

"If the court determines that he has so benefited, the court shall, [before sentencing or otherwise dealing with him in respect of the offence or, as the case may be, any of the offences concerned,] determine in accordance with section 4 of this Act the amount to be recovered in his case by virtue of this section". [If the court proceeds under s.5A, B or C the words in square brackets should be omitted].

When one therefore looks at s.4(1), the "amount to be recovered" is to be equated with "the amount the Crown Court assesses to be the value of the defendant's proceeds of drug trafficking".

Note the words in square brackets. There will often be cases where an accused no longer holds capital and/or savings to that extent. The Act does not seek to make him bankrupt in those circumstances but, by s.4(3) of the DTOA, the "amount to be recovered" shall be the amount that can be "realised".

Determination of Benefit

The court must first determine whether the defendant has "benefited" from drug trafficking. If it is obvious that the defendant has obtained no benefit then nothing is to be gained by expending court time and money proceeding any further. The legislature may have originally contemplated that cases in which there was no discernible benefit would be weeded out speedily and expeditiously. Frequently the prosecution indicates to the court, upon conviction, that the defendant has received no benefit and the court is invited to make a nil confiscation order. In the author's experience the Customs and Excise often take a sensible, realistic and robust view in this regard.

In *R*. v. *Dickens* [1990] 2 Q.B. 102 Lord Lane C.J. appears to have had this approach in mind when he said (at p. 106):

"... the judge has to make a preliminary assessment as to whether it is or is likely to be a 'benefit' case or not. No doubt the evidence from the trial, if there has been one, or from a recital of the facts if there has been a plea, will be enough for him to form such a preliminary assessment".

This approach did not always find favour with the judiciary on the grounds that it was for the court to determine in every case whether the accused has benefited from drug trafficking or not; the court can only do this if it is fully informed of the defendant's financial affairs during the relevant period.

There are two broad ways in which pointless enquiries can be weeded out. First, by adopting the approach of Lord Lane C.J. in *Dickens* (see above) and by clarifying the circumstances in which the assumption may be invoked. Secondly, by abolishing the mandatory requirement to embark on a DTOA enquiry in every case where a defendant fails to be sentenced for a drug trafficking offence. The Home Office Working Group 1991 was unanimously in favour of the continuation of mandatory confiscation orders (May 1991, para. 2.5) but suggested that the way in which the court determines whether to invoke the assumption should be reformed. They considered that one approach would be to provide that "once an individual had been convicted of drug trafficking, the court should be required to assume that all property appearing to it to be in his possession (or which appears to have passed through his hands over the last six years, etc.) represents the proceeds of drug trafficking. *Only the application of the prosecutor could relieve the court from the requirement to make these assumptions although the court would retain the discretion to make the assumptions if it wished, even if the prosecutor recommended against.* Once the assumptions had been made, it would be up to the defendant to seek to persuade the court that the assumptions were inappropriate, either in regard to the whole of his property or specific items of it" [emphasis added, para. 2.6].

The question is whether the amendments made under the 1993 Act have that effect. Section 1 of the DTOA (as amended by s.7(1) of the Criminal Justice Act 1993) does give the prosecutor a discretion which may be overridden by the court. However, that discretion does not relate to the making of assumptions but solely as to whether to ask the court to embark upon an enquiry under the DTOA. It therefore follows that the Legislature did not adopt the recommendation of the Working Group that confiscation proceedings should be mandatory.

The Working Party also recommended that the DTOA should be amended to ensure that the court would make the assumptions in all cases, unless satisfied, from arguments produced by the defendant or any other information available to it, either during the trial or otherwise, that it would be inappropriate to do so. An example of this would be where the case was of such a minor nature that the procedure would not, in the judge's view, be warranted. The judge would, of course, not apply the assumptions where it was obvious that they were incorrect. Where the court concluded that the assumptions should not be applied, it would be required to state its reasons *and those reasons would be subject to challenge in a higher court* (emphasis added, para. 2.8).

The effect of s.2 of the DTOA, as amended by s.9 of the 1993 Act, is to provide that the court must make the assumptions unless (a) the assumption in question is shown to be incorrect in the defendant's case, or (b) the court is satisfied that there would be a serious risk of injustice in the case if the assumption were to be made. Note the phrase "serious risk". It could, perhaps, be argued that one of the considerations which the court would be entitled to take into account, when deciding whether to embark upon an enquiry under s.1(1) of the DTOA (as amended), is the appropriateness of making any of the assumptions under the Act for the reasons given, *inter alia*, by the Working Group (para. 2.8, above). It is not clear whether such an approach would be contrary to the intention of the Legislature. The Parliamentary debates provide little assistance on this point and it would have been a simple matter for the draughtsman to have included in s.2 a provision not dissimilar to that introduced into s.1(1) of the DTOA by s.7(1) of the 1993 Act. The absence of such a provision is not conclusive. The statutory exceptions set out in s.2(2A) of the DTOA (see s.9(3) of the Criminal Justice Act 1993) are not free of difficulty. Who raises an issue under s.2(2A)(b)? Would *any* risk of injustice (which is not merely fanciful) be regarded by the courts as a "serious" one given the consequences that will flow from the making of an assumption? Even if the reasons stated for not applying the assumptions under s.2(2B) of the DTOA are erroneous, that does not seem to entitle the prosecution to apply for reassessment under s.5B of the DTOA (see s.12 of the 1993 Act), nor is it clear that the prosecutor would be entitled to seek Judicial Review of a judge's decision in the light of his stated reasons.

Under the Scottish legislation, the High Court is not required, as a first step, to determine whether the defendant has benefited from drug trafficking. This is because the making of a confiscation order is in any event discretionary. The High Court is swiftly directed to assess the value of the defendant's proceeds of drug trafficking in accordance with s.3 of the Criminal Justice (Scotland) Act 1987.

Definition of Benefit
The phrase "benefited from drug trafficking" is a term which falls to be construed in accordance with s.1(3) of the DTOA (*supra*), and see s.38(2). A benefit under the 1993 Act continues to have the following features:
   (i) it must be a payment or other reward;
   (ii) it must be received by a person;
   (iii) the payment must be received in connection with drug trafficking;
   (iv) the drug trafficking must have been carried on by the recipient or another;
   (v) the recipient must know that the payment or reward was made "in connection with drug trafficking" (*R.* v. *Richards* [1992] 2 All E.R. 573).

(2) QUANTIFYING THE DEFENDANT'S PROCEEDS OF DRUG TRAFFICKING
The second step is for the court to assess the value of the defendant's proceeds of drug trafficking. Note the word "value". What has to be recovered prima facie is the value of the defendant's proceeds of drug trafficking (s.4 of the DTOA) and not necessarily the value of tangible assets known to exist in the hands of the defendant.

The initial calculation involves aggregating all gross receipts received in connection with drug trafficking and then revaluing the total amount if necessary under s.5(5) of the DTOA to reflect inflation, profitable investment or market fluctuation. The severity of that calculation may be mitigated by the provisions of s.4(3), which provide that the amount to be recovered under the confiscation order is the amount that might be realised if that amount is less than the value of the defendant's proceeds of drug trafficking. The court is concerned with "proceeds", not profit, and therefore the expense involved in buying, selling, transporting or distributing the drug is irrelevant and the court can make no deduction in respect of drug proceeds reinvested in another purchase of drugs (see *R.* v. *Smith* (*Ian*) [1989] 1 W.L.R. 765; *R.* v. *McDonald* (*Gregor Ian*) (1990) 12 Cr.App.R.(S.) 457; and *R.* v. *Comiskey* (1991) 193 Cr.App.R. 227).

A "payment" or "other reward" may be cash but it may also be a benefit in kind, *e.g.* an airline ticket (see *R.* v. *Osei* [1988] Crim.L.R. 775). A payment or reward may also be a "gift", a chose in action or another intangible (see s.38(1) of the DTOA). It does not matter when the payment or reward was received by the defendant. There is no time limit as to how far back the prosecution may scan. Thus, payments made before the commencement of the Act are included. The payment must be actually received by the defendant; presumably an offer to advance a payment or reward cannot be taken into account; and similarly a payment which has been misdirected (*i.e.* forwarded to another individual in error) cannot feature in the calculation. It does not matter whether the payment is in connection with the defendant's drug trafficking or someone else's (see s.2(1)(a) of the DTOA).

The practical effect of s.2(1) of the DTOA may be summarised as follows. If the prosecution can prove that a payment or reward was received by the defendant at any time and if it can be proved to be connected with drug trafficking, then such a payment represents the "proceeds" of drug trafficking for the purposes of the Act. Obviously, there will be many occasions when the prosecution cannot prove the link between a payment and a drug trafficking offence—however suspicious the circumstances of its receipt may seem. Parliament therefore requires the court to make certain "assumptions" concerning the origin of property received by the accused in the circumstances set out in s.2(3) of the DTOA and the court may take into account any statement tendered by the prosecution as to any matters relevant "to the assessment of the value" of the defendant's proceeds of drug trafficking (s.3(1) of the DTOA).

Although the DTOA provides that a defendant may also tender a statement to the Crown Court (s.3(4)) it seems that the contents of that statement should be confined to matters relevant to determining "the amount that might be realised" rather than the value of any payments or rewards received by him; assessing the statement is to be conclusive of the matters to which it relates within the terms of s.3(4).

The assumptions

Section 2(2) of the DTOA (as amended by s.9 of the 1993 Act) provides:
"The Court shall, for the purpose of determining whether the defendant has benefited from drug trafficking and, if he has, of assessing the value of his proceeds of drug trafficking, make the required assumptions".

New subss. (2A) and (2B) provide:
(2A) The court shall not make any required assumption if—
   (a) that assumption is shown to be incorrect in the defendant's case; or
   (b) the court is satisfied that there would be a serious risk of injustice in his case if the assumption were to be made.
(2B) Where the court does not apply one or more of the required assumptions it shall state its reasons.

By section 2(3) (as amended by s.9 of the 1993 Act) the required assumptions are:
"(a) that any property appearing to the court—
   (i) to have been held by [the defendant] at any time since his conviction, or
   (ii) to have been transferred to him at any time since the beginning of the period of six years ending when the proceedings were instituted against him,
was received by him, at the earliest time at which he appears to the court to have held it, as a payment or reward in connection with drug trafficking carried on by him,
(b) that any expenditure of his since the beginning of that period was met out of payments received by him in connection with drug trafficking carried on by him, and
(c) that, for the purpose of valuing any property received or assumed to have been received by him at any time as such a reward, he received the property free of any other interests in it".

If the court makes any of the assumptions specified in s.2(3) of the DTOA then (as is apparent from the wording of that section), it will be made on the basis that the defendant has received a payment or reward in connection with drug trafficking carried on by him and by no-one else.

Previously, the court had a discretion whether or not to invoke any of the statutory assumptions but the DTOA, as originally drafted, did not indicate the circumstances in which it was appropriate to apply them and there existed a conflict of authority (see *R.* v. *Redbourne* (1990) 96 Cr.App.R. 201, and see *R.* v. *Rose* [1993] Crim.L.R. 407. See also "Making Statutory Assumptions Under the Drug Trafficking Offences Act" (R. Fortson, *Archbold News*, Issue No. 5, May 28, 1993); and the Report of the Home Office Working Group on the Drug Trafficking Offences Act 1986 (1991) (para. 2.6)).

By virtue of s.2 of the DTOA, the trial judge should not make any of the assumptions specified in s.2(3) to the extent that "any of the assumptions are shown to be incorrect in the defendant's case", or if "the court is satisfied that there would be a serious risk of injustice in his case if the assumptions were to be made" (s.2(2A)(b) of the DTOA).

Shown to be Incorrect

As originally drafted, the only exception to appear in s.2(2) of the DTOA was to the extent that "any of the assumptions are shown to be incorrect in the defendant's case". It follows that the working of s.2(2A)(a) of the DTOA is essentially the same. In *R.* v. *Dickens* [1990] 2 Q.B. 102, it was held that the burden of proving an assumption to be incorrect falls on the defendant. With this proposition the Home Office Working Group appears to have no quarrel (see paras. 2.8 and 2.10(iv)).

One reading of s.2(2A)(a) of the DTOA suggests that this need not necessarily be so if the words "the defendant's case" as they appear in s.2(2A)(a) are to be treated as being synonymous in meaning with the words "in the case against the defendant". It would have been very easy for the draftsman simply to have used the words "shown to be incorrect by the defendant". If the evidence in the case, no matter who adduces it, shows an assumption to be incorrect, then the court may not make it.

In para. 2.10(iv) of their Report (1991), the Home Office Working Group suggested that the onus should be on the defendant to rebut the assumption, but (somewhat inconsistently) they also suggested that the court need not make the assumption if "for any other reason" it would not be appropriate to do so (para. 2.10(ii)).

In *R.* v. *Johnson* [1991] 2 Q.B. 249 the appellant received a cheque for £6,750 which had been credited into her account. A few days later the bank debited the account on the basis that the cheque was dishonoured on presentation. The court was entitled to make the assumption that the appellant received a payment in connection with drug trafficking but the cheque was plainly of no value as it was dishonoured, and thus the assumption (if made) would be shown to be incorrect by proof (whoever adduced the evidence) that the cheque had no value. Again, a motor car was bought by the appellant for £6,000 of which £5,600 was obtained by way of a loan from a finance house. The judge was entitled to make the assumption, prima facie, that she held the car and received it as a payment or reward in connection with drug trafficking carried on by her. However, there was no evidence that the money from the finance company was tainted and so the assumption would again be shown to be incorrect in the defendant's case.

Serious Risk of Injustice

Would *any* risk of injustice (which is not merely fanciful) be regarded by the courts as "serious" given the consequences that will flow from the making of an assumption? Even if the reasons stated for not applying the assumptions under s.2(2B) of the DTOA are erroneous, that does not seem to entitle the prosecution to apply for re-assessment under new s.5B of the DTOA (see s.12 of the 1993 Act), nor is it clear that the prosecutor would be entitled to seek Judicial Review of a judge's decision in the light of his stated reasons.

Weight Attaching to an Assumption

In *R.* v. *Redbourne* [1992] 1 W.L.R. 1182, the Court of Appeal also considered what the effect of the assumptions would be if they were not rebutted by or on behalf of the defendant. The short answer is that an assumed fact must be treated as being true. There would be little point in making an assumption if such a result were not to follow. The point is reinforced by the wording of s.2(2A) of the DTOA which includes a proviso in respect of the converse case where an assumption is shown to be "incorrect" in the defendant's case.

Although not expressly clarified by the DTOA, there is now clear authority that the prosecution has the task of proving both the fact that the defendant has benefited from drug trafficking and the extent of that benefit (*R.* v. *Dickens* [1990] 2 Q.B. 102 and *R.* v. *Enwezor* (1991) 93 Cr.App.R. 233). The 1993 Act does not alter the earlier position as to the incidence of proof.

The following example demonstrates the relevant principles now to be applied: suppose D is shown to have received a payment of £1,000 one year prior to proceedings being instituted against him for a drug trafficking offence. The burden rests on the prosecution to prove to the civil standard, that D received it in connection with drug trafficking carried on by him or another (s.2(1) of the DTOA) and that he therefore benefited to the sum of £1,000 (s.1(3)). Assuming there was no direct evidence that D received the money in connection with drug trafficking (but the prosecution can show that D was unemployed at the material time with no known sources of legitimate income) then the judge is entitled to find as a fact that the sum was "transferred to [the defendant]" during the relevant period (s.2(3)(a)(ii) of the DTOA) and that accordingly he "held it" at that moment (see s.38(7) and (10) of the DTOA). That fact alone is enough to enable the court to make the assumption under s.2(3)(a)(ii). Accordingly, the judge must assume that the sum was accordingly "received" by the defendant as a payment or reward in connection with drug trafficking carried on by the defendant (s.2(3)(a)(ii)).

In *R.* v. *Enwezor* (1991) 93 Cr.App.R. 233 the judge made a confiscation order of £20,000. A total of £11,000 had been paid into a building society account in the name of the appellant's sister. The appellant contended that the payments were made by various people coming from Nigeria and not (as alleged) by himself. The trial judge ruled that the payments into the account were gifts caught by the Act which represented the proceeds of drug trafficking and that the appellant had benefited by that amount. The judge said that "it is plain from the general tenor and working of the Act that the ordinary criminal burden and standard of proof is not applicable". He accordingly made his determination on the basis of the civil standard of proof. The judge added that "if the criminal standard of proof had applied I would not have found . . . against him". It was held on appeal that the judge was entitled to rely on the assumptions under s.2(2) and (3) of the DTOA but that the correct standard of proof was the criminal standard and that since the judge would have reached a different conclusion on that basis the appeal would be allowed.

In the light of s.1(7A) (inserted by s.7(2) of the 1993 Act) the result in *Enwezor* would be different.

Evidential Considerations

The defendant is of course entitled to call evidence during the hearing and he may seek an adjournment for that purpose (*R.* v. *Nicholson* (1990) 12 Cr.App.R.(S.) 58; and see *R.* v. *Jenkins* (*Paul*) (1990) 12 Cr.App.R.(S.) 582). If the defendant fails to keep proper records, but he has acquired and spent large sums of money (the origin of which he is not able to explain), then he runs the risk that the court will make findings adverse to him on the basis of the statutory assumptions under s.2(2) and (3) of the DTOA (see *R.* v. *Small* (*Michael*) (1989) 88 Cr.App.R. 184).

Joint Beneficiaries

Where two or more defendants have been engaged in a joint enterprise to commit a drug trafficking offence but one defendant is shown to have received more payments during the relevant period than the other, the court must determine the total value of the benefits received jointly and then determine the value of the benefit received by each of the defendants. In the absence of any evidence on the point, the sentencer may (but is not obliged to) assume that the defendants shared equally (see *R.* v. *Porter* (*Jeremy*) [1990] 1 W.L.R. 1260, but contrast that decision with *R.* v. *Chrastny* (*No. 2*) [1991] 1 W.L.R. 1385). There is nothing in the 1993 Act which alters the previous position.

Assets Held Abroad

By s.38(3), the DTOA applies to property whether it is situated in England and Wales or elsewhere (*R.* v. *Hopes* (1989) 11 Cr.App.R.(S.) 38).

The DTOA applies to all unlawful drug trafficking ventures wherever they are carried out (see s.38(1)) and the Act applies in respect of property held by the defendant anywhere in the world (see s.38(3)). The burden will therefore rest on the defendant to liquidate his assets or face the alternative of serving a consecutive sentence in default.

The approach adopted in *Hopes* appears to have differed from that in *R.* v. *Bragason* (1988) 10 Cr.App.R.(S.) 258 where the court assessed B's proceeds of drug trafficking at £15,000 but certified that the amount which might be realised from the assets which he held "in the jurisdiction" as nil. It is not clear whether the sentencer thought that it was necessary to assess the value of assets held by the defendant in England and Wales but, if he did, he was clearly in error (see also s.38(3) of the DTOA).

Ramifications of s.2(3) of the DTOA

Even if a defendant is convicted of supplying drugs over a very short period of time, the court is required (in appropriate cases) to assume that all property transferred to the defendant over the preceding six years (prior to the moment when proceedings were instituted against him) was a payment or reward made in connection with drug trafficking carried on by the defendant and moreover, that any expenditure made by the defendant over that period, came out of the proceeds of drug trafficking. Where property is proved to have been received by an accused and where there is no evidence at all to suggest that when he received it, the accused (or the transferor) were engaged in drug trafficking, then such a lack of evidence may of itself be the best evidence to show that the "assumptions", which the court can make under s.2(2) of the DTOA, are incorrect.

(3) Assessing The Amount That Might Be Realised

What is to be recovered by the court, under a confiscation order, is the amount which the Crown Court assesses to be the value of the defendant's proceeds of drug trafficking (s.4(1) of the DTOA). This figure represents the ideal.

However, the reality of the situation will often be that the defendant only has assets for a value which is lower than the amount which the court assesses to be the value of the defendant's proceeds of drug trafficking. The court may therefore reduce the value of the confiscation order and recover the lesser amount or a "nominal amount" (see s.4(3) as amended), but only within the terms of ss.4(3), 5(1) and (3) of the DTOA. The circumstances in which the court can confiscate a lesser amount are very limited and the following points should be borne in mind.

First, there exists no provision under the DTOA for reducing the amount on grounds of personal hardship. Accordingly, no reduction can be made on the basis that the only realisable asset held by the defendant is the matrimonial home (but see *R.* v. *Keston* (1990) 12 Cr.App.R. (S.) 93 where a contrary impression is given). On the other hand, it remains to be seen whether (by virtue of s.1(1) of the DTOA, as amended by s.7(1) of the 1993 Act) decisions taken by prosecutors and by the courts not to proceed under the DTOA, are influenced by considerations of hardship.

Secondly, the court must confiscate the full amount (being the defendant's proceeds of drug trafficking) unless it is satisfied that the lesser amount represents the "amount that might be realised" under s.4(3) of the DTOA. In those circumstances the court must make an order for the lesser amount. There is no halfway house.

"The amount that might be realised" is defined by s.5(3) of the DTOA. It is not the same thing as "realisable property" which is separately defined by s.5(1). In the majority of cases the practical effect is that the "amount that might be realised" under s.4 will be the value of the "realisable property", but this need not necessarily be so (see *R.* v. *Carroll* (*Thomas Anthony*) (1992) 13 Cr.App.R.(S.) 236).

Thirdly, any "realisable property" which forms part of the determination of the "amount that might be realised" under ss.4(3) and 5(3) of the DTOA need not, of itself, have been acquired with the proceeds of drug trafficking because the definition of "realisable property" in s.5(1) includes legitimately acquired property (*R.* v. *Chrastny* (*No. 2*) [1991] 1 W.L.R. 1385).

Fourthly, the burden will normally be on the defendant to satisfy the court of the matters referred to in s.4(3) of the DTOA but it would seem that in appropriate cases, the court may, of its own volition, make a determination under that subsection (see *R.* v. *Keston* (1990) 12 Cr.App.R.(S.) 93; *R.* v. *Comiskey* (1991) 93 Cr.App.R. 227; *R.* v. *Ilsemann* (*Horst Reiner*) (1990) 12 Cr.App.R.(S.) 398; and *R.* v. *Carroll* (*Thomas Anthony*) 1992 13 Cr.App.R.(S.) 236). The court is not obliged to determine the extent of the defendant's realisable assets in every case where the court proposes to make a confiscation order. This is because the Act places the burden on the defendant to satisfy the order or serve a consecutive sentence of imprisonment in default of payment (see *R.* v. *Ilsemann* (*Horst Reiner*) (1990) 12 Cr.App.R.(S.) 398).

The criteria
Section 4(3) of the DTOA (as amended) provides:
"If the court is satisfied that the amount that might be realised at the time the confiscation order is made [(or) a 'determination is made'] is less than the amount the court assesses to be the value of his proceeds of drug trafficking, the amount to be recovered in the defendant's case under the confiscation order shall be:
  (a) the amount appearing to the court to be the amount that might be so realised, or
  (b) a nominal amount, where it appears to the court (on the information available to it at the time) that the amount that might be realised is nil."

Definition of "Realisable Property"
Section 5(1) of the DTOA provides:
"In this Act, 'realisable property' means, subject to subsection (2) below—
  (a) any property held by the defendant; and
  (b) any property held by a person to whom the defendant has directly or indirectly made a gift caught by this Act."
"Realisable property" therefore includes property held by the defendant (s.5(1)(a) of the DTOA) but also gifts caught by the Act which are held by any person (s.5(1)(b)). Powers of the High Court are exercisable over realisable property (see ss.8, 9 and 11 of the DTOA).

Definition of the "amount that might be realised"
Section 5(3) of the DTOA (as amended) provides:
"For the purposes of [...] this Act the amount that might be realised at the time a confiscation order is made against the defendant is:
  (a) the total of the values at that time of all the realisable property held by the defendant less
  (b) where there are obligations having priority at that time the total amounts payable in pursuance of such obligations,
together with the total of the values at that time of all gifts caught by this Act".
Section 5(3) is concerned with values not limited to the value of realisable property. The draftsmen did not refer to "realisable property" in s.4 of the DTOA and this omission is deliberate. The Act contemplates a situation in which the defendant made gifts "caught" by the Act (as defined by s.5(9)), the value of which may be assessed for the purposes of ss.4 and 5(3), but which fall outside the strict definition of "realisable property" as set out in s.5(1) of the DTOA.

In *R.* v. *Dickens* [1990] 2 Q.B. 102, the Court of Appeal referred to the fact that "realisable property" and "amount that might be realised" were separately defined under the DTOA and meant two very different things. Lord Lane C.J. said (at p. 111):
"... the phrase 'realisable property' does not appear in s.4 of the Act and in particular does not appear in s.4(3). If Parliament had wished the confiscation order to be confined to the defendant's 'realisable property' as defined by s.5(1), then it would undoubtedly have said so in s.4(3), which it did not. We have no doubt that that was deliberate and was designed to ensure that drug traffickers could not protect the assets they had acquired through drug trafficking by 'giving' those assets to others".

Accordingly, the judge was entitled to look at the value of the gift made by D to his wife. That gift was caught by the DTOA (s.5(9)) and its value fell within the definition of "the amount that might be realised" (s.5(3)) for the purposes of s.4(3). The fact that the gift to the wife could no longer be physically realised was irrelevant.

Who raises the issue under s.4(3) of the DTOA?

In theory the court need only make two determinations before making a confiscation order. First, whether the defendant has benefited from drug trafficking and secondly, to assess the value of the defendant's proceeds of drug trafficking. In practice, the court will often need to go on and assess the amount that might actually be realised under s.4(3). However, the opening words, "If the court is satisfied ..." poses the question as to whether the court, of its own motion, should initiate the third stage or whether it is the defendant who must take the initiative and satisfy the court on a balance of probabilities that a lesser amount should be confiscated. In *R.* v. *Johnson* (1991) 2 Q.B. 249, Neill L.J. said (at p. 259):

"It is only necessary to make a calculation in accordance with s.4(3) of the 1986 Act if it appears that the amount that might be realised at the time that the confiscation order is made is less than the amount the court assesses to be the value of the defendant's proceeds of drug trafficking. In the present case it is accepted on behalf of the appellant that her proceeds were not less than £1,300."

Those last few words imply that it is for the defendant to initiate a determination under s.4(3) of the DTOA. However, *R.* v. *Keston* (1990) 12 Cr.App.R.(S.) 93 (wrongly referred to as *Preston* in [1990] Crim.L.R. 528) can be read as implying that in every case the court should determine "the amount that might be realised" under s.4(3). However, the judgment does not, in terms, go so far and such a statement would be at variance with *R.* v. *Johnson* [1991] 2 Q.B. 249, *R.* v. *Comiskey* (1991) 93 Cr.App.R. 227, *R.* v. *Ilsemann* (*Horst Reiner*) (1990) 12 Cr.App.R.(S.) 398 and *R.* v. *Carroll* (*Thomas Anthony*) (1992) 13 Cr.App.R.(S.) 99.

In *R.* v. *Dickens* [1990] 2 Q.B. 102 the Court of Appeal did remark that determining the "amount that might be realised" may overlap with the determination of the defendant's proceeds of drug trafficking.

In *R.* v. *Comiskey* (1991) 12 Cr.App.R.(S.) 562, Tucker J. asked whether there was anything to cause the judge to be satisfied that the amount that might be realised was less than the value of the defendant's proceeds of drug trafficking in circumstances where the appellant did not give evidence during the DTOA enquiry or call evidence.

The burden is certainly not on the Crown to satisfy the court under s.4(3) but, the mere fact that the defendant is normally in a better position to shoulder the burden does not therefore preclude the court, of its own motion, following the steps in s.4(3) (see the judgment of Tucker J. in *Comiskey* (at p. 567).

The authorities therefore seem to show that, under the Act, either the defendant or the court may take the initiative to make a determination under ss.4(3) and 5(3). Each case depends on its own facts. What has not been conclusively decided is whether the defendant carries merely an evidential burden under s.4(3) or whether he must go on and discharge the persuasive burden as well.

Evidential or persuasive burden under s.4(3) of the DTOA?

This is not a straightforward issue: see Fortson, *Law on the Misuse of Drugs and Drug Trafficking Offences* (Sweet & Maxwell 1992, 2ed., paras. 12–84). Given that the "amount to be recovered" under s.4(3) is the "amount that might be realised", it follows that any question as to the standard of proof is to be resolved by new s.1(7A) of the DTOA (see s.7(2) of the 1993 Act). Arguably s.1(7A) does not go far enough to make it plain whether the defendant always carries the persuasive burden but, in practice, the net effect is that the defendant will generally have the task of discharging not only the evidential burden but also the persuasive burden because, in reality, how else is he to satisfy the court of the relevant matters in s.4(3)? On first principles, evidence of any witness (including therefore a defendant) which is unchallenged, is to be accepted as representing the truth of the matter testified on pain of punishment for perjury if the evidence subsequently transpires to be false. In *R.* v. *Johnson* [1991] 2 Q.B. 249, the Court of Appeal seems to have followed this approach (see *R.* v. *McDonald* (*Gregor Ian*) (1990) 12 Cr.App.R.(S.) 457).

The approach suggested above would result in little or no prejudice to the prosecution because where the court makes a confiscation order and later discovers that assets are available to the court which were originally unknown, then the court may vary the order under s.47 of the Supreme Court Act 1981 within the relevant time-limit (see *R.* v. *Miller* (*Tony*) (1991) 92 Cr.App.R. 191 and the provisions of the Criminal Justice (International Co-operation) Act 1990, s.16).

Quantifying the amount that might be realised

The "amount that might be realised" is defined by s.5(3) of the DTOA (as amended):

"For the purposes of [. . .] this Act the amount that might be realised at the time a confiscation order is made against the defendant is—

   (a) the total of the values at that time of all the realisable property held by the defendant less

   (b) where there are obligations having priority at that time the total amounts payable in pursuance of such obligations,

together with the total of values at that time of all gifts caught by this Act."

The calculation therefore involves the sum of the value of "realisable property" (defined by s.5(1)) plus the value of gifts caught by the Act (see s.5(9)) but excludes the total value of payments made in pursuance of obligations "having priority". Such obligations are specified in s.5(7) (as amended by s.12 of the 1993 Act) as follows:

"For the purposes of subsection (3) above, an obligation has priority at any time if it is an obligation of the defendant to—

   (a) pay an amount due in respect of a fine, or other order of a court, imposed or made on conviction of any offence, where the fine was imposed or order made before the confiscation order [(or) "determination"], or

   (b) pay any sum which would be included among the preferential debts (within the meaning given by section 386 of the Insolvency Act 1986) in the defendant's bankruptcy commencing on the date of the confiscation order or winding up under an order of the court made on that date".

Obligations having priority: s.5(3) and (7) of the DTOA

See *R. v. McDonald (Gregor Ian)* (1990) 12 Cr.App.R.(S.) 457.

Valuation and Revaluations

Provisions dealing with the revaluation of property and gifts to take account of changes in the value of money, successful investment and so on, are to be found in s.5(4) to (6).

The obvious importance of putting before the court up-to-date and accurate information regarding values and expenses cannot be too strongly emphasised if a fair order is to be made (*R. v. Lemmon (Kevin)* (1992) 13 Cr.App.R.(S.) 66).

It is not necessary that the assets must be proved to be the proceeds of drug trafficking for the purposes of ss.4(3) and 5(3) except in the case of gifts made more than six years prior to the institution of proceedings against him (see ss.5(1)(b) and 38(ii)); see also *R. v. Chrastny (No. 2)* [1991] 1 W.L.R. 1385 and *R. v. Chapman, The Times*, November 18, 1991).

Establishing an Interest in Property

Realisable property also includes a beneficial interest created under a resulting or constructive trust (see *R. v. Robson (Steven Kenneth)* (1991) 92 Cr.App.R. 1; see also *Eves v. Eves* [1975] 1 W.L.R. 1338 and *Grant v. Edwards* [1986] Ch. 638). In the latter two cases the court concluded that a beneficial interest was conferred in circumstances where the beneficiary had acted to her detriment. Accordingly, in *Robson*, the court reduced the confiscation order to £1,490.

Value of the Drugs

There is already clear authority for the proposition that proceeds which have been invested in buying drugs, which have then been sold and the proceeds of that sale rolled over into yet another purchase of drugs, all count towards the determination of the benefit received (*R. v. Smith (Ian)* [1989] 1 W.L.R. 765; see also *R. v. Butler* [1993] Crim.L.R. 320).

Actual value of property

There is authority for the proposition that the combined effect of s.5(1) and (3) of the DTOA is to suggest that what the court has to have regard to in determining the "amount that might be realised" is the actual property held by the defendant or by a person to whom he has given it (*R. v. Comiskey* (1991) 93 Cr.App.R. 227).

(4) THE SCOTTISH APPROACH

Most of the provisions of the DTOA do not apply to Scotland: see s.40. A Bill to recover the proceeds of drug trafficking was considered by the Scottish Grand Committee and the First Scottish Standing Committee in 1987. In May of that year, the Criminal Justice (Scotland) Act 1987 received Royal Assent. The Scottish model is also draconian but, unlike the Crown Court in England, the power of the High Court of Justiciary to make a confiscation order is discretionary. The court is not obliged to embark upon an investigation as to the extent of an accused's proceeds of drug trafficking every time the accused is convicted of a drug trafficking offence. Indeed the High Court of Justiciary can only exercise its discretion upon the application of the prosecutor who must make his application prior to sentence or before any part of it has been pronounced (Criminal Justice (Scotland) Act 1987, s.1(1)). The Government's view was that relatively few orders will be made in Scotland each year and this view is certainly being confirmed in practice. One merit of the Scottish model is the considerable saving of court time in cases where it is obvious from the outset that the defendant has no assets capable of being realised and where, after investigation by the court, a nil confiscation order is the only realistic order which the court can make. There is also force in the argument that the courts should be primarily concerned with serious cases of drug trafficking and this was one of the reasons why s.1 of the DTOA has now been modified (s.7(1) of the 1993 Act).

In England, even a solitary incident at the lowest end of the gravity scale was sufficient to trigger proceedings under the DTOA.

English courts remain obliged to make an order (if they can) for the total amount which the court assesses to be the value of the defendant's proceeds of drug trafficking (or the value of the accused's realisable property plus the value of the gifts caught by the Act). In Scotland such a figure represents not a mandatory amount to be confiscated, but a ceiling, which the High Court of Justiciary may confiscate. The overriding task of the High Court (if it makes an order) is to require the defendant to pay "such amount as the Court considers appropriate" which does not exceed that ceiling. The discretionary power of the court to determine an "appropriate" amount enables the court to arrive at a decision which does not deprive the defendant of all his assets with the consequential hardship which may descend upon innocent third parties.

Confiscation orders

Confiscation orders

7.—(1) In section 1 of the Drug Trafficking Offences Act 1986 (confiscation orders), in subsection (1), for "the court" there shall be substituted "then—

> (a) if the prosecutor asks it to proceed under this section, or
> (b) if the court considers that, even though the prosecutor has not asked it to do so, it is appropriate for it to proceed under this section,
>
> it".

(2) After subsection (7) of that section there shall be inserted—

> "(7A) The standard of proof required to determine any question arising under this Act as to—
>
> (a) whether a person has benefited from drug trafficking, or
> (b) the amount to be recovered in his case by virtue of this section,
>
> shall be that applicable in civil proceedings.".

(3) In subsection (3) of section 4 of the Act of 1986 (amount to be recovered under confiscation order), for the words from "the amount appearing" to the end there shall be substituted "—

> (a) the amount appearing to the court to be the amount that might be so realised, or
> (b) a nominal amount, where it appears to the court (on the information available to it at the time) that the amount that might be so realised is nil".

DEFINITIONS
"amount that might be realised": s.4(3) of the DTOA.
"amount to be recovered": ss.4(1) and 38(2) of the DTOA.
"benefited from drug trafficking": ss.1(3) and s.38(2) of the DTOA.
"drug trafficking": s.38(1) of the DTOA.
"nominal amount": s.7(3).
"standard of proof": s.7(3); s.1(7A) of the DTOA.

GENERAL NOTE

Subs. (1)
The effect of this provision has been largely dealt with above. In addition, it should be noted that the amendments to s.1(1) of the DTOA may also serve as a tactical device. In *R.* v.

Atkinson [1992] Crim.L.R. 749 and *R.* v. *Finch* [1992] Crim.L.R. 901, it was held that a defendant who agrees a "s.3 statement" or a schedule of assets; with the prosecution does not prevent the court making up its own mind and confiscating a higher figure. This was because the court was obliged to follow the steps set out in the DTOA as originally drafted. It follows that where (for example) a defendant gave considerable assistance to law enforcement agencies, he could not be "rewarded" by way of a "concession" made by the prosecution not to confiscate assets under a confiscation order which would result in the loss of his home or prized motor vehicle. The court was bound to confiscate such assets if it could. However, the effect of s.1(1) (as amended by s.7(1) of the Criminal Justice Act 1993) is to leave that possibility open although, clearly, the court has the final say by virtue of what is now s.1(1)(*b*) of the DTOA (see s.7(1) of the 1993 Act).

It is also anticipated that "minor cases" that do not attract a confiscation hearing under the new arrangements will continue to be dealt with by means of fines, forfeiture, orders and imprisonment (see *Hansard*, H.L. Vol. 222, col. 866).

Subs. (2)

Note the commentary, above, in respect of the standard of proof.

The effect of new s.1(7A) of the DTOA is to overrule the decisions of *R.* v. *Dickens* [1990] 2 Q.B. 102 and *R.* v. *Enwezor* (1991) 93 Cr.App.R. 233 in so far as they held that the criminal standard of proof applied at any stage of the proceedings (*Hansard*, H.L. Vol. 539, col. 1383).

The Home Office Working Group in their Report on the DTOA 1986 (1991) recommended that the civil standard of proof was the appropriate one. This seems to have been the Government's intention when the DTOA was being debated as a Bill. Lord Glenarthur (in proposing what is now s.2), said:

"The burden will remain on the prosecution, in the usual way, to prove beyond reasonable doubt that the defendant is guilty of the offence of which he is charged. Once a person has been convicted of a drug trafficking offence however, the onus *may* be placed on him to show which, if any, of his assets were *legitimately acquired* .... Such information is, however, very clearly within the knowledge of the offender ..." (emphasis added). (*Hansard*, H.L. Vol. 472, col. 92).

This approach was permitted by Art. 7 of the Vienna Convention 1988 which provides that "Each Party may consider ensuring that the onus of proof be reversed regarding the lawful origin of alleged proceeds or other property liable to confiscation, to the extent that such action is consistent with the principles of its domestic law and with the nature of the judicial and other proceedings."

The views of the Working Group are in marked contrast to the Home Affairs Committee who (in their 7th Report on *Drug Trafficking and Related Serious Crime*, 1989), accepted that a shift to the civil standard of proof would represent a "far reaching change in English criminal law" and they required further evidence of its necessity. The National Drugs Intelligence Coordinator did not "appear to favour this solution" (para. 8.2). The Home Office Affairs Committee recommended that the Home Office set up a Working Group whose membership consisted of representatives from the Home Office, H.M. Customs and Excise, the National Drugs Intelligence Unit, the Crown Prosecution Service and members representing the Association of Chief Police Officers. The views of the Criminal Bar Association were sought, by the Home Office, upon publication of the 1991 Report. For their part, the Criminal Bar Association expressed disquiet at such a shift. The views of other interested parties and bodies were also sought by the Home Office. It is apparent that at least one judge endorsed the recommendation of the Working Group that the civil standard should apply to decide the benefit, and the amount of the benefit and that the court should make the assumptions in all cases unless they are rebutted by the defendant (Standing Committee B, col. 79, June 8, 1993). It is not clear to what extent this represented the views of the majority of the judiciary.

Although the application of the criminal standard of proof was not welcomed by the Government, or by the law enforcement agencies, it is difficult to test objectively (and not just by anecdotal accounts) whether the criminal standard has in practice made the task of confiscating drug profits more difficult. Certainly, the result in *R.* v. *Enwezor* (1991) 93 Cr.App.R. 233 would have been different if the civil standard had been upheld but, in the majority of cases, the task of the prosecution was "considerably lightened" by the assumption which the court previously had a discretion to make (see Lord Lane C.J. in *R.* v. *Dickens* [1990] 2 Q.B. 102). That task would now be lightened still further given the mandatory effect of s.2(2) of the DTOA as amended by s.9(2)(a) of the 1993 Act. Note that an assumption made under s.2(3) of the DTOA proceeds on the basis that the payment or expenditure was made in connection with drug trafficking carried on by the defendant and by no one else. The making of an assumption results in a grave finding of fact and thus, given both the consequences of such a finding, as well as the 'stigma' which it inevitably attracts, it is conceivable that the courts will require a high degree of probability in any event.

As Lord Ackner pointed out during the debates, proof on the civil basis varies in its weight according to what has to be proved (*Hansard*, H.L. Vol. 540, col. 1472) and see the judgment of Denning L.J. in *Bater* v. *Bater* [1951] P. 35, 36–7. See also *Blyth* v. *Blyth* (*No. 2*) [1966] A.C. 643.

A proposed amendment to the Bill, substituting the phrase "a balance of probabilities" in place of "the civil standard", was withdrawn (*Hansard*, H.L. Vol. 540, col. 1474).

Note that what is now s.1(7A) of the DTOA is limited to two broad questions only. The "amount to be recovered" is a term of art employed in ss.1(4) and 4(3) of the DTOA. That term is to be distinguished from the "amount that might be realised" which is another term of art—employed in ss.4(3) and 5. Given that the "amount to be recovered" could be assessed to be the "amount that might be realised" it follows that any question as to the standard of proof applicable to an assessment under s.4(3) is the civil standard by virtue of s.1(7A).

Subs. (3)
See the general commentary in relation to this provision. In the ordinary way the amount to be recovered is the amount the court assesses to be the defendant's proceeds of drug trafficking. Usually, the defendant will not be able to pay the full amount and thus the court will realistically look to confiscate the "amount that might be realised". Frequently that figure is nil. Originally, when the DTOA was enacted, the prosecution could not apply to vary the order if assets held by the defendant (at the time the order was made) subsequently came to light or the value had subsequently increased. This was remedied by s.16 of the Criminal Justice (International Co-operation) Act 1991. However, s.16 of the 1990 Act only bites if "an amount" was determined under s.4(3) of the DTOA and thus s.16 could not apply where the amount was nil. Assets originally hidden, and which subsequently surfaced after a nil order was made, escaped the s.16 procedure. For this reason s.7(3) of the 1993 Act was introduced to fill that loop-hole.

Postponed determinations

8. The following section shall be inserted in the Drug Trafficking Offences Act 1986, after section 1—

"Postponed determinations
1A.—(1) Where the Crown Court is acting under section 1 of this Act but considers that it requires further information before—
    (a) determining whether the defendant has benefited from drug trafficking, or
    (b) determining the amount to be recovered in his case by virtue of section 1 of this Act,
it may, for the purpose of enabling that information to be obtained, postpone making the determination for such period as it may specify.
    (2) More than one postponement may be made under subsection (1) above in relation to the same case.
    (3) Unless it is satisfied that there are exceptional circumstances, the court shall not specify a period under subsection (1) above which—
    (a) by itself, or
    (b) where there have been one or more previous postponements under subsection (1) above or (4) below, when taken together with the earlier specified period or periods,
exceeds six months beginning with the date of conviction.
    (4) Where the defendant appeals against his conviction, the court may, on that account—
    (a) postpone making either or both of the determinations mentioned in subsection (1) above for such period as it may specify, or
    (b) where it has already exercised its powers under this section to postpone, extend the specified period.
    (5) A postponement or extension under subsection (1) or (4) above may be made—

(a) on application by the defendant or the prosecutor, or

(b) by the court of its own motion.

(6) Unless the court is satisfied that there are exceptional circumstances, any postponement or extension under subsection (4) above shall not exceed the period ending three months after the date on which the appeal is determined or otherwise disposed of.

(7) Where the court exercises its power under subsection (1) or (4) above, it may nevertheless proceed to sentence, or otherwise deal with, the defendant in respect of the relevant offence or any of the relevant offences.

(8) Where the court has so proceeded, section 1 of this Act shall have effect as if—

(a) in subsection (4), the words from "before sentencing" to "offences concerned" were omitted, and

(b) in subsection (5)(c), after "determining" there were inserted "in relation to any offence in respect of which he has not been sentenced or otherwise dealt with".

(9) In sentencing, or otherwise dealing with, the defendant in respect of the relevant offence or any of the relevant offences at any time during the specified period, the court shall not—

(a) impose any fine on him, or

(b) make any such order as is mentioned in section 1(5)(b)(ii) or (iii) of this Act.

(10) In this section—

(a) "the relevant offence" means the drug trafficking offence in respect of which the defendant appears (as mentioned in section 1(1) of this Act) before the court;

(b) references to an appeal include references to an application under section 111 of the Magistrates' Courts Act 1980 (statement of case by magistrates' court).

(11) In this section "the date of conviction" means—

(a) the date on which the defendant was convicted, or

(b) where he appeared to be sentenced in respect of more than one conviction, and those convictions were not all on the same date, the date of the latest of those convictions.".

DEFINITIONS

"amount to be recovered": s.4(1) of the DTOA.
"benefited from drug trafficking": ss.1(3) and 38(2) of the DTOA.
"date of conviction": s.8; s.1A(11) of the DTOA.
"relevant offence": s.8; s.1A(10) of the DTOA.

GENERAL NOTE

Previously the court was bound to determine the amount to be recovered under a confiscation order (and to make such an order if possible) before proceeding to sentence. This frequently led to long delays between conviction and sentence, but the inevitable desire to keep the delay to a minimum occasionally resulted in further assets being revealed after the confiscation was made. Lengthy and costly DTOA enquiries were also futile if the relevant conviction was quashed on appeal. Accordingly, s.8 amends s.1 of the DTOA and enables the court to postpone the determination of the question of benefit or the amount to be recovered under a confiscation order where the defendant has appealed against his conviction or where the court requires further information. Maximum periods are imposed by the relevant provisions.

S.1A(1) and (4) of the DTOA

In statutorily prescribed circumstances the period of postponement may be extended. The court may proceed to sentence the defendant notwithstanding a period of postponement or extension (s.1A of the DTOA).

S.1A(1) to (7) of the DTOA

It would seem that the power to postpone or grant an extension of time (even where the defendant appeals against his conviction) rests with the Crown Court. Unless there are "exceptional circumstances" the period of postponement may be for any period not exceeding six months, and the court may order one or several postponements providing the total period does not exceed six months from the date of conviction (see s.1A(3) and (11) of the DTOA). Where the defendant faced more than one trial (*e.g.* as a result of separate committals or separate trials ordered on severance of an indictment) the period of postponement runs from his latest conviction for a drug trafficking offence (s.1A(11) of the DTOA). (See also Standing Committee B, col. 62, May 27, 1993). This applies whether or not the convictions occurred at the same or different Crown Courts (Standing Committee B, *ibid.*).

In theory these provisions serve to present something of an administrative nightmare. Suppose D is convicted of a relevant offence. He is to be tried two months later at another court for another drug trafficking offence and that second trial is expected (and does) last for three months, to be followed by a third trial. In theory a series of postponements could be ordered until such time as the last conviction is served whereupon subsequent postponements must not exceed six months from the latest date of conviction. What would be the effect if the defendant (during the specified period) was committed for trial and convicted of another drug trafficking offence shortly before the expiration of the original six month period? Presumably the clock again starts from zero from the date of the latest conviction by virtue of s.11.

S.1A(9) of the DTOA
The purpose of this provision is merely to ensure that assets to monies are confiscated under the DTOA machinery.

S.1A(11) of the DTOA
Where the defendant appeals against a conviction the court may, for that reason alone, postpone a determination (as above). Where the period of six months has expired, the period may be further extended (s.1A(4)(b) of the DTOA but once the appeal is heard, the Crown Court must proceed with the DTOA enquiry within three months *unless* there are "exceptional circumstances" justifying a longer period. It is not easy to predict instances which the court could properly treat as "exceptional" but it is foreseeable that a lack of court time may be held to be one such exception (consider *R.* v. *Norwich Crown Court* (1993) 97 Cr.App.R. 145 and *R.* v. *Governor of Winchester Prison*, ex p. *Roddie*; *R.* v. *Southampton Crown Court*, ex p. *Roddie* [1991] 1 W.L.R. 303.

Assumptions about proceeds of drug trafficking

9.—(1) Section 2 of the Drug Trafficking Offences Act 1986 (assessing proceeds of drug trafficking) shall be amended as follows.
(2) In subsection (2)—
(a) for "may" there shall be substituted "shall"; and
(b) for the words from "following" to the end there shall be substituted "required assumptions".
(3) After subsection (2), there shall be inserted—
"(2A) The court shall not make any required assumption if—
(a) that assumption is shown to be incorrect in the defendant's case, or
(b) the court is satisfied that there would be a serious risk of injustice in his case if the assumption were to be made.
(2B) Where the court does not apply one or more of the required assumptions it shall state its reasons.".
(4) In subsection (3)—
(a) for "Those" there shall be substituted "The required"; and
(b) in paragraph (a)(i), for "him" there shall be substituted "the defendant".

DEFINITIONS
"proceeds of drug trafficking": ss.2(1)(a) and 38(2) of the DTOA.
"required assumptions": s.9(2); s.2(2A) of the DTOA.

GENERAL NOTE
This section should be read in conjunction with s.1(7A) of the DTOA inserted by s.7(2) of the 1993 Act (standard of proof). Once again Members of Parliament sought clarification and evidence that amendments to s.2 of the DTOA were necessary (Standing Committee B, col.

66, May 27, 1993). However, the Home Office did not maintain statistics on the number of cases in which assumptions had not been applied although the Minister of State for the Home Office referred to a "wealth of anecdotal evidence" that the previous provisions were unsatisfactory. The reasoning appears to have been that in cases where the prosecution could not determine whether property passing through the defendant's hands was legitimately acquired or not, then the prosecution could progress no further because there is no obligation on the offender to account for such property given that s.3(3) of the DTOA specifically does not require the defendant to account for an allegation that property represents the proceeds of drug trafficking. The 1993 Act does not amend s.3(3) of the DTOA to that extent but it does insert s.3A (by s.10(5)), which empowers the court to order the defendant to give it such information as may be specified in the order (s.3A(2)) and if the defendant fails, without reasonable excuse, to comply with that order then the court may draw such inference "as it considers appropriate" (s.3A(5)). If it is permissible to ask the defendant whether or not he admits that the property represents the proceeds of drug trafficking then it would seem to be open to the court (in appropriate cases) to draw an adverse inference if he fails to answer the question. Arguably, s.3A(5) of the DTOA is more "open-ended" than s.3(3) and thus the two provisions would not actually be in conflict. The reason for making assumptions mandatory would thus seem to be designed (in part) to lever the defendant into disclosing the origin of the property received by him—a lever which is then extended by s.3A(2) and (5).

Provision of information

10.—(1) Section 3 of the Drug Trafficking Offences Act 1986 (statements relating to drug trafficking) shall be amended in accordance with subsections (2) to (4).

(2) For subsections (1) and (2), there shall be substituted—

"(1) Where the prosecutor asks the court to proceed under section 1 of this Act or applies to the court under section 4A, 5A, 5B or 5C of this Act he shall give the court, within such period as it may direct, a statement of matters which he considers relevant in connection with—

(a) determining whether the defendant has benefited from drug trafficking, or

(b) assessing the value of his proceeds of drug trafficking.

(1A) In this section such a statement is referred to as a "prosecutor's statement".

(1B) Where the court proceeds under section 1 of this Act without the prosecutor having asked it to do so, it may require him to give it a prosecutor's statement, within such period as it may direct.

(1C) Where the prosecutor has given a prosecutor's statement—

(a) he may at any time give the court a further such statement, and

(b) the court may at any time require him to give it a further such statement, within such period as it may direct.

(1D) Where any prosecutor's statement has been given and the court is satisfied that a copy of the statement has been served on the defendant, it may require the defendant—

(a) to indicate to it, within such period as it may direct, the extent to which he accepts each allegation in the statement, and

(b) so far as he does not accept any such allegation, to give particulars of any matters on which he proposes to rely.

(1E) Where the court has given a direction under this section it may at any time vary it by giving a further direction.

(2) Where the defendant accepts to any extent any allegation in any prosecutor's statement, the court may, for the purposes of—

(a) determining whether the defendant has benefited from drug trafficking, or

(b) assessing the value of his proceeds of drug trafficking,

treat his acceptance as conclusive of the matters to which it relates.".

(3) In subsection (3), for "statement" there shall be substituted "prosecutor's statement in question".

(4) For subsection (5) there shall be substituted—

"(5) An allegation may be accepted, or particulars of any matter may be given, for the purposes of this section in such manner as may be prescribed by rules of court or as the court may direct.".

(5) The following section shall be inserted in the Act of 1986, after section 3—

"Provision of information by defendant

3A.—(1) This section applies where—

    (a) the prosecutor has asked the court to proceed under section 1 of this Act or has applied to the court under section 5A, 5B or 5C of this Act, or

    (b) no such request has been made but the court is nevertheless proceeding, or considering whether to proceed, under section 1.

(2) For the purpose of obtaining information to assist it in carrying out its functions, the court may at any time order the defendant to give it such information as may be specified in the order.

(3) An order under subsection (2) above may require all, or any specified part, of the required information to be given to the court in such manner, and before such date, as may be specified in the order.

(4) Crown Court Rules may make provision as to the maximum or minimum period that may be allowed under subsection (3) above.

(5) If the defendant fails, without reasonable excuse, to comply with any order under this section, the court may draw such inference from that failure as it considers appropriate.

(6) Where the prosecutor accepts to any extent any allegation made by the defendant in giving to the court information required by an order under this section, the court may treat that acceptance as conclusive of the matters to which it relates.

(7) For the purposes of this section, an allegation may be accepted in such manner as may be prescribed by rules of court or as the court may direct.".

(6) In section 5(3) of the Act of 1986 the words "sections 3 and 4 of" shall be omitted.

DEFINITIONS
    "benefited from drug trafficking": ss.1(3) and 38(2) of the DTOA.
    "drug trafficking": s.38(1) of the DTOA.
    "proceeds of drug trafficking": ss.2(1)(a) and 38(2) of the DTOA.
    "prosecutor's statement": s.3(1A) of the DTOA.
    "value of proceeds of drug trafficking": ss.2(1)(b) and 38(2) of the DTOA.

GENERAL NOTE

Evidence
    The judge is entitled to rely on the evidence given during the trial. The prosecution is not obliged to call or recall that evidence again during the drug trafficking investigation (*R.* v. *Jenkins* (*Paul*) (1990) 12 Cr.App.R.(S.) 582). The prosecution may rely and call evidence in respect of any statement or notice served by them in accordance with s.3 of the DTOA. As the Court of Appeal in *R.* v. *Comiskey* (1991) 93 Cr.App.R. 227 remarked:
    "Section 3 of the Act provides convenient and effective machinery for ascertaining matters relevant to the courts' determination of the amount to be paid under a confiscation order. It is very desirable that those responsible for the prosecution of offences should make full use of this".
    The court also pointed out the desirability, in appropriate cases, of inviting the defendant to indicate to what extent he accepts the Crown's allegations or, if he does not do so, to indicate any matters he proposes to rely on (see now s.3(1D) of the DTOA). Previously, a statement made out of court by a person not called as a witness cannot be admitted, except in accordance with established principles of admissibility at common law or under statute: see *R.* v. *Chrastny* (*No. 2*) [1991] 1 W.L.R. 1385.

It may be for this reason that allegations accepted or matters indicated for the purposes of s.3 of the DTOA which formerly could be presented either orally "before the court", or in writing in accordance with the Crown Court Rules (*i.e.* the old s.5(5)), may now be presented as "the court may direct" (s.3(5) of the DTOA, as amended by s.10(4) of the 1993 Act).

Putting the relevant party to "strict proof" of their case will often result in the contents of any statement tendered to the other side not being admitted for a variety of reasons, *e.g.* the statement infringes the hearsay rule. Where, for example, a prosecutor is in possession of information alleging that on certain dates valuable property was given to the accused, he may seek to embody those allegations in a statement which he can then serve on the defence by way of s.9 of the Criminal Justice Act 1967, in the hope that the statement will be accepted. In fact, if put to strict proof, the prosecutor might find that he cannot prove the contents at all.

Under the 1993 Act the procedure for the provision of information has been strengthened. The procedure applies not only to the usual situation where the court proceeds under s.1 of the DTOA following a conviction for a drug trafficking offence, but also where the court is asked to proceed under s.1 when it originally declined to do so (s.5 of the DTOA); or where the court is asked to reassess whether the defendant has benefited from drug trafficking (s.5B of the DTOA); or where the court revises its assessment of the proceeds of any trafficking (s.5 of the DTOA); and in cases where the defendant has died or absconded (s.4A of the DTOA). These new provisions were inserted by ss.12 and 14 of the 1993 Act.

Section 3(1) of the DTOA refers to a "statement of matters" which is the same thing as the "prosecutor's statement", the court may order him to serve one (s.3(1B)). Section 3(1D) is essentially the same provision as the old s.3(2) and what is now s.3(2) re-enacts s.3(1) as originally drafted.

Section 3 of the DTOA asks the court to adopt an inquisitorial role. The defendant may therefore be asked to state those matters (if any) which he proposes to rely on to refute an allegation contained in the statement tendered. The penalty, for a failure to comply with s.3, is set out in s.3(3). The defendant may thus be treated as accepting every allegation in the prosecutor's statement in question apart from: (a) any allegation in respect of which he has complied with the requirement; and (b) any allegation that he has benefited from drug trafficking or that any payment or other reward was "received by him in connection with drug trafficking" carried on by him or another.

Although it is obvious from the wording of s.3(3)(b) of the DTOA that the legislature was not prepared to go so far as to say that a defendant's non-compliance with the requirements of s.2 should be construed as an admission that he either benefited from drug trafficking, or that any payment or reward received by him represents the proceeds of that activity, the reality of the situation is that once the prosecution has established that the defendant has received property, it is open to the court to see if it may assume that the payment was received in connection with drug trafficking by virtue of s.2(2) and (3) of the DTOA.

Subs. (5)
Reference to this has been made in the notes to s.9 of the 1993 Act.

Subs. (6)
This merely tidies up the legislation having regard to the wide powers which the court now has to vary, and to confiscate, assets in the hands of a defendant, absconder or a deceased defendant.

Variation of confiscation orders

11.—(1) Section 14 of the Drug Trafficking Offences Act 1986 (variation of confiscation orders) shall be amended as follows.

(2) In subsection (1) (variation on application of defendant), after "defendant" there shall be inserted "or a receiver appointed under section 8 or 11 of this Act, or in pursuance of a charging order, made".

(3) In subsection (3), for "defendant" there shall be substituted "person who applied for it".

(4) The following shall be inserted at the end—

"(5) Rules of court may make provision—
(a) for the giving of notice of any application under this section; and
(b) for any person appearing to the court to be likely to be affected by any exercise of its powers under this section to be given an opportunity to make representations to the court.".

Variation by a Defendant or by a Receiver

Formerly, s.14 of the DTOA was limited to the defendant alone to apply for a variation of a confiscation order made under the 1986 Act. Two major changes have been introduced into this provision. First the application may be made either by the defendant or by a receiver appointed under s.8 or 11 of the DTOA (s.11(2) of the Criminal Justice Act 1993). Secondly, it addresses the concern expressed by members of the judiciary (among others) in respect of the interests of third parties who seemed (under the DTOA as originally drafted) no to have any *locus standi* in confiscation proceedings before the Crown Court. By contrast, third party representation was expressly catered for in the DTOA in respect of High Court proceedings where property was sought to be realised by a receiver (s.11 of the DTOA) or on an application to discharge or to vary a restraint or charging order under s.9 of the DTOA (*cf.* Standing Committee B, col. 81, June 8, 1993).

Variation by the Defendant

A variation of a confiscation order is to be carefully distinguished from an appeal against the making of an order. Where a defendant complains that the court erred in the determination of the order, *e.g.* in the assessment of the proceeds of drug trafficking, then the appropriate course is to appeal against the making of the order because such an order is a sentence for the purposes of ss.9 and 11 of the Criminal Appeal Act 1968 (see *R.* v. *Johnson* [1991] 2 Q.B. 249).

However, a variation of a confiscation order under DTOA is confined to a reduction in the amount of the order in cases where the defendant's realisable property is inadequate to satisfy the making of an order. Thus s.14(1) of the DTOA (as amended by s.11(1) of the 1993 Act) provides:

"If, on an application by the defendant or a receiver appointed under s.8(11) of this Act, or in pursuance of a Charging Order, made in respect of a confiscation order, the High Court is satisfied that the realisable property is inadequate for the payment of any amount remaining to be recovered under the order the court shall issue a certificate to that effect, giving the court's reasons".

Note that the High Court can do no more than to issue a certificate and to give its reasons for so doing. It cannot vary the order under s.14. Clearly if the defendant has been adjudged bankrupt then the court must take into account the extent to which his property will be distributed amongst his creditors. The court must also guard against the manipulative defendant who has taken steps to prevent the court seizing his assets (see s.14(2) of the DTOA).

By s.14(3), where a certificate has been issued under s.14(1), the *person who applied for it* (see s.11 of the 1993 Act) "may apply to the Crown Court for the amount to be recovered under the order to be reduced". The powers of the Crown Court are set out in s.14(4) of the DTOA.

It would seem that the Crown Court is obliged to substitute a lesser amount although the actual figure is entirely a matter for the court to decide. Even if the High Court were to quantify the amount by which the realisable property is inadequate to satisfy the order, the Crown Court is not obliged to vary the order to that extent but must substitute a lesser amount "as the court thinks just in all the circumstances of the case".

Nothing in s.14 of the DTOA requires the prosecution to be put on notice of an application under that section which, may therefore be made *ex parte*. However, it is difficult to imagine many applications proceeding on that basis and it is submitted that the appropriate course is for the prosecutor to be notified.

Revised assessment of proceeds of drug trafficking

12. The following sections shall be inserted in the Drug Trafficking Offences Act 1986, after section 5—

"Reconsideration of case where court has not proceeded under section 1

5A.—(1) This section applies where the defendant has appeared before the Crown Court to be sentenced in respect of one or more drug trafficking offences but the court has not proceeded under section 1 of this Act.

(2) If the prosecutor has evidence—

(a) which was not available to him when the defendant appeared to be sentenced (and accordingly was not considered by the court), but

(b) which the prosecutor believes would have led the court to determine that the defendant had benefited from drug trafficking if—

    (i) the prosecutor had asked the court to proceed under section 1 of this Act, and

    (ii) the evidence had been considered by the court,

he may apply to the Crown Court for it to consider the evidence.

(3) The court shall proceed under section 1 of this Act if, having considered the evidence, it is satisfied that it is appropriate to do so.

(4) In considering whether it is appropriate to proceed under section 1, the court shall have regard to all the circumstances of the case.

(5) Where, having decided to proceed under section 1, the court proposes to make a confiscation order against the defendant, it shall order the payment of such amount as it thinks just in all the circumstances of the case.

(6) In considering the circumstances of any case the court shall have regard, in particular, to the amount of any fine imposed on the defendant in respect of the offence or offences in question.

(7) Where the court is proceeding under section 1 of this Act, by virtue of this section, subsection (4) of that section shall have effect as if the words "before sentencing or otherwise dealing with him in respect of the offence or, as the case may be, any of the offences concerned" were omitted.

(8) The court may take into account any payment or other reward received by the defendant on or after the date of conviction, but only if the prosecutor shows that it was received by the defendant in connection with drug trafficking carried on by the defendant or another on or before that date.

(9) In considering any evidence under this section which relates to any payment or reward to which subsection (8) above applies, the court shall not make the assumptions which would otherwise be required by section 2 of this Act.

(10) No application shall be entertained by the court under this section if it is made after the end of the period of six years beginning with the date of conviction.

(11) In this section "the date of conviction" means—

(a) the date on which the defendant was convicted, or

(b) where he appeared to be sentenced in respect of more than one conviction, and those convictions were not all on the same date, the date of the latest of those convictions.

Re-assessment of whether defendant has benefited from drug trafficking

5B.—(1) This section applies where the court has made a determination ("the section 1(2) determination") under section 1(2) of this Act that the defendant has not benefited from drug trafficking.

(2) If the prosecutor has evidence—

(a) which was not considered by the court in making the section 1(2) determination, but

(b) which the prosecutor believes would have led the court to determine that the defendant had benefited from drug trafficking if it had been considered by the court,

he may apply to the Crown Court for it to consider that evidence.

(3) If, having considered the evidence, the court is satisfied that it would have determined that the defendant had benefited from drug trafficking if that evidence had been available to it, the court—

(a) shall—

(i) make a fresh determination under subsection (2) of section 1 of this Act; and

(ii) make a determination under subsection (4) of that section of the amount to be recovered by virtue of that section; and

(b) may make an order under that section.

(4) Where the court is proceeding under section 1 of this Act, by virtue of this section, subsection (4) of that section shall have effect as if the words "before sentencing or otherwise dealing with him in respect of the offence or, as the case may be, any of the offences concerned" were omitted.

(5) The court may take into account any payment or other reward received by the defendant on or after the date of the section 1(2) determination, but only if the prosecutor shows that it was received by the defendant in connection with drug trafficking carried on by the defendant or another on or before that date.

(6) In considering any evidence under this section which relates to any payment or reward to which subsection (5) above applies, the court shall not make the assumptions which would otherwise be required by section 2 of this Act.

(7) Where the High Court—

(a) has been asked to proceed under section 4A of this Act in relation to a defendant who has absconded, but

(b) has decided not to make a confiscation order against him, this section shall not apply at any time while he remains an absconder.

(8) No application shall be entertained by the court under this section if it is made after the end of the period of six years beginning with—

(a) the date on which the defendant was convicted; or

(b) where he appeared to be sentenced in respect of more than one conviction, and those convictions were not all on the same date, the date of the latest of those convictions.

Revised assessment of proceeds of drug trafficking

5C.—(1) This section applies where the court has made a determination under section 1(4) of this Act of the amount to be recovered in a particular case by virtue of that section ("the current section 1(4) determination").

(2) Where the prosecutor is of the opinion that the real value of the defendant's proceeds of drug trafficking was greater than their assessed value, the prosecutor may apply to the Crown Court for the evidence on which the prosecutor has formed his opinion to be considered by the court.

(3) In subsection (2) above—

"assessed value" means the value of the defendant's proceeds of drug trafficking as assessed by the court under section 4(1) of this Act; and

"real value" means the value of the defendant's proceeds of drug trafficking which took place—

(a) in the period by reference to which the current section 1(4) determination was made; or

(b) in any earlier period.

(4) If, having considered the evidence, the court is satisfied that the real value of the defendant's proceeds of drug trafficking is greater than their assessed value (whether because the real value was higher at the time of the current section 1(4) determination than was thought or because the value of the proceeds in question has subsequently

increased), the court shall make a fresh determination under subsection (4) of section 1 of this Act of the amount to be recovered by virtue of that section.

(5) Where the court is proceeding under section 1 of this Act, by virtue of this section, subsection (4) of that section shall have effect as if the words "before sentencing or otherwise dealing with him in respect of the offence or, as the case may be, any of the offences concerned" were omitted.

(6) Any determination under section 1(4) of this Act by virtue of this section shall be by reference to the amount that might be realised at the time when the determination is made.

(7) For any determination under section 1(4) of this Act by virtue of this section, section 2(5) of this Act shall not apply in relation to any of the defendant's proceeds of drug trafficking taken into account in respect of the current section 1(4) determination.

(8) In relation to any such determination—

  (a) sections 3(4)(a), 4(2) and 5(7) of this Act shall have effect as if for "confiscation order" there were substituted "determination";

  (b) section 4(3) of this Act shall have effect as if for "confiscation order is made" there were substituted "determination is made"; and

  (c) section 5(3) of this Act shall have effect as if for "a confiscation order is made against the defendant" there were substituted "of the determination".

(9) The court may take into account any payment or other reward received by the defendant on or after the date of the current section 1(4) determination, but only if the prosecutor shows that it was received by the defendant in connection with drug trafficking carried on by the defendant or another on or before that date.

(10) In considering any evidence under this section which relates to any payment or reward to which subsection (9) above applies, the court shall not make the assumptions which would otherwise be required by section 2 of this Act.

(11) If, as a result of making the fresh determination required by subsection (4) above, the amount to be recovered exceeds the amount set by the current section 1(4) determination, the court may substitute for the amount to be recovered under the confiscation order which was made by reference to the current section 1(4) determination such greater amount as it thinks just in all the circumstances of the case.

(12) Where the court varies a confiscation order under subsection (11) above, it shall substitute for the term of imprisonment or of detention fixed under section 31(2) of the Powers of Criminal Courts Act 1973 in respect of the amount to be recovered under the order a longer term determined in accordance with that section (as it has effect by virtue of section 6 of this Act) in respect of the greater amount substituted under subsection (11) above.

(13) Subsection (12) above shall apply only if the effect of the substitution is to increase the maximum period applicable in relation to the order under section 31(3A) of the Act of 1973.

(14) Where a confiscation order has been made in relation to any defendant by virtue of section 4A of this Act, this section shall not apply at any time while he is an absconder.

(15) No application shall be entertained by the court under this section if it is made after the end of the period of six years beginning with—

  (a) the date on which the defendant was convicted; or

(b) where he appeared to be sentenced in respect of more than one conviction, and those convictions were not all on the same date, the date of the latest of those convictions.".

DEFINITIONS
  "assessed value": s.12; s.5C(3) of the DTOA.
  "benefited from drug trafficking": ss.1(3) and 38(2) of the DTOA.
  "confiscation order": Sched. 5; ss.1(8) and 38 of the DTOA.
  "date of conviction": s.12; s.5A of the DTOA.
  "drug trafficking": s.38(1) of the DTOA.
  "drug trafficking offence": s.38(1) of the DTOA.
  "real value": s.12; s.5C(3) of the DTOA.

GENERAL NOTE

Variation and re-assessment by prosecution
  As originally drafted, the DTOA allowed a defendant to apply for a downward variation of the confiscation order but it did not give the court a power to vary or to reassess the amount to be recovered under a confiscation order if assets (or evidence relevant to determinations made under the Act) come to light after the making of an order. Reform, in this area, has been piecemeal which aggravates an already confused and difficult area of the law. There are three determinations to consider. First, whether the defendant has benefited from drug trafficking at all. If the answer is in the negative a "nil order" is made. Secondly, the amount which represents the total *proceeds* of the defendant's drug trafficking. Thirdly, the "amount that might be realised" under ss.4(3) and 5(3) of the DTOA. If that figure is nil then, again, a "nil order" is made. The Criminal Justice (International Co-operation) Act 1990 amended the law in respect of the third determination but it did not touch the first two (and see para. 4.1 of the Working Group Report (1991)).
  Reforms introduced by s.12 of the 1993 Act therefore address the problems associated with the first two determinations. (a) Section 12 introduces s.5A into the DTOA and empowers the Crown Court to embark upon a drug trafficking enquiry when it had earlier declined to do so. This provision is particularly significant given that by s.1(1) of the DTOA (as amended now by s.7(1) of the 1993 Act) a court may not be asked to proceed under s.1 of the DTOA in every case; (b) by s.5B of the DTOA, the court, which *did* embark upon an enquiry but nevertheless concluded that there was no benefit received by the defendant, can now reassess that determination if new evidence becomes available; (c) by s.5C of the DTOA, the court may reassess the value of the defendant's *proceeds* of drug trafficking if new evidence comes to light. Prosecutors will be anxious to keep this figure under review because it represents the maximum that can be recovered under a confiscation order. Accordingly, where the prosecutor successfully applies to the Crown Court for an increased confiscation order on the basis that there were more realisable assets in existence than at first known (*i.e.* under s.15 of the Criminal Justice (International Co-operation) Act 1990) it follows that the new order cannot exceed the amount originally determined to be the value of the defendant's proceeds of drug trafficking.
  Common to each of these new provisions (ss.5A, 5B and 5C) is a six year time-limit which runs from the date of the defendant's last conviction for a drug trafficking offence in respect of which he appeared before the Crown Court to be sentenced at the time the confiscation order was made.
  These provisions have been attacked as "hounding" a man who has been convicted (*Hansard*, H.L. Vol. 539, col. 1357) and it is perhaps to this end that s.5A(4) of the DTOA was enacted (in so far as that subsection affects s.5A) but even where a court is required to make a determination under s.5B or 5C, the court is not entitled to rely on any of the statutory assumptions under s.2 of the DTOA (and similarly in respect of s.5A). Furthermore, under both s.5A and 5C the court appears to be entitled to mitigate the amount to be confiscated as is "just in all the circumstances" (see s.5A(5) and 5C(11)).
  By an ingenious route, the prosecution in *R.* v. *Miller (Tony)* (1991) 92 Cr.App.R. 191 successfully applied for a variation of the order by invoking the provisions of s.47 of the Supreme Court Act 1981 in circumstances where further assets held by the defendant at the time the order was made, were discovered. This route might not be appropriate in all cases and, in any event, the procedure is subject to time limits (normally 28 days) (see also *R.* v. *Onwuka* (1992) 95 Cr.App.R. 47).
  In 1990, Parliament enacted the Criminal Justice (International Co-operation) Act 1990 and took the opportunity to amend the law. Parliament did not, technically speaking, amend the

DTOA itself but, by s.16 of the 1990 Act, the prosecution is now entitled to apply for a variation in the limited circumstances specified below:

"(1) This section has effect where by virtue of s.4(3) of the Drug Trafficking Offences Act 1986 (insufficient realisable property), the amount which a person is ordered to pay by a confiscation order is less than the amount assessed to be the value of his proceeds of drug trafficking.

(2) If, on an application made in accordance with subsection (3) below, the High Court is satisfied that the amount that might be realised in the case of the person in question is greater than the amount taken into account in making the confiscation order (whether it was greater than was thought when the order was made or has subsequently increased) the court shall issue a certificate to that effect, giving the court's reasons.

(3) An application under subsection (2) above may be made either by the prosecutor or by a receiver appointed under the said Act of 1986 in relation to the realisable property of the person in question.

(4) Where a certificate has been issued under subsection (2) above the prosecutor may apply to the Crown Court for an increase in the amount to be recovered under the confiscation order; and on that application the court may—

    (a) substitute for that amount such amount (not exceeding the amount assessed as the value referred to in subsection (1) above) as appears to the court to be appropriate having regard to the amount now shown to be realisable; and

    (b) increase the term of imprisonment or detention fixed in respect of the confiscation order under subsection 2) of section 31 of the Powers of Criminal Courts Act 1973 (imprisonment in default of payment) if the effect of the substitution is to increase the maximum period applicable in relation to the order under subsection (3A) of that section."

Similar amendments were made to the Scottish Law by s.17 of the 1990 Act (see s.1(1)(b) of the Criminal Justice (Scotland) Act 1987).

It will be seen from the wording of s.16 of the 1990 Act that the High Court is not itself empowered to vary the order. It can do no more than to certify that the facts set out in s.16(2) exist and to leave it to the Crown Court to substitute an amount that is "appropriate" (s.16(4)(a)) and to increase the default period accordingly (s.16(4)(b)).

Note that s.16 of the 1990 Act does not apply to property which comes into the possession of the defendant after the order is made. Furthermore, an application made under s.16 is subject to a ceiling, namely, the amount which the Crown Court assessed to be the proceeds of the defendant's drug trafficking. That figure will often be calculated on the basis of what was believed to be the defendant's financial position, over the relevant period, at the time the original order was made. The Home Office Working Group on Confiscation suggests that the Crown Court should be empowered to make a fresh order on the basis of a reassessment of the extent of the defendant's benefit.

Under both s.14 of the DTOA and s.16 of the Criminal Justice (International Co-operation) Act 1990, it is necessary to go to the High Court first and not straight to the Crown Court. It is not clear why the legislature thought this route to be desirable or necessary. An initial reaction is that the provisions were intended to confer upon the High Court a supervisory role and thus safeguard the interests of persons likely to be affected by a successful application, but the terms of ss.14 and 16, *supra* impose a mandatory obligation on the High Court to issue a certificate upon making the requisite findings of fact for the purposes of s.14(1) and s.16(2). Neither of these two sections gives any indication or guidance as to the burden or standard of proof.

S.5A of the DTOA

Under this provision the court may be asked, by the prosecutor, to embark upon a drug trafficking enquiry if evidence was not previously available to him which he believes would have led the court to conclude that the defendant had benefited from drug trafficking. Under s.1(1) of the DTOA, as amended by s.7(1) of the 1993 Act, the court is not obliged to proceed under the 1986 Act and this could be for a number of reasons (including tactical ones) in circumstances where the prosecutor did have compelling evidence when the defendant was due to be sentenced but decided not to rely on it. If the prosecutor subsequently changes direction, he can only go back to the Crown Court if he has something else which was not available to him originally. A safeguard (if one were needed) is provided by s.5A(3) and (4) and the court is entitled to have regard to all the circumstances of the case before concluding that it would be "appropriate" to proceed under s.1 of the DTOA (s.5A(3) of the DTOA).

If the court relies on payments received by the defendant *on or after* the date of conviction then the prosecution must prove (to the civil standard: s.1(7A) of the DTOA) that (a) he received the payment; (b) that he received it in connection with drug trafficking carried on by him or by another; and (c) that the drug trafficking activity occurred *before* the date of conviction (see s.5A(8) and (11)). Presumably the reasoning behind this approach is that the conviction should be seen as marking the end of the defendant's drug trafficking career, for confiscation purposes, and that the use of the assumptions is justified where payments are received up and until the moment of conviction.

Where a determination is made under s.1(4) of the DTOA, the court is only obliged to order a payment that is "just" in all the circumstances. The court is required to have "regard" (but not necessarily to leave out of account) any fine paid by the defendant (s.5A(6) of the DTOA) and presumably other financial or forfeiture orders as well.

S.5B of the DTOA

By s.5B(2), the court appears to be required to form an opinion based on hindsight, *i.e.* that it "would have" determined that the defendant had benefited from drug trafficking if the evidence which ultimately came to light had been available to it. Payments received by the defendant after the date on which the court originally concluded he received no benefit, may be taken into account but the prosecution will not be able to rely on the statutory assumptions.

S.5C of the DTOA

There appears to be a difference of scope in the ambit of these provisions when s.5C(2) is read in contrast with s.5C(4). Section 5C(2) seems to look to the "real value" as it should have been assessed at the time the order was made but the conclusion which the court is actually entitled to make under s.5C(4), includes any *increased value* of the proceeds in question. Be that as it may, the governing provision is s.5C(4). The court therefore looks at the current value of the proceeds (which were ascertained by the date the confiscation order was originally made) (s.5C(4)) plus, any payment received by the defendant *on or after* that date, which were the fruits of drug trafficking carried on by the defendant or another *before* that moment (s.5C(9)). The prosecution cannot rely on the statutory assumptions (s.5C(10)). However, the "amount to be recovered", under a fresh confiscation order, is prima facie the "amount that might be realised" (see ss.4(3), 5(3) and 5C(6)). It follows that if the defendant's finances have improved by the date of the subsequent determination, it is the higher figure which is relevant. Given that the court is being asked to make a fresh confiscation order it follows that s.2(5) of the DTOA must be disregarded and that is what s.5C(7) achieves. Even if, prima facie, the "amount to be recovered" (being the "amount that might be realised") is greater than it was originally assessed to be, nevertheless, the court need only order such greater amount as it thinks just in all the circumstances of the case.

Availability of powers and satisfaction of orders

13.—(1) In section 6 of the Drug Trafficking Offences Act 1986 (default in complying with confiscation order: application of procedure for enforcing fines), the following subsection shall be added at the end—

"(7) Where the defendant serves a term of imprisonment or detention in default of paying any amount due under a confiscation order, his serving that term does not prevent the confiscation order from continuing to have effect, so far as any other method of enforcement is concerned.".

(2) Section 7 of the Act of 1986 (cases in which restraint orders and charging orders may be made) shall be amended as set out in subsections (3) to (5).

(3) The following subsection shall be substituted for subsection (1)—

"(1) The powers conferred on the High Court by sections 8(1) and 9(1) of this Act are exercisable where—

(a) proceedings have been instituted in England and Wales against the defendant for a drug trafficking offence or an application has been made by the prosecutor in respect of the defendant under section 16 of the Criminal Justice (International Co-operation) Act 1990 (increase in realisable property) or section 4A, 5A, 5B or 5C of this Act,

(b) the proceedings have not, or the application has not, been concluded, and

(c) the court is satisfied that there is reasonable cause to believe—

(i) in the case of an application under section 5C of this Act or section 16 of the Act of 1990, that the court will be satisfied

as mentioned in section 5C(4) of this Act or, as the case may
be, section 16(2) of the Act of 1990, or
    (ii) in any other case, that the defendant has benefited from
drug trafficking.".
  (4) The following subsection shall be substituted for subsection (2)—
    "(2) Those powers are also exercisable where—
    (a) the court is satisfied that, whether by the laying of an information
      or otherwise, a person is to be charged with a drug trafficking
      offence or that an application of a kind mentioned in subsection
      (1)(a) above is to be made in respect of the defendant, and
    (b) the court is also satisfied as mentioned in subsection (1)(c)
      above.".
  (5) The following subsections shall be added at the end—
    "(5) Where the court has made an order under section 8(1) or 9(1) of
this Act in relation to a proposed application by virtue of subsection (2)
above, the court shall discharge the order if the application is not made
within such time as the court considers reasonable.
    (6) The court shall not exercise powers under section 8(1) or 9(1) of
this Act, by virtue of subsection (1) above, if it is satisfied that—
    (a) there has been undue delay in continuing the proceedings or
      application in question; or
    (b) the prosecutor does not intend to proceed.".
  (6) In section 8 of the Act of 1986 (restraint orders), the following
subsection shall be substituted for subsection (5)—
    "(5) A restraint order—
    (a) may be discharged or varied in relation to any property, and
    (b) shall be discharged on the conclusion of the proceedings or of the
      application in question.".
  (7) In section 9 of the Act of 1986 (charging orders), the following
subsection shall be substituted for subsection (7)—
    "(7) In relation to a charging order, the court—
    (a) may make an order discharging or varying it, and
    (b) shall make an order discharging it—
        (i) on the conclusion of the proceedings or of the application
      in question, or
        (ii) on payment into court of the amount payment of which
      is secured by the charge.".
  (8) In section 11 of the Act of 1986 (realisation of property), the following
subsection shall be substituted for subsection (1)—
    "(1) Where a confiscation order—
    (a) has been made under this Act,
    (b) is not satisfied, and
    (c) is not subject to appeal,
the High Court or a county court may, on an application by the prosecutor, exercise the powers conferred by subsections (2) to (6) below.".
  (9) In section 15 of the Act of 1986 (bankruptcy of defendant), the
following shall be substituted for paragraphs (a) and (b) of subsection (6)—
    "(a) no order shall be made under section 339 or 423 of that Act
      (avoidance of certain transactions) in respect of the making of
      the gift at any time when—
        (i) proceedings for a drug trafficking offence have been
      instituted against him and have not been concluded;
        (ii) an application has been made in respect of the defen-
      dant under section 4A, 5A, 5B or 5C of this Act or section 16
      of the Criminal Justice (International Co-operation) Act 1990
      and has not been concluded; or
        (iii) property of the person to whom the gift was made is
      subject to a restraint order or charging order; and

(b) any order made under section 339 or 423 after the conclusion of the proceedings or of the application shall take into account any realisation under this Act of property held by the person to whom the gift was made.".

(10) In section 16 of the Act of 1986 (sequestration in Scotland), the following shall be substituted for paragraphs (a) and (b) of subsection (6)—

"(a) no decree shall be granted under section 34 or 36 of that Act (gratuitous alienations and unfair preferences) in respect of the making of the gift at any time when—

(i) proceedings for a drug trafficking offence have been instituted against him and have not been concluded;

(ii) an application has been made in respect of the defendant under section 4A, 5A, 5B or 5C of this Act or section 16 of the Criminal Justice (International Co-operation) Act 1990 and has not been concluded; or

(iii) property of the person to whom the gift was made is subject to a restraint order or charging order; and

(b) any decree made under section 34 or 36 after the conclusion of the proceedings or of the application shall take into account any realisation under this Act of property held by a person to whom the gift was made.".

(11) In section 38 of the Act of 1986 (interpretation), the following subsections shall be substituted for subsection (12)—

"(12) Proceedings for a drug trafficking offence are concluded—

(a) when the defendant is acquitted on all counts;

(b) if he is convicted on one or more counts, but the court decides not to make a confiscation order against him, when it makes that decision; or

(c) if a confiscation order is made against him in those proceedings, when the order is satisfied.

(12A) An application under section 4A, 5A or 5B of this Act is concluded—

(a) if the court decides not to make a confiscation order against the defendant, when it makes that decision; or

(b) if a confiscation order is made against him as a result of that application, when the order is satisfied.

(12B) An application under section 16 of the Criminal Justice (International Co-operation) Act 1990 (increase in realisable property) or section 5C of this Act is concluded—

(a) if the court decides not to vary the confiscation order in question, when it makes that decision; or

(b) if the court varies the confiscation order as a result of the application, when the order is satisfied.

(12C) For the purposes of this Act, a confiscation order is satisfied when no amount is due under it.

(12D) For the purposes of sections 15 and 16 of this Act, a confiscation order is also satisfied when the defendant in respect of whom it was made has served a term of imprisonment or detention in default of payment of the amount due under the order.".

DEFINITIONS

"charging order": s.9(2) of the DTOA.

"confiscation order": Sched. 5; ss.1(8) and 38(1) of the DTOA.

"drug trafficking": s.38(1) of the DTOA.

"drug trafficking offence": s.38(1) of the DTOA.

"gift": s.5(9) of the DTOA.

"proceedings for a drug trafficking offence are concluded": ss.13(11) and 38(12) of the DTOA.

"property": s.38(1) of the DTOA.

"realisable property": s.5(1) of the DTOA.
"restraint order": s.8(1) of the DTOA.

GENERAL NOTE

The broad approach is that the amount of a confiscation order shall be treated as if the amount were a fine imposed on him by the Crown Court (see s.6(1) of the DTOA). It follows that a term of imprisonment must be imposed in default of payment.

The plain purpose of the DTOA was that a person convicted of a drug trafficking offence should be deprived of the proceeds to the extent that they were realisable. Committing a defendant to prison by way of a "warrant of commitment" under s.6(2) of the DTOA is a course of last resort. The magistrates (who may issue such a warrant) should therefore consider all other methods of enforcing payment prior to the issue of a warrant (see *R.* v. *Harrow Justices*, ex p. *D.P.P.* [1991] 1 W.L.R. 395).

Originally, the practical consequences flowing from the defendant's commitment to prison were three-fold. First, the period to be served in default relieved the defendant of the requirement to satisfy that proportion of the order which remained outstanding. The defendant therefore effectively "served" his way out of paying the order and so defeated the primary purpose of the Act. Secondly, a warrant, once issued, cannot be withdrawn by the magistrates' court: *R.* v. *Newport Pagnell Justices*, ex p. *Smith* (1988) 152 J.P. 475. Thirdly, proceedings for the purposes of the DTOA were "concluded" upon the defendant serving a term of imprisonment in default (s.38(12) of the DTOA as amended by Sched. 5, para. 16 of the Criminal Justice Act 1988). Section 38(12) has now been substantially amended by s.13(11) of the 1993 Act. Powers conferred on the High Court in respect of the making of a restraint or charging order, or the realisation of property by the appointment of a receiver, are only exercisable where proceedings are not concluded (see DTOA, ss.7 to 13, as amended).

Even where monies had actually been taken from the defendant at the time of his arrest, it was a mandatory requirement of s.6 of the DTOA that a term of imprisonment be imposed in default of payment of the sums confiscated (*R.* v. *Popple*; *R.* v. *Smith*; *R.* v. *Walker* (1992) 156 J.P. 910). This is because Customs and Excise officers, for example, did not have power to pay money in satisfaction of a confiscation order without first obtaining the defendant's consent or applying to a magistrates' court for a distress warrant.

By s.6(2) of the DTOA, a term of imprisonment (or detention) ordered to be served in default of payment, shall run after the defendant has served any sentences of imprisonment which were imposed in respect of the offences for which he appeared at the Crown Court.

Following the Seventh Report of the Home Office Affairs Committee, "*Drug Trafficking and Related Serious Crime*" (1989), the Home Office Working Group (1991) expressed concern that trafficking could obstruct the satisfaction of a confiscation order by shifting funds. Once he had served a term of imprisonment in default, his property would not be liable to confiscation wherever it was situated. The Group therefore recommended that a term of imprisonment served in default should not expunge what ought to be regarded as a "debt" (para. 3.11). Accordingly, new s.6(7) was inserted into the DTOA by s.13(1) of the 1993 Act.

The remaining provisions are primarily designed to bring the DTOA into line following the changes which have been introduced by the other provisions of the 1993 Act. As originally drafted the circumstances in which proceedings for a drug trafficking offence were to be treated as "concluded" were relatively straightforward because the machinery for varying a confiscation was limited only to an application made by the defendant under s.14 of the DTOA (s.38(12) of the DTOA).

Not only will proceedings now not be concluded upon serving a sentence in default of payment (s.6(7) of the DTOA) but the ability of the prosecution to seek a re-determination of issues under s.1 of the DTOA, over a period of six years from the date of the relevant conviction or determination (see s.12 of the 1993 Act) means that the machinery necessary to enforce the satisfaction of the order had to be redefined. Thus;

  (a) the powers of the High Court under ss.8(1) and 9(1) of the DTOA are extended to applications brought by the prosecutor under s.16 of the Criminal Justice (International Co-operation) Act 1990; s.4A of the DTOA (defendant who has died or absconded); ss.5A, 5B and 5C of the DTOA (redetermination under s.1 of the DTOA); and s.7(1) of the DTOA as amended by s.13(3) of the Criminal Justice Act 1993;

  (b) the same powers exist even if any such applications are to be made (s.7(2) of the DTOA as amended) subject to the safeguards set out in s.7(5) of the DTOA (added by s.13(5) Criminal Justice Act 1993);

  (c) restraint orders under s.8 of the DTOA may be varied, etc. (s.8(5) of the DTOA amended by s.13(6) of the Criminal Justice Act 1993);

  (d) similarly, changing orders may be varied, etc. (s.9(7) of the DTOA amended by s.13(7) of the Criminal Justice Act 1993);

(e) powers under s.11 of the DTOA may be exercised where an order is not satisfied (see s.13(8) of the Criminal Justice Act 1993);

(f) there are further rules relevant to bankruptcy (or, in Scotland, sequestration) (s.13(9) and (10));

(g) the circumstances, in respect of proceedings for "drug trafficking offences", which can be said to be "concluded", are redefined (s.38(12) of the DTOA, as amended by s.13(11) of the Criminal Justice Act 1993).

APPOINTMENT AND POWERS OF A RECEIVER

In summary, once a confiscation order has been made which is not subject to appeal and which has not been satisfied, the High Court may, on the application of the prosecutor, appoint a receiver to realise any realisable property (s.11(5) of the DTOA) with a view to satisfying the confiscation order (s.13(2) of the DTOA) and to apply the property so realised on the defendant's behalf towards the satisfaction of the order (s.12(1) of the DTOA). A reasonable opportunity must be given for persons holding any interest in the property to make representations to the court (s.11(8) of the DTOA). Sums remaining in the hands of the receiver after the satisfaction of a confiscation order must be distributed among the holders of property in such proportions as the court shall direct (s.12(2) of the DTOA). The material powers conferred on a receiver are set out in s.11 of the DTOA (as amended by s.13(8) of the 1993 Act).

Note that under s.11(1)(c) of the DTOA (see s.13(8) of the 1993 Act), a receiver cannot be appointed if the order is subject to appeal (see s.38(13) of the DTOA as amended by Sched. 5 to the Criminal Justice Act 1988).

Again, by s.11(1)(b) of the DTOA, a receiver can only be appointed if the confiscation order "is not satisfied". By s.38(12) proceedings in England and Wales for an offence are concluded on the occurrence of one of the events set out in that section (as amended by s.13(11) of the 1993 Act).

The Powers of the High Court or the receiver must be exercised within the framework set out in s.13 of the DTOA.

Death or absence of defendant

Defendant who has died or absconded

14.—(1) The following sections shall be inserted in the Drug Trafficking Offences Act 1986, after section 4—

"Powers of High Court where defendant has died or absconded

4A.—(1) Subsection (2) below applies where a person has been convicted of one or more drug trafficking offences.

(2) If the prosecutor asks it to proceed under this section, the High Court may exercise the powers of the Crown Court under this Act to make a confiscation order against the defendant if satisfied that the defendant has died or absconded.

(3) Subsection (4) below applies where proceedings for one or more drug trafficking offences have been instituted against a person but have not been concluded.

(4) If the prosecutor asks it to proceed under this section, the High Court may exercise the powers of the Crown Court under this Act to make a confiscation order against the defendant if satisfied that the defendant has absconded.

(5) The power conferred by subsection (4) above may not be exercised at any time before the end of the period of two years beginning with the date which is, in the opinion of the court, the date on which the defendant absconded.

(6) In any proceedings on an application under this section—

(a) sections 2(2) and 3(1D), (2) and (3) shall not apply,

(b) the court shall not make a confiscation order against a person who has absconded unless it is satisfied that the prosecutor has taken reasonable steps to contact him, and

(c) any person appearing to the court to be likely to be affected by the making of a confiscation order by the court shall be entitled to appear before the court and make representations.

Effect of conviction where High Court has acted under section 4A

4B.—(1) Where the High Court has made a confiscation order by virtue of section 4A of this Act, the Crown Court shall, in respect of the offence or any of the offences concerned—

(a) take account of the order before—
  (i) imposing any fine on him, or
  (ii) making any order involving any payment by him, or
  (iii) making any order under section 27 of the Misuse of Drugs Act 1971 (forfeiture orders) or section 43 of the Powers of Criminal Courts Act 1973 (deprivation orders), and

(b) subject to paragraph (a) above, leave the order out of account in determining the appropriate sentence or other manner of dealing with the defendant.

(2) Where the High Court has made a confiscation order by virtue of section 4A of this Act and the defendant subsequently appears before the Crown Court to be sentenced in respect of one or more of the offences concerned, section 1(1) of this Act shall not apply so far as his appearance is in respect of that offence or those offences.".

(2) In section 6 of the Act of 1986 (application of procedure for enforcing fines), in subsection (6), after the words "made by", where they first occur, there shall be inserted "the High Court, by virtue of section 4A of this Act, or by".

(3) The following subsection shall be added at the end of section 6 of the Act of 1986—

"(8) Where the High Court makes a confiscation order by virtue of section 4A of this Act in relation to a defendant who has died, subsection (1) above shall be read as referring only to sections 31(1) and 32(1) of the Act of 1973.".

DEFINITIONS
"confiscation order": Sched. 5.
"defendant": Sched. 5.
"drug trafficking offence": s.38(1) of the DTOA.
"proceedings . . . concluded": s.13(11); s.38(12) of the DTOA.

GENERAL NOTE
As the law stood, where a defendant either died or absconded before a confiscation order was made, the court was powerless to make a confiscation order. An indication of the sort of problems that can arise where a defendant absconds were demonstrated in *R. v. Chrastny (No. 2)* [1991] 1 W.L.R. 1385. In that case the court had to determine whether property held jointly by the husband and wife (both of whom had been jointly charged with a drug trafficking offence) was "realisable" for the purposes of s.4(3) of the DTOA, in circumstances where the wife had been convicted but where the husband had absconded. The court answered that question affirmatively. If the husband were to be apprehended, tried and convicted then the court could not include in any confiscation order against him, property realised to satisfy the order payable by his wife because the property was no longer under his control (*per Glidewell* L.J. at 1394). The Home Office Working Group on Confiscation identified three situations to which different considerations may apply but which originally fell outside the ambit of the DTOA namely (1) death after conviction but before a confiscation order is made; (2) the defendant absconds after conviction but before the order is made; and (3) the defendant either dies or absconds before conviction.

Death or Absconding After Conviction
The Working Group, in their Report on the Drug Trafficking Offences Act 1986 (1991), saw no reason to distinguish between the two cases (in principle) and stated that it should be possible to make confiscation orders in each case (para. 5.6). The DTOA (as amended by ss.14–16 of the 1993 Act) follows that approach. Thus, s.4A(1) of the DTOA requires a confiscation for a drug trafficking offence. However, only the High Court may make a confiscation order and accordingly the prosecutor must apply to that court upon evidence being adduced, to the satisfaction of the High Court, that the defendant has either died or absconded. Section 4A(3), (4) and (5) of the DTOA does not apply if the defendant is deceased. The difference between s.4A(1) and s.4A(3) is that s.4A(1) is applicable where there is a *conviction*, whereas s.4A(3) applies even if there is no conviction but proceedings have been instituted (see s.38(11) of the DTOA). However, subss. (3), (4) and (5) of s.4A of the DTOA are linked and

should therefore be read together. Those three provisions form a set, which apply only to absconders, whether or not they are convicted of an offence. The result is that a confiscation order may not be made until two years after the date on which the defendant (in the opinion of the court) absconded.

It is not clear what the position would be if a defendant inexplicably went "missing", *e.g.* after a boating trip in mysterious circumstances pending the DTOA enquiry. Would the court treat him as having "absconded" or must the court wait seven years until he could be presumed dead? Note the obligation imposed on the prosecution by s.4A(6)(b) of the DTOA. Note that the statutory assumptions do not apply under s.4A (see s.4A(6)(1)).

Note that the court is required to make a confiscation order before sentencing the absent defendant (s.4B(1) of the DTOA).

Where an absconder returns, the High Court may cancel the confiscation order if there has been undue delay on the part of the prosecution in pursuing proceedings under s.4A(4) of the DTOA (see s.19B(2)(a) of the DTOA inserted by s.15 of the 1993 Act).

Defendant Dies or Absconds before Conviction

Note that subss. (3), (4) and (5) of s.4A of the DTOA are linked to form a set of provisions (see above). Accordingly, only as against him can the High Court exercise the powers of the Crown Court to make a confiscation order (subject to s.4A(6) of the DTOA). The Working Group sought views as to whether the courts should be empowered to commence proceedings against persons who died or absconded prior to conviction (para. 5.9) but Parliament clearly took the view that it would be too drastic a step to extend the provisions of s.4A to those who died and who could never answer the indictment which they faced.

Where an absconder is acquitted (whether in his absence or otherwise) the court by which the defendant was acquired (*e.g.* the Crown Court) may cancel the confiscation order (s.19A(1) and (2) of the DTOA inserted by s.5 of the 1993 Act) and apply for compensation if he has suffered loss as is just in all circumstances of the case (s.19A(3) and (4) of the DTOA inserted by s.15 of the 1993 Act).

Note the power of the High Court to vary confiscation orders upon the application of the defendant, which was made under s.4A of the DTOA (see s.19C of the DTOA, inserted by s.15 of the 1993 Act).

Compensation

15. The following sections shall be inserted in the Drug Trafficking Offences Act 1986, after section 19—

"Compensation etc. where absconder is acquitted

19A.—(1) This section applies where—

(a) the High Court has made a confiscation order by virtue of section 4A(4) of this Act, and

(b) the defendant is subsequently tried for the offence or offences concerned and acquitted on all counts.

(2) The court by which the defendant is acquitted shall cancel the confiscation order.

(3) The High Court may, on the application of a person who held property which was realisable property, order compensation to be paid to the applicant if it is satisfied that the applicant has suffered loss as a result of the making of the confiscation order.

(4) The amount of compensation to be paid under this section shall be such as the court considers just in all the circumstances of the case.

(5) Rules of court may make provision—

(a) for the giving of notice of any application under this section; and

(b) for any person appearing to the court to be likely to be affected by any exercise of its powers under this section to be given an opportunity to make representations to the court.

(6) Any payment of compensation under this section shall be made by the Lord Chancellor out of money provided by Parliament.

(7) Where the court cancels a confiscation order under this section it may make such consequential or incidental order as it considers appropriate in connection with the cancellation.

Power to discharge confiscation order and order compensation where absconder returns

19B.—(1) This section applies where—

(a) the High Court has made a confiscation order by virtue of section 4A(4) of this Act in relation to an absconder,

(b) the defendant has ceased to be an absconder, and

(c) section 19A of this Act does not apply.

(2) The High Court may, on the application of the defendant, cancel the confiscation order if it is satisfied that—

(a) there has been undue delay in continuing the proceedings in respect of which the power under section 4A(4) of this Act was exercised; or

(b) the prosecutor does not intend to proceed with the prosecution.

(3) Where the High Court cancels a confiscation order under this section it may, on the application of a person who held property which was realisable property, order compensation to be paid to the applicant if it is satisfied that the applicant has suffered loss as a result of the making of the confiscation order.

(4) The amount of compensation to be paid under this section shall be such as the court considers just in all the circumstances of the case.

(5) Rules of court may make provision—

(a) for the giving of notice of any application under this section; and

(b) for any person appearing to the court to be likely to be affected by any exercise of its powers under this section to be given an opportunity to make representations to the court.

(6) Any payment of compensation under this section shall be made by the Lord Chancellor out of money provided by Parliament.

(7) Where the court cancels a confiscation order under this section it may make such consequential or incidental order as it considers appropriate in connection with the cancellation.

Variation of confiscation orders made by virtue of section 4A

19C.—(1) This section applies where—

(a) the High Court has made a confiscation order by virtue of section 4A(4) of this Act, and

(b) the defendant has ceased to be an absconder.

(2) If the defendant alleges that—

(a) the value of his proceeds of drug trafficking in the period by reference to which the determination in question was made (the "original value"), or

(b) the amount that might have been realised at the time the confiscation order was made,

was less than the amount ordered to be paid under the confiscation order, he may apply to the High Court for it to consider his evidence.

(3) If, having considered that evidence, the court is satisfied that the defendant's allegation is correct it—

(a) shall make a fresh determination under subsection (4) of section 1 of this Act, and

(b) may, if it considers it just in all the circumstances, vary the amount to be recovered under the confiscation order.

(4) For any determination under section 1 of this Act by virtue of this section, section 2(5) of this Act shall not apply in relation to any of the defendant's proceeds of drug trafficking taken into account in determining the original value.

(5) Where the court varies a confiscation order under this section—

(a) it shall substitute for the term of imprisonment or of detention fixed under section 31(2) of the Powers of Criminal Courts Act 1973 in respect of the amount to be recovered under the order a shorter term determined in accordance with that section (as it has effect by virtue of section 6 of this Act) in respect of the lesser amount; and

(b) on the application of a person who held property which was realisable property, it may order compensation to be paid to the applicant if—

    (i) it is satisfied that the applicant has suffered loss as a result of the making of the confiscation order; and

    (ii) having regard to all the circumstances of the case, the court considers it to be appropriate.

(6) The amount of compensation to be paid under this section shall be such as the court considers just in all the circumstances of the case.

(7) Rules of court may make provision—

(a) for the giving of notice of any application under this section; and

(b) for any person appearing to the court to be likely to be affected by any exercise of its powers under this section to be given an opportunity to make representations to the court.

(8) Any payment of compensation under this section shall be made by the Lord Chancellor out of money provided by Parliament.

(9) No application shall be entertained by the court under this section if it is made after the end of the period of six years beginning with the date on which the confiscation order was made.".

DEFINITIONS

"amount that might be realised": ss.4(3) and 5(3) of the DTOA.
"confiscation order": Sched. 5.
"defendant": Sched. 5.
"proceeds of drug trafficking": s.2(1)(a) of the DTOA.
"realisable property": s.5(1) of the DTOA.

GENERAL NOTE

In 1989 the National Drugs Intelligence co-ordinator informed the Home Affairs Committee on Drug Trafficking and Related Serious Crime that at least £1,800m. (derived from drug trafficking) was circulating in the U.K. Money being laundered is now thought to be as high as £57m. a year from drug sales in America and Europe alone. Despite the DTOA, the U.K. continues to be a major centre for money laundering. In the same year, the Home Office told the Committee that the DTOA has promoted drug traffickers to adopt greater sophistication in their efforts to launder the proceeds, so that money laundering is "probably the most organised aspect of drug trafficking" (see the Home Affairs Committee 7th Report (1989)). The Home Office indicated that although the evidence of links between organised crime and drug trafficking was largely anecdotal, "there is an undoubted link between the two". The link is said to be evident between the drugs trade and the financing of wars and terrorism but usually the link is much more basic and symptomatic of general criminal activity committed by drug traffickers. There is much in the 1993 Act which represents the views and the concerns of the Legislature expressed when the DTOA was being debated as a Bill. It is plain from the *Hansard* Reports that Parliament regard the DTOA as marking only the first step in the fight against organised crime and not solely against drug trafficking. The extent to which other areas of the law in 1986 required reform (*e.g.* extradition, banking and international co-operation in respect of the gathering and calling of evidence) meant that the DTOA could not embrace every activity that was either linked (or akin) to drug trafficking and money laundering. Parliament was also mindful that the Criminal Justice Bill (now the Criminal Justice Act 1988) was being drafted but had to be considered by Parliament. Lord Harris of Greenwich explained the problem when he said ". . . it is an illusion to imagine that drug trafficking can be treated as an isolated crime . . . we are confronted with the existence of highly sophisticated criminal syndicates. The operators move effectively from one form of serious crime to another; from drug trafficking to armed robbery, from counterfeit currency operations to large-scale fraud and then back again to drug trafficking" (*Hansard*, H.L. Vol. 474, col. 1115).

The object of money laundering is to transfer the proceeds of crime through the financial sector so that it re-emerges back into legitimate commercial or financial concerns controlled or directed by the participants in the criminal enterprise. The methods by which proceeds are concealed are many and varied ranging from the setting up of so-called "paper trails" (designed to "lose" the proceeds in a diverse and confusing "maze" of translations) to the use of various shields—whether jurisdictional or rooted in privilege and confidentiality.

Organised crime exploits the three elements of business: supply, demand and profit, and the law enforcement agencies (while traditionally deployed to tackle the first two elements) are devoting more resources to tackling the profit element for two reasons: (a) funds removed from circulation cannot be reused to finance further criminal enterprises; and (b) it removes the incentive to commit crime.

Given that drug trafficking and money laundering operate on an international scale, many of the provisions of the DTOA (and subsequent legislation) are the product of diplomatic efforts and rooted in several Treaties, Conventions, Bi-lateral Agreements and (now) European Directives: see the European Convention on Mutual Assistance 1957 (which the U.K. was not able to ratify until the enactment of the Criminal Justice (International Co-operation) Act 1990); the United Nations Convention Against Illicit Traffic In Narcotic Drugs and Psychotropic Substances 1988 (the "Vienna Convention", ratified by the U.K. in 1991); the Council of Europe Convention on Laundering, Search, Seizure and Confiscation of the Proceeds of Crime 1990 (yet to be ratified by the U.K.). See also the European Council Directive (91/308/E.E.C.). Note also s.26 of the DTOA (as amended) and the Drug Trafficking Offences Act 1986 (Designated Countries and Territories) Order 1990 (S.I. 1990 No. 1199) (as amended by S.I. 1991 No. 1465). Orders made in Scotland under the Criminal Justice (Scotland) Act 1987 may now be enforced in England and Wales (see the Drug Trafficking Offences (Enforcement in England and Wales) Order 1988 (S.I. 1988 No. 593).

The Financial Action Task Force ("FATF") made a number of radical proposals in 1990 which go beyond those agreed at the 1988 United Nations Convention. FATF recommended that member states should address their money laundering provisions to various major crimes and not just drug trafficking. It also suggested that rules of secrecy or confidentiality held by various financial institutions should be qualified so as to permit suspicious transactions to be reported to the authorities.

These proposals were already in Parliament's mind in 1986 (see *Hansard*, H.L. Vol. 474, col. 1094) and s.24 of the DTOA makes it an offence to assist another to retain the benefit of drug trafficking in circumstances where the defendant knew or even suspected that the assisted person has benefited from drug trafficking. Section 24 does not impose an obligation to disclose a suspicion but where a person or body (*e.g.* a bank) discloses suspicions to the authorities he will have the protections afforded to him by s.24(3) (*e.g.* against breach of contract) and he may continue to act for the person under suspicion (*e.g.* not closing his bank account) within the limits set out in s.24(3) (see also the Wilton Park Paper No. 65, 919930 (HMSO)).

For over 20 years, the U.S. has been developing powerful anti-money laundering laws both by way of its legislation and at common law. The Bank Secrecy Act 1970 (U.S.) applies to financial institutions and businesses which accept large sums of cash. A "financial institution" is very broadly defined (*U.S.* v. *Rigdon* (1989) 874 F.2d 774; *U.S.* v. *Clines* (1992) 958 F.2d 578). The BSA requires businesses and individuals to submit Currency Transaction Reports (CTRs) as well as various reports of currency instruments, foreign bank accounts, and cash payments over \$10,000 U.S. in a trade or business. Businesses and their employees may be required to lodge Criminal Referral Forms (CRFs) in respect of any "known or suspected criminal violation . . . committed against (or through) a bank" used to facilitate a criminal transaction. Failure to file a CRF may result in so-called civil penalties being assessed against the institution, its officers or employees. Data and intelligence gleaned from these records are collated on a databases utilised by FINCEN (Financial Crimes Enforcement Network). The Anti-Abuse Act 1988 (U.S.) includes a requirement upon the Secretary to the Treasury to negotiate with other countries to ensure that they have adequate records on international currency transactions, which might be taken as a requirement for mandatory reporting along U.S. lines.

The Money Laundering Control Act (1986) (U.S.), creates a number of offences in respect of the knowing participation by any person in transactions with persons who derive their money from specified unlawful activities, *e.g.* drug trafficking.

Forfeiture, under U.S. legislation, is permitted under the BSA, the MLCA, the Comprehensive Drug Abuse Prevention and Control Act, the Controlled Substances Act the Racketeer-Influenced and Corrupt Organisations (RICO) and the Continuing Criminal Enterprise statutes. Of particular interest here are two concepts. First, some statutory provisions enjoy a reduced standard of proof requiring the government to prove only a "probable" cause to believe "that a substantial connection exists between the property to be forfeited" and the act which contravenes the statute: *U.S.* v. *Four Million Dollars* (1985) 762 F.2d 895. Secondly, there is the "Relation-Back Doctrine" which is based on the fiction that illegally obtained property vests in the government at the time of the offence.

Developments in the U.S. have to some extent been mirrored elsewhere as a large number of countries have collaborated to combat drug trafficking and money laundering. These two activities now have to be seen in the context of each other.

The American model was considered by the House of Lords in 1986 (*Hansard*, H.L. Vol. 474, col. 1112) when it was pointed out that American law was not confined to drug trafficking. The British Government was not then prepared to move in the direction of the American model although the then Parliamentary Under-Secretary had indicated that "there might be movement in the future" (*Hansard*, H.L. Vol. 474, col. 1116).

Significantly, Art. 5(1) of the Vienna Convention 1988 provides that each party is to adopt such measures as may be necessary to enable confiscation of ". . . (a) the proceeds derived from offences established in accordance with Art. 3, para. 1, or property the value of which corresponds to that of such proceeds . . .", while Art. 5(3) requires each party to empower its courts to order that bank, financial or commercial records be made available or seized. Provision for the reversal of the burden of proof is made by Art. 7: "each Party may consider ensuring that the onus of proof be reversed regarding the lawful origin of alleged proceeds or other property liable to confiscation, to the extent that such action is consistent with the principles of its domestic law and with the nature of the judicial and other proceedings".

Article 3 of the 1988 Convention also requires Member States to make the concealment or disguising of the proceeds of drug trafficking an offence without reference (as appears in s.24 of the DTOA) to "facilitating" or "assisting" the drug trafficker. Article 3 also requires the creation of an offence of handling the proceeds of drug trafficking.

Accordingly, the Home Affairs Committee in their Seventh Report (Vol I; session 1988–89) recommended that English law be amended so that the U.K. could ratify Art. 3.

The U.S. authorities made representations to the Home Affairs Committee that the U.K. should introduce money laundering measures similar to those already operating in the U.S. The 1993 Act suggests that the Government are moving in that direction but the severity of American law should not be under-estimated both in terms of the draconian effect of their law and the vigorous way it is enforced with very heavy penalties for non-compliance (see also the European Council Directive (91/308/EEC)).

Offences Relevant to Part II

The relevant offences are now:

(a) Assisting another to retain the benefit of drug trafficking "knowing or suspecting" that the assisted person is a drug trafficker or who has benefited from drug trafficking (s.24 of the DTOA 1986);

(b) Prejudicing an investigation (s.31 of the DTOA 1986);

(c) Concealing, disguising, transferring or removing the proceeds of drug trafficking; the offence being committed by the trafficker himself (s.14(1) of the Criminal Justice (International Co-operation) Act 1990);

(d) The same conduct as in (c) above but committed by another to assist any person to avoid prosecution for a drug trafficking offence or the making of enforcement of a confiscation order (s.14(2) of the Criminal Justice (International Co-operation) Act 1990);

(e) Acquisition, possession or use of proceeds of drug trafficking (s.23A of the DTOA (inserted by s.16 of the Criminal Justice Act 1993));

(f) Failing to disclose knowledge of suspicion of money-laundering (s.26B of the Drug Trafficking Offences Act inserted by s.18 of Criminal Justice Act 1993);

(g) Disclosing information to another which is likely to prejudice an investigation or proposed investigation (s.26C of the DTOA, inserted by s.18 of the Criminal Justice Act 1993).

Offences similar to (f) and (g) are introduced into Scottish law by s.19 of the 1993 Act.

Offences

Acquisition, possession or use of proceeds of drug trafficking

16.—(1) The following section shall be inserted in the Drug Trafficking Offences Act 1986 at the appropriate place—

"Acquiring etc. property derived from drug trafficking

Acquisition, possession or use of proceeds of drug trafficking
23A.—(1) A person is guilty of an offence if, knowing that any

property is, or in whole or in part directly or indirectly represents, another person's proceeds of drug trafficking, he acquires or uses that property or has possession of it.

(2) It is a defence to a charge of committing an offence under this section that the person charged acquired or used the property or had possession of it for adequate consideration.

(3) For the purposes of subsection (2) above—

(a) a person acquires property for inadequate consideration if the value of the consideration is significantly less than the value of the property; and

(b) a person uses or has possession of property for inadequate consideration if the value of the consideration is significantly less than the value of his use or possession of the property.

(4) The provision for any person of services or goods which are of assistance to him in drug trafficking shall not be treated as consideration for the purposes of subsection (2) above.

(5) Where a person discloses to a constable a suspicion or belief that any property is, or in whole or in part directly or indirectly represents, another person's proceeds of drug trafficking, or discloses to a constable any matter on which such a suspicion or belief is based—

(a) the disclosure shall not be treated as a breach of any restriction upon the disclosure of information imposed by statute or otherwise; and

(b) if he does any act in relation to the property in contravention of subsection (1) above, he does not commit an offence under this section if—

(i) the disclosure is made before he does the act concerned and the act is done with the consent of the constable, or

(ii) the disclosure is made after he does the act, but on his initiative and as soon as it is reasonable for him to make it.

(6) For the purposes of this section, having possession of any property shall be taken to be doing an act in relation to it.

(7) In proceedings against a person for an offence under this section, it is a defence to prove that—

(a) he intended to disclose to a constable such a suspicion, belief or matter as is mentioned in subsection (5) above, but

(b) there is reasonable excuse for his failure to make the disclosure in accordance with paragraph (b) of that subsection.

(8) In the case of a person who was in employment at the relevant time, subsections (5) and (7) above shall have effect in relation to disclosures, and intended disclosures, to the appropriate person in accordance with the procedure established by his employer for the making of such disclosures as they have effect in relation to disclosures, and intended disclosures, to a constable.

(9) A person guilty of an offence under this section is liable—

(a) on summary conviction, to imprisonment for a term not exceeding six months or a fine not exceeding the statutory maximum or to both, or

(b) on conviction on indictment, to imprisonment for a term not exceeding fourteen years or a fine or to both.

(10) No constable or other person shall be guilty of an offence under this section in respect of anything done by him in the course of acting in connection with the enforcement, or intended enforcement, of any provision of this Act or of any other enactment relating to drug trafficking or the proceedings of such trafficking.".

(2) In section 2(4) of the Act of 1986 (circumstances where assumptions are not to be made), after first "section" there shall be inserted "23A or".

DEFINITIONS
"drug trafficking": s.38(1) of the DTOA.
"inadequate consideration": s.16; s.23A of the DTOA.
"possession": s.23A(6) of the DTOA; s.42A(6) of the Criminal Justice (Scotland) Act 1987.
"proceeds of drug trafficking": s.2(1)(a) of the DTOA.
"property": s.38(1) of the DTOA.

GENERAL NOTE
This section should be read and compared with s.14(3) of the Criminal Justice (International Co-operation) Act 1990 since both were drafted to deal with property coming to the hands of another which represents in whole, or in part, directly or indirectly, the proceeds of drug trafficking. The offence under s.14(3) of the 1990 Act (repealed by Sched. 6, Pt. I of the 1993 Act) was narrower in the sense that it was confined to property which had been "acquired" presumably in the sense that the recipient acquired an interest in the property or was held by the recipient on more than a merely temporary or short-term basis. By contrast, s.23A of the DTOA includes any acquisition, but the section also includes the *possession* or *use of* that property. Presumably, the defendant (in order to be in possession) must know that he has it (see *Warner* v. *Metropolitan Police Commissioner* [1969] 2 A.C. 256), and this seems to be supported by s.23A(6) of the DTOA which appears to define possession in terms of "doing an act in relation to" the property. This may mean no more than that a person exercises control over the property in question.
An essential exemption is given by s.23A(10) of the DTOA to persons who deal with the property in connection with the investigation, defection or judicial proceedings relating to drug trafficking matters by virtue of any enactment.
On the other hand, s.23A is narrower than s.14(3) of the 1990 Act in terms of the *mens rea* required to be proved. Under s.14(3) it was enough if a defendant acquired property "knowing or having reasonable grounds to suspect" its drug trafficking origins. The objective element does not appear in s.23A and what is required is actual knowledge; suspicion is not enough.

S.23A(2) of the DTOA
Under s.14(3) of the 1990 Act the burden was on the prosecution to prove that the defendant acquired the property for "no or inadequate consideration" but this last ingredient is omitted from s.23A. Instead, the burden is on the defendant to prove that he provided "adequate consideration". Presumably it will be for the jury to decide whether the consideration provided is in fact "adequate" having regard to s.23A(3) but it is likely that it will fall to the courts to decide what that phrase means. Section 23A(3) of the DTOA provides two instances where consideration is "inadequate" but is this subsection a closed category? If a person pays an excessive price for the property is the consideration to be regarded as being "adequate"? By s.38(1) of the DTOA, "property" includes money. If services are provided in consideration for a substantial sum of drug money, how is it to be determined that the value of the service was not worth what was claimed or charged? (see *Hansard*, H.C. Vol. 222, col. 907, Sir Ivan Lawrence, Q.C.). In the majority of cases issues as to value and ambiguity may be resolved with expert help.
The upshot of s.23A seems to be that it will be lawful to use a drug trafficker's villa or motor vehicle providing an adequate sum is paid for it—but it will be an offence if he pays too little or nothing. It seems that knowledge of the origins of the property will not taint the consideration nor will it negate the defence.
Section 23A(2) should be read in conjunction with s.23A(4).

S.23A(4) of the DTOA
This provision is designed to achieve the same result as s.14(5) of the 1990 Act (s.14(5) is repealed by Sched. 6, Pt. I of the 1993 Act). The provisions of s.23A are designed to *exclude* persons who provide goods or services to another so long as the goods or services supplied were not of "assistance to him in drug trafficking" (see s.23A(4) of the DTOA). If the goods or services are of assistance to him then s.23A(4) creates a fiction and deems the supply not to be adequate consideration. Section 23A(4) is intended to protect trades-people who are paid for goods and services from the proceeds of drug trafficking (see Standing Committee B, col. 93, June 8, 1993). It is not clear whether the defendant must know or intend that the goods or services supplied "are of assistance to him in drug trafficking" for the purposes of s.23A(4).

S.23A(5) and (7) of the DTOA
This follows the model provided by s.24(3) of the DTOA; and see Sched. 7 to the Prevention

of Terrorism (Temporary Provisions) Act 1989. Section 23A(5) and (7) are designed to protect persons (particularly those employed in the financial sector) from any action for breach of contract, confidence or a duty arising out of their obligations to their clients.

Both s.23A(5) and s.24(3) of the DTOA refer to the disclosure of "suspicions". There would seem to be two reasons why disclosure based on "suspicion" is said to be irrelevant. First, disclosure based on any higher standard would present individuals with a difficult issue of fact to resolve. How much information do they need to satisfy themselves before they could (or are required to) disclose a belief? (see *Hansard*, H.L. Vol. 474, col. 1114). Secondly, law enforcement agencies act on suspicion and accordingly a lot of intelligence could be lost if all that could be disclosed were beliefs. The Government considered that it would be "up to the policemen, the professions, [and] the investigators to decide whether or not [the suspicion] was true" (*per* Earl Ferrers, *Hansard*, H.L. Vol. 540, col. 753).

S.23A(7) of the DTOA
This follows the model in s.24(4)(c) of the DTOA.

S.23A(10) of the DTOA
This provision is very widely drawn. It is not clear whether legal advisers (whether prosecuting or defending) are included in this provision.

Acquisition, possession or use of proceeds of drug trafficking: Scotland

17.—(1) The following section shall be inserted in the Criminal Justice (Scotland) Act 1987, after section 42—

> **"Acquisition, possession or use of proceeds of drug trafficking**
>
> 42A.—(1) A person is guilty of an offence if, knowing that any property is, or in whole or in part directly or indirectly represents, another person's proceeds of drug trafficking, he acquires or uses that property or has possession of it.
>
> (2) It is a defence to a charge of committing an offence under this section that the person charged acquired or used the property or had possession of it for adequate consideration.
>
> (3) For the purposes of subsection (2) above—
>
>   (a) a person acquires property for inadequate consideration if the value of the consideration is significantly less than the value of the property; and
>
>   (b) a person uses or has possession of property for inadequate consideration if the value of the consideration is significantly less than the value of his use or possession of the property.
>
> (4) The provision for any person of services or goods which are of assistance to him in drug trafficking shall not be treated as consideration for the purposes of subsection (2) above.
>
> (5) Where a person discloses to a constable or to a person commissioned by the Commissioners of Customs and Excise a suspicion or belief that any property is, or in whole or in part directly or indirectly represents, another person's proceeds of drug trafficking, or discloses to a constable or a person so commissioned any matter on which such a suspicion or belief is based—
>
>   (a) the disclosure shall not be treated as a breach of any restriction upon the disclosure of information imposed by statute or otherwise; and
>
>   (b) if he does any act in relation to the property in contravention of subsection (1) above, he does not commit an offence under this section if—
>
>   (i) the disclosure is made before he does the act concerned and the act is done with the consent of the constable or person so commissioned, or
>
>   (ii) the disclosure is made after he does the act, but on his initiative and as soon as it is reasonable for him to make it.

(6) For the purposes of this section having possession of any property shall be taken to be doing an act in relation to it.

(7) In proceedings against a person for an offence under this section, it is a defence to prove that—

(a) he intended to disclose to a constable or a person so commissioned such a suspicion, belief or matter as is mentioned in subsection (5) above; but

(b) there is reasonable excuse for his failure to make the disclosure in accordance with paragraph (b) of that subsection.

(8) In the case of a person who was in employment at the relevant time, subsections (5) and (7) above shall have effect in relation to disclosures, and intended disclosures, to the appropriate person in accordance with the procedure established by his employer for the making of such disclosures as they have effect in relation to disclosures, and intended disclosures, to a constable or a person so commissioned.

(9) A person guilty of an offence under this section is liable—

(a) on summary conviction, to imprisonment for a term not exceeding six months or to a fine not exceeding the statutory maximum or to both; or

(b) on conviction on indictment, to imprisonment for a term not exceeding fourteen years or to a fine or to both.

(10) No constable, person so commissioned or other person shall be guilty of an offence under this section in respect of anything done by him in the course of acting in connection with the enforcement, or intended enforcement, of any provision of this Act or of any other enactment relating to drug trafficking or the proceeds of such trafficking.".

(2) In section 3(3) of the Act of 1987 (circumstances where assumptions are not to be made), after the word "section" where it first occurs there shall be inserted the words "42A or".

DEFINITIONS

"drug trafficking": s.38(1) of the DTOA.
"inadequate consideration": s.16; s.23A of the DTOA.
"possession": s.23A(6) of the DTOA; s.42A(6) of the Criminal Justice (Scotland) Act 1987.
"proceeds of drug trafficking": s.2(1)(a) of the DTOA.
"property": s.38(1) of the DTOA.

GENERAL NOTE

See the commentary to s.16 above.

Offences in connection with laundering money from drug trafficking

18.—(1) The following sections shall be inserted in the Drug Trafficking Offences Act 1986, after section 26A— •

"Offences in connection with money laundering

Failure to disclose knowledge or suspicion of money laundering

26B.—(1) A person is guilty of an offence if—

(a) he knows, or suspects, that another person is engaged in drug money laundering,

(b) the information, or other matter, on which that knowledge or suspicion is based came to his attention in the course of his trade, profession, business or employment, and

(c) he does not disclose the information or other matter to a constable as soon as is reasonably practicable after it comes to his attention.

(2) Subsection (1) above does not make it an offence for a professional legal adviser to fail to disclose any information or other matter which has come to him in privileged circumstances.

(3) It is a defence to a charge of committing an offence under this section that the person charged had a reasonable excuse for not disclosing the information or other matter in question.

(4) Where a person discloses to a constable—

(a) his suspicion or belief that another person is engaged in drug money laundering, or

(b) any information or other matter on which that suspicion or belief is based,

the disclosure shall not be treated as a breach of any restriction imposed by statute or otherwise.

(5) Without prejudice to subsection (3) or (4) above, in the case of a person who was in employment at the relevant time, it is a defence to a charge of committing an offence under this section that he disclosed the information or other matter in question to the appropriate person in accordance with the procedure established by his employer for the making of such disclosures.

(6) A disclosure to which subsection (5) above applies shall not be treated as a breach of any restriction imposed by statute or otherwise.

(7) In this section, "drug money laundering" means doing any act which constitutes an offence under—

(a) section 23A or 24 of this Act; or

(b) section 14 of the Criminal Justice (International Co-operation) Act 1990 (concealing or transferring proceeds of drug trafficking);

or, in the case of an act done otherwise than in England and Wales, would constitute such an offence if done in England and Wales.

(8) For the purposes of subsection (7) above, having possession of any property shall be taken to be doing an act in relation to it.

(9) For the purposes of this section, any information or other matter comes to a professional legal adviser in privileged circumstances if it is communicated, or given, to him—

(a) by, or by a representative of, a client of his in connection with the giving by the adviser of legal advice to the client;

(b) by, or by a representative of, a person seeking legal advice from the adviser; or

(c) by any person—

(i) in contemplation of, or in connection with, legal proceedings; and

(ii) for the purpose of those proceedings.

(10) No information or other matter shall be treated as coming to a professional legal adviser in privileged circumstances if it is communicated or given with a view to furthering any criminal purpose.

(11) A person guilty of an offence under this section shall be liable—

(a) on summary conviction, to imprisonment for a term not exceeding six months or a fine not exceeding the statutory maximum or to both, or

(b) on conviction on indictment, to imprisonment for a term not exceeding five years or a fine or to both.

Tipping-off

26C.—(1) A person is guilty of an offence if—

(a) he knows or suspects that a constable is acting, or is proposing to act, in connection with an investigation which is being, or is about to be, conducted into drug money laundering, and

(b) he discloses to any other person information or any other matter which is likely to prejudice that investigation, or proposed investigation.

(2) A person is guilty of an offence if—

(a) he knows or suspects that a disclosure ("the disclosure") has been made to a constable under section 23A, 24 or 26B of this Act, and

(b) he discloses to any other person information or any other matter which is likely to prejudice any investigation which might be conducted following the disclosure.

(3) A person is guilty of an offence if—

(a) he knows or suspects that a disclosure of a kind mentioned in section 23A(8), 24(4A) or 26B(5) of this Act ("the disclosure") has been made, and

(b) he discloses to any person information or any other matter which is likely to prejudice any investigation which might be conducted following the disclosure.

(4) Nothing in subsections (1) to (3) above makes it an offence for a professional legal adviser to disclose any information or other matter—

(a) to, or to a representative of, a client of his in connection with the giving by the adviser of legal advice to the client; or

(b) to any person—

(i) in contemplation of, or in connection with, legal proceedings; and

(ii) for the purpose of those proceedings.

(5) Subsection (4) above does not apply in relation to any information or other matter which is disclosed with a view to furthering any criminal purpose.

(6) In proceedings against a person for an offence under subsection (1), (2) or (3) above, it is a defence to prove that he did not know or suspect that the disclosure was likely to be prejudicial in the way mentioned in that subsection.

(7) In this section "drug money laundering" has the same meaning as in section 26B of this Act.

(8) A person guilty of an offence under this section shall be liable—

(a) on summary conviction, to imprisonment for a term not exceeding six months or a fine not exceeding the statutory maximum or to both, or

(b) on conviction on indictment, to imprisonment for a term not exceeding five years or a fine or to both.

(9) No constable or other person shall be guilty of an offence under this section in respect of anything done by him in the course of acting in connection with the enforcement, or intended enforcement, of any provision of this Act or of any other enactment relating to drug trafficking or the proceeds of such trafficking.".

(2) In section 24 of the Drug Trafficking Offences Act 1986 (assisting another to retain the benefit of drug trafficking), in subsection (3)(a) for the word "contract" there shall be substituted "statute or otherwise".

(3) In section 24 of the Act of 1986, the following subsection shall be inserted after subsection (4)—

"(4A) In the case of a person who was in employment at the relevant time, subsections (3) and (4) above shall have effect in relation to disclosures, and intended disclosures, to the appropriate person in accordance with the procedure established by his employer for the making of such disclosures as they have effect in relation to disclosures, and intended disclosures, to a constable.".

DEFINITIONS
"drug money laundering": s.26B(7) of the DTOA.
"privileged circumstances": s.26B(9) and (10) of the DTOA.

GENERAL NOTE

S.26B of the DTOA
Section 26B creates a new offence in English law. Although s.24 of the DTOA (and s.23A of that Act) both include provisions to protect those who disclose their suspicions concerning drug trafficking carried on by another, in neither provision is there an actual obligation to make a disclosure. By contrast, s.26B makes it an offence to *fail* to disclose to a constable (or to an "appropriate person" (s.26B(5)) as soon as reasonably practicable, knowledge or even a suspicion that a person is engaged in drug-money laundering, where that knowledge or suspicion is gained in the course of a person's employment. Protection is afforded to legal advisers who give legal advice on a "privileged occasion" as defined by s.26B(9) but not if information is received or given to further "any criminal purpose"—not just drug trafficking (s.26B(10)).
The history of this offence has its roots in American law (see the commentary to s.16). When the DTOA was being debated as a Bill, Lord Denning moved an amendment (No. 30; subsequently withdrawn: *Hansard*, H.L. Vol. 472, col. 1185) which proposed that the Secretary of State be empowered to draw up a scheme requiring banks and financial institutions to report to various authorities any deposit of or a transaction in currency exceeding a certain sum. This, in turn, was modelled on the American Bank Secrecy Act.
Following publication of the *Guidance Notes on Money Laundering for Banks and Building Societies*, on December 10, 1990, the number of suspicious transactions amounted to some 12,000 cases without mandatory legislation (*Hansard*, H.L. Vol. 539, cols. 1373 and 1385). The Home Affairs Committee had previously expressed concern that financial institutions would adopt an approach that was too passive and which would require the Government to "take the initiative" (para. 8 of their Seventh Report, 1988–89). In the light of agreements reached by the Council of Europe Convention on Laundering, Tracing, Seizure and Confiscation of Proceeds of Crime 1990) and the Council Directive 91/308/E.E.C., s.26B of the DTOA was enacted.
By Art. 6 of the above Directive, Member States are required to ensure that credit and financial institutions, their directors and employees co-operate fully with the authorities by informing them of "any fact which might be an indication of money laundering". By Art. 7 such institutions are required to "refrain from carrying out transactions which they know or suspect to be related to money laundering until they have appraised the authorities".
By Art. 9, a disclosure in good faith to the authorities "shall not constitute a breach of any restriction on disclosure of information imposed by contract or by any legislative, regulatory or administrative provision". The provisions of that Directive are to extend in whole, or in part, to professions and various undertakings "likely to be used for money laundering purposes" (Art. 12).
Section 26B is not, by itself, as extensive in its scope as the Directive permits since s.26B is limited to drug-money laundering only.
The reasons for including a mere suspicion in the provision are essentially the same as those relevant to s.23A of the DTOA (*i.e.* s.23A(5) and (7)) (as inserted by s.16 of the 1993 Act). See the commentary to s.16 above.

S.26C of the DTOA
Section 26C of the DTOA creates three offences. First, it is an offence for a defendant who knows or suspects that an investigation into drug-money laundering is being conducted (or is about to be) to divulge that fact, or other information, which is likely to prejudice such an investigation (s.26C(1)). Secondly, if a disclosure of a suspicion (or information) has been lawfully disclosed to a constable (*e.g.* by a bank) under s.23A, s.24 or s.26B then it is an offence if that fact is disclosed to another and which is likely to prejudice an investigation which might be conducted on the basis of the original disclosure (s.26C(2)). Third, the same offence as in s.26C(2), above, but where the original disclosure was made to an "appropriate person" (*e.g.* an employer).
There is an exemption in the case of legal advisers (within the terms of s.26C(4) and (5)).
It is a defence to each of the three offences if the defendant proves that he did not know or suspect that the disclosure was likely to be prejudicial (s.26C(6)).

Offences in connection with laundering money from drug trafficking: Scotland

19.—(1) The following sections shall be inserted after section 43 of the Criminal Justice (Scotland) Act 1987—

"Failure to disclose knowledge or suspicion of money laundering

43A.—(1) A person is guilty of an offence if—

(a) he knows, or suspects, that another person is engaged in drug money laundering,

(b) the information, or other matter, on which that knowledge or suspicion is based came to his attention in the course of his trade, profession, business or employment, and

(c) he does not disclose the information or other matter to a constable or to a person commissioned by the Commissioners of Customs and Excise as soon as is reasonably practicable after it comes to his attention.

(2) Subsection (1) above does not make it an offence for a professional legal adviser to fail to disclose any information or other matter which has come to him in privileged circumstances.

(3) It is a defence to a charge of committing an offence under this section that the person charged had a reasonable excuse for not disclosing the information or other matter in question.

(4) Where a person discloses to a constable or a person so commissioned—

(a) his suspicion or belief that another person is engaged in drug money laundering, or

(b) any information or other matter on which that suspicion or belief is based,

the disclosure shall not be treated as a breach of any restriction imposed by statute or otherwise.

(5) Without prejudice to subsection (3) or (4) above, in the case of a person who was in employment at the relevant time, it is a defence to a charge of committing an offence under this section that he disclosed the information or other matter in question to the appropriate person in accordance with the procedure established by his employer for the making of such disclosures.

(6) A disclosure to which subsection (5) above applies shall not be treated as a breach of any restriction imposed by statute or otherwise.

(7) In this section "drug money laundering" means doing any act which constitutes an offence under—

(a) section 42A or 43 of this Act; or

(b) section 14 of the Criminal Justice (International Co-operation) Act 1990 (concealing or transferring proceeds of drug trafficking),

or, in the case of an act done otherwise than in Scotland, would constitute such an offence if done in Scotland.

(8) For the purposes of subsection (7) above, having possession of any property shall be taken to be doing an act in relation to it.

(9) For the purposes of this section, any information or other matter comes to a professional legal adviser in privileged circumstances if it is communicated, or given, to him—

(a) by, or by a representative of, a client of his in connection with the giving by the adviser of legal advice to the client;

(b) by, or by a representative of, a person seeking legal advice from the adviser; or

(c) by any person—

(i) in contemplation of, or in connection with, legal proceedings; and

(ii) for the purpose of those proceedings.

(10) No information or other matter shall be treated as coming to a professional legal adviser in privileged circumstances if it is communicated or given with a view to furthering any criminal purpose.

(11) A person guilty of an offence under this section shall be liable—

(a) on summary conviction, to imprisonment for a term not exceeding six months or a fine not exceeding the statutory maximum or to both, or

(b) on conviction on indictment, to imprisonment for a term not exceeding five years or a fine, or to both.

Tipping-off

43B.—(1) A person is guilty of an offence if—

(a) he knows or suspects that a constable or a person commissioned by the Commissioners of Customs and Excise is acting, or is proposing to act, in connection with an investigation which is being, or is about to be, conducted into drug money laundering within the meaning of subsections (7) and (8) of section 43A of this Act; and

(b) he discloses to any other person information or any other matter which is likely to prejudice that investigation, or proposed investigation.

(2) A person is guilty of an offence if—

(a) he knows or suspects that a disclosure has been made to a constable, or a person so commissioned, under section 42A, 43 or 43A of this Act; and

(b) he discloses to any other person information or any other matter which is likely to prejudice any investigation which might be conducted following the disclosure.

(3) A person is guilty of an offence if—

(a) he knows or suspects that a disclosure of a kind mentioned in section 42A(8), 43(4A) or 43A(5) of this Act has been made; and

(b) he discloses to any person information or any other matter which is likely to prejudice any investigation which might be conducted following the disclosure.

(4) Nothing in subsections (1) to (3) above makes it an offence for a professional legal adviser to disclose any information or other matter—

(a) to, or to a representative of, a client of his in connection with the giving by the adviser of legal advice to the client; or

(b) to any person—

(i) in contemplation of, or in connection with, legal proceedings; and

(ii) for the purpose of those proceedings.

(5) Subsection (4) above does not apply in relation to any information or other matter which is disclosed with a view to furthering any criminal purpose.

(6) In proceedings against a person for an offence under subsection (1), (2) or (3) above, it is a defence to prove that he did not know or suspect that the disclosure was likely to be prejudicial in the way mentioned in that subsection.

(7) A person guilty of an offence under this section shall be liable—

(a) on summary conviction, to imprisonment for a term not exceeding six months or a fine not exceeding the statutory maximum or to both, or

(b) on conviction on indictment, to imprisonment for a term not exceeding five years or a fine, or to both.

(8) No constable, person so commissioned or other person shall be guilty of an offence under this section in respect of anything done by him in the course of acting in connection with the enforcement, or intended enforcement, of any provision of this Act or of any other

enactment relating to drug trafficking or the proceeds of such trafficking.".

(2) In section 43 of the Act of 1987 (assisting another to retain the proceeds of drug trafficking)—

(a) in subsection (3), after the words "trafficking or" there shall be inserted the words "discloses to a constable or a person so commissioned"; and

(b) in paragraph (a) of subsection (3), for the word "contract" there shall be substituted "statute or otherwise".

(3) After subsection (4) of that section, there shall be inserted the following subsection—

"(4A) In the case of a person who was in employment at the relevant time, subsections (3) and (4) above shall have effect in relation to disclosures, and intended disclosures, to the appropriate person in accordance with the procedure established by his employer for the making of such disclosures as they have effect in relation to disclosures, and intended disclosures, to a constable or a person commissioned as aforesaid.".

DEFINITIONS
"drug-money laundering": s.26B(7) of the DTOA.
"privileged circumstances": s.26B(9) and (10) of the DTOA.

GENERAL NOTE
This section introduces provisions, similar to s.18 above, into the Criminal Justice (Scotland) Act 1987.

Prosecution by order of the Commissioners of Customs and Excise

20.—(1) The following section shall be inserted in the Drug Trafficking Offences Act 1986, after section 36—

"Prosecution by order of the Commissioners of Customs and Excise
36A.—(1) Proceedings for an offence to which this section applies ("a specified offence") may be instituted by order of the Commissioners.

(2) Any proceedings for a specified offence which are so instituted shall be commenced in the name of an officer.

(3) In the case of the death, removal, discharge or absence of the officer in whose name any proceedings for a specified offence were commenced, those proceedings may be continued by another officer.

(4) Where the Commissioners investigate, or propose to investigate, any matter with a view to determining—

(a) whether there are grounds for believing that a specified offence has been committed, or

(b) whether a person should be prosecuted for a specified offence, that matter shall be treated as an assigned matter within the meaning of the Customs and Excise Management Act 1979.

(5) Nothing in this section shall be taken—

(a) to prevent any person (including any officer) who has power to arrest, detain or prosecute any person for a specified offence from doing so; or

(b) to prevent a court from proceeding to deal with a person brought before it following his arrest by an officer for a specified offence, even though the proceedings have not been instituted by an order made under subsection (1) above.

(6) In this section—

"the Commissioners" means the Commissioners of Customs and Excise;

"officer" means a person commissioned by the Commissioners; and

"specified offence" means—

> (a) an offence under section 23A, 24, 26B, 26C or 31 of this Act or section 14 of the Criminal Justice (International Co-operation) Act 1990 (concealing or transferring proceeds of drug trafficking);
>
> (b) attempting to commit, conspiracy to commit or incitement to commit, any such offence; or
>
> (c) any other offence of a kind prescribed in regulations made by the Secretary of State for the purposes of this section.

(7) The power to make regulations under subsection (6) above shall be exercisable by statutory instrument.

(8) Any such instrument shall be subject to annulment in pursuance of a resolution of either House of Parliament.".

(2) The following section shall be inserted in the Criminal Justice (Scotland) Act 1987, after section 40—

"Prosecution by order of the Commissioners of Customs and Excise

40A.—(1) Summary proceedings for a specified offence may be instituted by order of the Commissioners and shall, if so instituted, be commenced in the name of an officer.

(2) In the case of the death, removal, discharge or absence of the officer in whose name any proceedings for a specified offence were commenced, those proceedings may be continued by another officer.

(3) Where the Commissioners investigate, or propose to investigate, any matter with a view to determining—

> (a) whether there are grounds for believing that a specified offence has been committed, or

(b) whether a person should be prosecuted for a specified offence, that matter shall be treated as an assigned matter within the meaning of the Customs and Excise Management Act 1979.

(4) Nothing in this section shall be taken—

> (a) to prevent any person (including any officer) who has power to arrest, detain or prosecute any person for a specified offence from doing so; or
>
> (b) to prevent a court from proceeding to deal with a person brought before it following his arrest by an officer for a specified offence, even though the proceedings have not been instituted by an order made under subsection (1) above.

(5) In this section—

> "the Commissioners" means the Commissioners of Customs and Excise,
>
> "officer" means a person commissioned by the Commissioners; and
>
> "specified offence" means—
>
> > (a) an offence under section 42, 42A, 43, 43A or 43B of this Act or section 14 of the Criminal Justice (International Co-operation) Act 1990 (concealing or transferring proceeds of drug trafficking);
> >
> > (b) attempting to commit, conspiracy to commit or incitement to commit, any such offence; or
> >
> > (c) any other offence of a kind prescribed in regulations made by the Secretary of State for the purposes of this section.

(6) Regulations under subsection (5) above shall be made by statutory instrument subject to annulment in pursuance of a resolution of either House of Parliament.".

DEFINITIONS
   "the Commissioner": s.36A(6) of the DTOA.
   "officer": s.36A(6) of the DTOA.
   "specified offence": s.36A(6) of the DTOA.

Enforcement

Enforcement of certain orders

21.—(1) In section 9 of the Criminal Justice (International Co-operation) Act 1990 (enforcement of overseas forfeiture orders), in subsection (1)(b), the words "or intended for use" shall be inserted after "used".

   (2) In section 24A of the Drug Trafficking Offences Act 1986 (recognition and enforcement of certain orders), the following shall be substituted for subsection (6)—

   "(6) An Order in Council under this section shall be subject to annulment in pursuance of a resolution of either House of Parliament.".

   (3) The same subsection as is inserted in section 24A of the Act of 1986 by subsection (2) shall be inserted in—

   (a) section 25 of that Act (but in substitution for subsection (4));
   (b) section 26 of that Act (but in substitution for subsection (5));
   (c) section 29 of the Criminal Justice (Scotland) Act 1987 (but in substitution for subsection (4));
   (d) section 30 of the Act of 1987 (but in substitution for subsection (5));
   (e) section 94 of the Criminal Justice Act 1988 (but in substitution for subsection (4));
   (f) section 95 of the Act of 1988 (but in substitution of subsection (3));
   (g) section 96 of the Act of 1988 (but in substitution for subsection (5));
   (h) section 9 of the Criminal Justice (International Co-operation) Act 1990 (but in substitution for subsection (5)).

Enforcement of Northern Ireland orders: drug trafficking

22.—(1) In section 25 of the Drug Trafficking Offences Act 1986 (enforcement of Northern (Ireland orders), in subsection (1), for "19" there shall be substituted "18" and the following subsection shall be inserted after subsection (3)—

   "(3A) An Order in Council under this section may, in particular, provide for section 18 of the Civil Jurisdiction and Judgments Act 1982 (enforcement of United Kingdom judgments in other parts of the United Kingdom) not to apply in relation to such orders as may be prescribed by the Order.".

   (2) In section 29 of the Criminal Justice (Scotland) Act 1987 (enforcement of Northern Ireland orders), the following subsection shall be inserted after subsection (3)—

   "(3A) An Order in Council under this section may, in particular, provide for section 18 of the Civil Jurisdiction and Judgments Act 1982 (enforcement of United Kingdom judgments in other parts of the United Kingdom) not to apply in relation to such orders as may be prescribed by the Order.".

Transfer of certain enforcement powers to the Commissioners of Customs and Excise

23.—(1) The functions of the Secretary of State under section 20 of the Criminal Justice (International Co-operation) Act 1990 (enforcement powers in relation to ships) are transferred to the Commissioners of Customs and Excise.

   (2) The following consequential amendments shall be made in the Act of 1990—

(a) in section 20, for "Secretary of State", "he" and "his", wherever they occur, there shall be substituted, respectively, "Commissioners of Customs and Excise", "they" and "their";

(b) in section 21(3), for "Secretary of State", where first occurring, there shall be substituted "Commissioners of Customs and Excise"; and

(c) in paragraph 2(2) of Schedule 3, for "Secretary of State" there shall be substituted "Commissioners of Customs and Excise".

(3) The transfer of functions effected by this section shall not affect the validity of any action taken or begun under section 20 of the Act of 1990 before the coming into force of this section.

Miscellaneous

Miscellaneous amendments

24.—(1) In section 8(6) of the Drug Trafficking Offences Act 1986 (restraint orders), for "the court may" there shall be substituted "the High Court or a county court may".

(2) In sections 12(1) and (2), 13(1), 15(2), 16(2), 17(2) and 19(2)(b)(i) of that Act after "High Court" there shall be inserted, in each case, "or a county court".

(3) In section 17A(2) of that Act (expenses of insolvency practitioner dealing with property subject to restraint order), for "(3)(za)" there shall be substituted "(4)".

(4) In section 18(2) of that Act (remuneration and expenses of receiver), for "(3B)" there shall be substituted "(5)".

(5) In section 27 of that Act (application for an order to make material available), in subsection (8) for "this section" there shall be substituted "subsection (1) above" and the following subsection shall be added at the end—

"(10) An application under subsection (1) or (5) above may be made ex parte to a judge in chambers.".

(6) In section 27(5) of that Act the words "or, as the case may be, the sheriff" (which are spent) shall be omitted.

(7) Section 38(1) of that Act (interpretation) shall be amended in accordance with subsections (8) and (9).

(8) In the definition of "drug trafficking", in paragraph (d), the words "or would be such an offence if it took place in England and Wales" shall be inserted at the end and the following paragraphs shall be inserted after paragraph (d)—

"(e) acquiring, having possession of or using property in circumstances which amount to the commission of an offence under section 23A of this Act or which would be such an offence if it took place in England and Wales;

(f) conduct which is an offence under section 14 (concealing or transferring proceeds of drug trafficking) of the Criminal Justice (International Co-operation) Act 1990 or which would be such an offence if it took place in England and Wales;

(g) using any ship for illicit traffic in controlled drugs in circumstances which amount to the commission of an offence under section 19 of the Act of 1990;".

(9) In the definition of "drug trafficking offence", the following paragraph shall be inserted after paragraph (c)—

"(cc) an offence under section 23A of this Act;".

(10) In section 18(4A) of the Civil Jurisdiction and Judgments Act 1982 (enforcement of United Kingdom judgments in other parts of the United Kingdom), after "High Court" there shall be inserted "or a county court".

(11) In section 116(2)(a) of the Police and Criminal Evidence Act 1984 (drug trafficking offences to be arrestable offences that are always serious), for "(d)" there shall be substituted "(dd)".

(12) Section 1 of the Criminal Justice (Scotland) Act 1987 (confiscation orders in relation to drug trafficking offences) shall be amended in accordance with subsections (13) to (15).

(13) In subsection (2) (offences in relation to which confiscation orders may be made), the following paragraph shall be inserted after paragraph (b)—

"(bb) an offence under section 42A of this Act;".

(14) In subsection (6) (definition of "drug trafficking"), after paragraph (e) there shall be inserted the following paragraphs—

"(f) acquiring, having possession of or using property in contravention of section 42A of this Act;

(g) concealing or transferring the proceeds of drug trafficking in contravention of section 14 of the Act of 1990;

(h) using any ship for illicit traffic in controlled drugs in contravention of section 19 of the Act of 1990;".

(15) After subsection (6) there shall be inserted the following subsection—

"(7) In paragraphs (e) to (g) of subsection (6) above, references to conduct in contravention of the enactments mentioned in those paragraphs include conduct which would contravene the enactments if it took place in Scotland.".

Appeal against order forfeiting drug trafficking cash

25.—(1) The following sections shall be inserted in the Criminal Justice (International Co-operation) Act 1990, after section 26—

"**Appeal against section 26 order**
26A.—(1) This section applies where an order for the forfeiture of cash ("the forfeiture order") is made under section 26 above by a magistrates' court.

(2) Any party to the proceedings in which the forfeiture order is made (other than the applicant for the order) may, before the end of the period of 30 days beginning with the date on which it is made, appeal to the Crown Court or, in Northern Ireland, to a county court.

(3) An appeal under this section shall be by way of a rehearing.

(4) On an application made by the appellant to a magistrates' court at any time, that court may order the release of so much of the cash to which the forfeiture order relates as it considers appropriate to enable him to meet his legal expenses in connection with the appeal.

(5) The court hearing an appeal under this section may make such order as it considers appropriate.

(6) If it upholds the appeal, the court may order the release of the cash, or (as the case may be) the remaining cash, together with any accrued interest.

(7) Section 26(3) applies in relation to a rehearing on an appeal under this section as it applies to proceedings under section 26.

Appeal against section 26 order: Scotland
26B. Any party to proceedings in which an order for the forfeiture of cash is made by the sheriff under section 26 above may appeal against the order to the Court of Session.".

(2) The Act of 1990 shall be further amended as follows.

(3) In section 26 (forfeiture of drug trafficking cash), after subsection (3) there shall be inserted the following subsection—

"(4) Proceedings on an application under this section to the sheriff shall be civil proceedings.".

(4) In section 28 (procedure), the words "or appeals" shall be inserted after the word "applications" in each place where it occurs in subsection (2).

(5) In section 30 (forfeited cash to be paid into the Consolidated Fund), the following subsection shall be added at the end—

"(3) Subsection (2) above does not apply—

(a) where an appeal is made under section 26A or 26B above, before the appeal is determined or otherwise disposed of; and

(b) in any other case—

(i) where the forfeiture was ordered by a magistrates' court, before the end of the period of 30 days mentioned in section 26A(2); or

(ii) where the forfeiture was ordered by the sheriff, before the end of any period within which, in accordance with rules of court, an appeal under section 26B must be made.".

(6) The amendments made by this section apply only in relation to orders under section 26 of the Act of 1990 made on or after the date on which this section comes into force.

Disclosure of information etc. received in privileged circumstances

26.—(1) In section 31 of the Drug Trafficking Offences Act 1986 (offence of prejudicing investigation), the following subsections shall be inserted after subsection (2)—

"(2A) Nothing in subsection (1) above makes it an offence for a professional legal adviser to disclose any information or other matter—

(a) to, or to a representative of, a client of his in connection with the giving by the adviser of legal advice to the client; or

(b) to any person—

(i) in contemplation of, or in connection with, legal proceedings; and

(ii) for the purpose of those proceedings.

(2B) Subsection (2A) above does not apply in relation to any information or other matter which is disclosed with a view to furthering any criminal purpose.".

(2) The same subsections as are inserted in section 31 of the Act of 1986 by subsection (1) shall be inserted in section 42 of the Criminal Justice (Scotland) Act 1987 (corresponding Scottish provision).

PART III

PROCEEDS OF CRIMINAL CONDUCT

GENERAL NOTE AND INTRODUCTION

Part III makes major changes to Pt. VI of the Criminal Justice Act 1988 but the 1988 Act remains considerably less "draconian" than the DTOA. The reason stems from the fact that the court retain a far greater degree of discretion in the making of orders under the CJA 1988.

Whereas the reforms and amendments made to the DTOA radically re-design the machinery for making and operating any confiscation orders, the basic structure of the 1988 Act remains largely unaltered although the powers of the court have been extended. The two principal changes to the machinery are, first, that the standard of proof applicable is the civil standard (s.71(7A) of the CJA 1988 inserted by s.27 of the 1993 Act) and second that the court may postpone a determination of the amount which may be recovered under the 1988 Act until the court has sentenced the defendant (s.72A of the CJA 1988 inserted by s.28 of the 1993 Act). Unlike the DTOA, there are no corresponding amendments made to the Criminal Justice Act 1988 which will empower the High Court to confiscate the benefits of an absconding or deceased defendant whether or not he was convicted of a relevant offence. Again, unlike the DTOA, no provision is made to enforce satisfaction of a confiscation order notwithstanding that the defendant has served a sentence of imprisonment in default of payment (see by contrast s.6(7) of the DTOA, inserted by s.13(1) of the 1993 Act).

However, the 1993 Act does introduce three "money laundering offences" into the CJA 1988, namely (1) "assisting another to retain the benefit of criminal conduct" (s.93A of the CJA 1988 inserted by s.29(1) of the 1993 Act which broadly mirrors s.24 of the DTOA); (2) the "acquisition, possession or use of the proceeds of criminal conduct" (s.93B of the CJA 1988, inserted by s.30 of the 1993 Act, which follows the model inserted into s.23A of the DTOA by s.16(1) of the 1993 Act); and (3) the "concealing or transferring of the proceeds of criminal conduct" (s.93C of the CJA 1988, inserted by s.31 of the 1993 Act and which is modelled on s.14(1) and (2) of the Criminal Justice (International Co-operation) Act 1990).

Disclosures of suspicions, or a belief, to law enforcement agencies, that property represents the proceeds of criminal conduct is encouraged (or arguably coerced) by making relevant disclosures a defence to a charge under ss.93A or 93B of the CJA 1988. However, the CJA 1988 falls short of the DTOA (as amended by s.18 of the 1993 Act) in that no corresponding offence has been created for *failing* to disclose knowledge or suspicion that a person is engaged in laundering the proceeds of criminal conduct. The reason for this may be explained on the basis that the statutory defences created under ss.93A and 93B provide a sufficient incentive, and secondly, that any suspicious conduct in respect of money laundering is just as likely to be reported on the basis that it *could* be the proceeds of drug trafficking even if, in reality, that ground was not well founded but the circumstances nevertheless revealed a non-drug trafficking offence. The Home Office Working Group on Confiscation in their Report on Pt. VI of the CJA 1988 (1992) recommended that a *failure* to report a suspicion of any criminal activity should be made a criminal offence (para. 2.48) but this has not been implemented. One reason may be that it was felt that the new offences under ss.93A and 93B go far enough both in terms of encouraging disclosures (in the face of the risk of prosecution for silence if what was done by the defendant comes within the ambit of either offence) and also in terms of meeting this country's obligations under the European Council Directive 91/308/EEC which provides that Member States shall ensure that credit and financial institutions, their directors and employees, co-operate fully with the authorities by disclosing suspicious transactions (Art. 6) and that such institutions and persons refrain from carrying out transactions which they know or suspect to be related to money laundering until they have made an appropriate disclosure (Art. 7). It will be seen that ss.93A(3)(b) and 93B(5)(b) of the CJA 1988 give effect to Art. 7. Immunity from civil action or prosecution arising out of proper disclosure is also given. However, the fact remains that the European Directive is itself limited in scope and the offence of *failing* to make a disclosure under s.26B of the DTOA (see s.18 of the 1993 Act), goes beyond what is obligatory under that Directive although Art. 15 permits Member States to adopt, or retain in force, "stricter provisions" in the field covered by the Directive.

Note that although the money laundering offences inserted by ss.29, 30 and 31 of the 1993 Act refer to "criminal conduct" this does not mean any offence but is a term of art defined by s.93A(7) of the CJA 1988 (inserted by s.29 of the 1993 Act) to mean an offence to which Pt. VI applies (*i.e.* an "indictable offence" in the Crown Court, or a Sched. 4 offence, in the Magistrates' Court) or conduct which "would constitute such an offence if it had occurred in England and Wales [or Scotland]". This seems to include transactions which originate abroad but involve conduct that would be a relevant offence if that conduct was committed here. In this connection see the commentary to Pt. I of the Act.

The Home Office Working Group, in their 1992 Report, examined whether the scope of the confiscation provisions under the 1988 Act should be identical or at least very closely aligned to the provisions of the DTOA. This was not an issue which the Working Group was able to resolve, not least because it would be difficult to define an appropriate category of offences which would justify the application of such draconian measures, as they exist under the DTOA (see para. 2.22 of the Report). Nevertheless, the Working Group recommended that "as a minimum", Pt. VI of the 1988 Act should be amended so that (i) the court should be under an obligation, rather than merely having the discretion, to make an order confiscating the proceeds of the immediate offence[s] where the prosecution has tendered a notice seeking this, and that other criteria are met; (ii) this obligation should apply in respect of any criminal offence to which the CJA 1988 applies, regardless of the amount of the benefit which the offender might have gained from involvement in this offence; and (iii) the court should be given the power to postpone the making of a confiscation order for up to six months after conviction (longer in exceptional circumstances) during which time the court may proceed to sentence the offender.

Parliament has not followed the first two recommendations. Accordingly, there remain major differences between the way in which the DTOA and Pt. VI of the CJA 1988 operate.

Under the 1988 Act, a court cannot make a confiscation order unless the prosecution have provided the requisite notice under s.72(1) and even when such a notice is provided, the court retains a discretion to make an order (s.72(2)). By contrast, even as amended, the DTOA compels the court to embark upon a confiscation enquiry if the prosecution asks it to do so (see s.1(1) of the DTOA as amended by s.7(1) of the 1993 Act). The court is not able to make any statutory assumptions, under Pt. VI of the 1988 Act, and no order may be made unless the benefit is at least the "minimum amount", presently £10,000 (s.71(7) of the CJA 1988) and, even then, the maximum amount to be confiscated is to be no greater than the amount that might be realised (see ss.71(6) and 74 of the CJA 1988)), or the value of the benefit, if this is the lesser sum (see s.71(6) of the CJA 1988), but ultimately, the court retains the overall discretion to order the confiscation of "such sum as the court thinks fit" (s.71(1) of the CJA 1988). There is thus no question of the defendant shouldering the burden of proving that the "amount that might be realised" is the appropriate sum to be confiscated rather than the full amount of his benefit (see, by contrast, s.4(3) of the DTOA).

The definition of "benefit" under the two Acts is wholly different since the 1988 Act focuses on property received or obtained by the defendant as a result of his own offending for which he falls to be sentenced by the court (s.71 of the CJA 1988). The court is not required (or permitted) to trawl back through the defendant's criminal career no matter how serious the offending was.

Another reason why much of Pt. VI of the CJA 1988 has been preserved, so as to be considerably less draconian, can be explained on the basis that many non-drug trafficking offences have identifiable victims who may be entitled to civil remedies and their civil rights are to be protected. This is supported by s.72(3) of the CJA 1988 which gives the court a discretion to take into account information that a victim has instituted civil proceedings (or intends to do so) against the defendant and thus will be compensated (and reimbursed on costs) out of the defendant's assets (and see s.72(7) of the CJA 1988 which clearly places compensation of the victim above the amount recoverable under a confiscation order).

The application of a civil standard of proof to confiscation proceedings has been a matter of considerable controversy particularly in so far as it affects proceedings under the DTOA. Arguably, it is easier to justify the civil standard for the purposes of Pt. VI of the 1988 Act on the grounds that the courts can only confiscate benefits which are connected with the offence (together with some other offence, if relevant) for which the defendant falls to be sentenced (s.71 of the CJA 1988). By that stage, the defendant's proceeds can be determined by reference to a conviction either on a plea of guilty or upon proof to the criminal standard. Assumptions, made under the DTOA, involve a finding of fact that any proceeds of drug trafficking, received in the hands of the defendant over the previous six years, were in connection with drug trafficking carried on by the defendant and by no-one else.

Confiscation orders

Confiscation orders

27.—(1) Section 71 of the Criminal Justice Act 1988 (confiscation orders) shall be amended as follows.

(2) The following subsection shall be inserted after subsection (7)—

"(7A) The standard of proof required to determine any question arising under this Part of this Act as to—

(a) whether a person has benefited as mentioned in subsection (2)(b)(i) above;

(b) whether his benefit is at least the minimum amount; or

(c) the amount to be recovered in his case by virtue of section 72 below,

shall be that applicable in civil proceedings.".

(3) The following subsection shall be inserted at the end—

"(10) Subsection (9) above is subject to section 93E below.".

DEFINITIONS
"benefited": s.71(4) of the CJA 1988.
"confiscation order": s.71(9) of the CJA 1988.
"minimum amount": s.71(7) of the CJA 1988.

GENERAL NOTE
See the General Note to Pt. II, above.
Reference to s.93E relates to an amendment made by s.33 of the 1993 Act which applies the provisions of ss.93A to D (inclusive) to the law of Scotland.

Postponed determinations

28. The following section shall be inserted in the Criminal Justice Act 1988, after section 72—

"**Postponed determinations**

72A.—(1) Where a court is acting under section 71 above but considers that it requires further information before—

(a) determining whether the defendant has benefited as mentioned in section 71(2)(b)(i) above;

(b) determining whether his benefit is at least the minimum amount; or

(c) determining the amount to be recovered in his case by virtue of section 72 above,

it may, for the purpose of enabling that information to be obtained, postpone making that determination for such period as it may specify.

(2) More than one postponement may be made under subsection (1) above in relation to the same case.

(3) Unless it is satisfied that there are exceptional circumstances, the court shall not specify a period under subsection (1) above which—

(a) by itself; or

(b) where there have been one or more previous postponements under subsection (1) above or (4) below, when taken together with the earlier specified period or periods,

exceeds six months beginning with the date of conviction.

(4) Where the defendant appeals against his conviction, the court may, on that account—

(a) postpone making any of the determinations mentioned in subsection (1) above for such period as it may specify; or

(b) where it has already exercised its powers under this section to postpone, extend the specified period.

(5) A postponement or extension under subsection (1) or (4) above may be made—

(a) on application by the defendant or the prosecutor; or

(b) by the court of its own motion.

(6) Unless the court is satisfied that there are exceptional circumstances, any postponement or extension under subsection (4) above shall not exceed the period ending three months after the date on which the appeal is determined or otherwise disposed of.

(7) Where the court exercises its power under subsection (1) or (4) above, it may nevertheless proceed to sentence, or otherwise deal with, the defendant in respect of the offence or any of the offences concerned.

(8) Where the court has so proceeded, section 72 above shall have effect as if—

(a) in subsection (4), the words from "before sentencing" to "offences concerned" were omitted; and

(b) in subsection (5), after "determining" there were inserted "in relation to any offence in respect of which he has not been sentenced or otherwise dealt with".

(9) In sentencing, or otherwise dealing with, the defendant in respect of the offence, or any of the offences, concerned at any time during the specified period, the court shall not—

(a) impose any fine on him; or

(b) make any such order as is mentioned in section 72(5)(b) or (c) above.

(10) In this section references to an appeal include references to an application under section 111 of the Magistrates' Courts Act 1980 (statement of case by magistrates' court).

(11) In this section "the date of conviction" means—

(a) the date on which the defendant was convicted of the offence concerned, or

(b) where he was convicted in the same proceedings, but on different dates, of two or more offences which may be taken together for the purposes of subsection (2) or, as the case may be, (3) of section 71 above, the date of the latest of those convictions.".

GENERAL NOTE

S.72A(1) and s.72A(4) of the CJA 1988

In statutorily prescribed circumstances the period of postponement may be extended. The court may proceed to sentence the defendant notwithstanding a period of postponement or extension (s.72A(7) of the CJA 1988).

S.72A(1) to (7) of the CJA 1988

It would seem that the power to postpone or grant an extension of time (even where the defendant appeals against his conviction) rests with the Crown Court. Unless there are "exceptional circumstances" the period of postponement may be for any period not exceeding six months and, the court may order one or several postponements providing the total period does not exceed six months from the date of conviction (see s.72A(3) and (11) of the CJA 1988). Where the defendant faced more than one trial (*e.g.* as a result of separate committals or separate trials ordered on severance of an indictment) the period of postponement runs from his latest conviction for a drug trafficking offence (see s.72A(11) of the CJA 1988). See also Standing Committee B, col. 62, May 27, 1993. This applies whether or not the convictions occurred at the same or different Crown Courts (Standing Committee B, *ibid.*).

In theory these provisions seem to have the potential for presenting something of an administrative nightmare. Suppose D is convicted of a relevant offence. He is to be tried two months later at another court for another offence and that second trial is expected to (and does) last for three months, to be followed by a third trial. In theory a series of postponements could be ordered until such time as the last conviction is served, whereupon subsequent postponements must not exceed six months from the latest date of conviction. What would be the effect if the defendant (during the specified period) was committed for trial and convicted of another offence shortly before the expiration of the original six month period? Presumably the clock starts from zero from the date of his latest conviction by virtue of s.72A.

S.72A(9) of the CJA 1988

The purpose of this provision is merely to ensure that assets and monies are seized by way of a confiscation order rather than by way of a fine.

S.72A(11) of the CJA 1988

Where the defendant appeals against a conviction the court may, for that reason alone, postpone a determination (as above). Where the period of six months has expired, the period may be further extended (s.72A(4)(b) of the CJA 1988) but once the appeal is heard, the court must proceed with confiscation proceedings within three months unless there are "exceptional circumstances" justifying a longer period. It is not easy to predict instances which the court could properly treat as "exceptional" but it is foreseeable that a lack of court time may be held to be one such exception (consider *R.* v. *Norwich Crown Court* [1993] 97 Cr.App.R. 145 and *R.* v. *Governor of Winchester Prison*, ex p. *Roddie*; *R.* v. *Southampton Crown Court*, ex p. *Roddie* [1991] 1 W.L.R. 303.

Money laundering and other offences

Assisting another to retain the benefit of criminal conduct

29.—(1) The following section shall be inserted in the Criminal Justice Act 1988, after section 93—

"Money laundering and other offences

Assisting another to retain the benefit of criminal conduct
93A.—(1) Subject to subsection (3) below, if a person enters into or is otherwise concerned in an arrangement whereby—

(a) the retention or control by or on behalf of another ("A") of A's proceeds of criminal conduct is facilitated (whether by concealment, removal from the jurisdiction, transfer to nominees or otherwise); or

(b) A's proceeds of criminal conduct—

(i) are used to secure that funds are placed at A's disposal; or

(ii) are used for A's benefit to acquire property by way of investment,

knowing or suspecting that A is a person who is or has been engaged in criminal conduct or has benefited from criminal conduct, he is guilty of an offence.

(2) In this section, references to any person's proceeds of criminal conduct include a reference to any property which in whole or in part directly or indirectly represented in his hands his proceeds of criminal conduct.

(3) Where a person discloses to a constable a suspicion or belief that any funds or investments are derived from or used in connection with criminal conduct or discloses to a constable any matter on which such a suspicion or belief is based—

(a) the disclosure shall not be treated as a breach of any restriction upon the disclosure of information imposed by statute or otherwise; and

(b) if he does any act in contravention of subsection (1) above and the disclosure relates to the arrangement concerned, he does not commit an offence under this section if—

(i) the disclosure is made before he does the act concerned and the act is done with the consent of the constable; or

(ii) the disclosure is made after he does the act, but is made on his initiative and as soon as it is reasonable for him to make it.

(4) In proceedings against a person for an offence under this section, it is a defence to prove—

(a) that he did not know or suspect that the arrangement related to any person's proceeds of criminal conduct; or

(b) that he did not know or suspect that by the arrangement the retention or control by or on behalf of A of any property was facilitated or, as the case may be, that by the arrangement any property was used, as mentioned in subsection (1) above; or

(c) that—

(i) he intended to disclose to a constable such a suspicion, belief or matter as is mentioned in subsection (3) above in relation to the arrangement; but

(ii) there is reasonable excuse for his failure to make disclosure in accordance with subsection (3)(b) above.

(5) In the case of a person who was in employment at the relevant time, subsections (3) and (4) above shall have effect in relation to disclosures, and intended disclosures, to the appropriate person in accordance with the procedure established by his employer for the making of such disclosures as they have effect in relation to disclosures, and intended disclosures, to a constable.

(6) A person guilty of an offence under this section shall be liable—

(a) on summary conviction, to imprisonment for a term not

exceeding six months or a fine not exceeding the statutory maximum or to both; or

(b) on conviction on indictment, to imprisonment for a term not exceeding fourteen years or a fine or to both.

(7) In this Part of this Act "criminal conduct" means conduct which constitutes an offence to which this Part of this Act applies or would constitute such an offence if it had occurred in England and Wales or (as the case may be) Scotland.".

(2) In section 102(1) of the Act of 1988 (interpretation of Part VI), the following definition shall be inserted after the definition of "interest"—

" "proceeds of criminal conduct", in relation to any person who has benefited from criminal conduct, means that benefit;".

(3) In section 102(2) of the Act of 1988, the following entry shall be inserted in the table after the entry relating to section 71(9)(a)—

"Criminal conduct   Section 93A(7)".

DEFINITIONS
"constable": s.102 of the CJA 1988.
"criminal conduct": s.93A(7) of the CJA 1988.
"proceeds of criminal conduct": s.29(2).

GENERAL NOTE
This provision is modelled on s.24 of the DTOA but whereas s.24 (as originally drafted) included a defence which was limited to a disclosure to a "constable", s.18(3) of the 1993 Act has widened the defence by adding subs. (4A) to s.24 of the DTOA to include disclosures made to an "appropriate person" in accordance with procedure established by his employer. This element is repeated in s.93A(5) of the CJA 1988, and see the Money Laundering Regulations 1993 (S.I. 1993 No. 1933). The prosecution must prove not only that the defendant entered into (or was otherwise concerned in) an arrangement described by s.93A(1) of the CJA 1988 but they must also prove "criminal conduct" on the part of A. It does not seem to be necessary for the prosecution to actually secure a conviction against A and it is questionable whether a conviction against A would be admissible in evidence against a defendant, charged under s.93A of the CJA 1988, in any event. The prosecution must therefore prove A's criminal conduct to the civil standard of proof.

At first sight, s.93A(1) and (4) of the CJA 1988 appear to be in conflict as to who shoulders the burden of proving *mens rea*. By s.93A(1) the burden seems to rest on the prosecution to prove that the defendant knew or suspected that A is a person who is or has been engaged in criminal conduct, or has benefited from criminal conduct, yet it is a defence if the defendant can prove that he did not "know or suspect" that the arrangement related to any person's proceeds of criminal conduct or that he did not know the effect of the arrangement.

However, there is no such conflict. It is not necessary for the prosecution to prove that the defendant knew the true purpose of the arrangement, only that he knew of A's criminal background or unlawful income. The burden is on the defendant to prove that he did not know of the nature of the arrangement or the effect of the arrangement. The prosecution must, of course, prove an association between A and the defendant (or that the latter was aware of A's identity) and deal with A as described in s.93A(1) of the CJA 1988.

Acquisition, possession or use of proceeds of criminal conduct

30. The following section shall be inserted in the Criminal Justice Act 1988, after section 93A—

"Acquisition, possession or use of proceeds of criminal conduct

93B.—(1) A person is guilty of an offence if, knowing that any property is, or in whole or in part directly or indirectly represents, another person's proceeds of criminal conduct, he acquires or uses that property or has possession of it.

(2) It is a defence to a charge of committing an offence under this section that the person charged acquired or used the property or had possession of it for adequate consideration.

(3) For the purposes of subsection (2) above—

(a) a person acquires property for inadequate consideration if the value of the consideration is significantly less than the value of the property; and

(b) a person uses or has possession of property for inadequate consideration if the value of the consideration is significantly less than the value of his use or possession of the property.

(4) The provision for any person of services or goods which are of assistance to him in criminal conduct shall not be treated as consideration for the purposes of subsection (2) above.

(5) Where a person discloses to a constable a suspicion or belief that any property is, or in whole or in part directly or indirectly represents, another person's proceeds of criminal conduct or discloses to a constable any matter on which such a suspicion or belief is based—

(a) the disclosure shall not be treated as a breach of any restriction upon the disclosure of information imposed by statute or otherwise; and

(b) if he does any act in relation to that property in contravention of subsection (1) above, he does not commit an offence under this section if—

(i) the disclosure is made before he does the act concerned and the act is done with the consent of the constable; or

(ii) the disclosure is made after he does the act, but on his initiative and as soon as it is reasonable for him to make it.

(6) For the purposes of this section, having possession of any property shall be taken to be doing an act in relation to it.

(7) In proceedings against a person for an offence under this section, it is a defence to prove that—

(a) he intended to disclose to a constable such a suspicion, belief or matter as is mentioned in subsection (5) above; but

(b) there is reasonable excuse for his failure to make the disclosure in accordance with paragraph (b) of that subsection.

(8) In the case of a person who was in employment at the relevant time, subsections (5) and (7) above shall have effect in relation to disclosures, and intended disclosures, to the appropriate person in accordance with the procedure established by his employer for the making of such disclosures as they have effect in relation to disclosures, and intended disclosures, to a constable.

(9) A person guilty of an offence under this section is liable—

(a) on summary conviction, to imprisonment for a term not exceeding six months or a fine not exceeding the statutory maximum or to both; or

(b) on conviction on indictment, to imprisonment for a term not exceeding fourteen years or a fine or to both.

(10) No constable or other person shall be guilty of an offence under this section in respect of anything done by him in the course of acting in connection with the enforcement, or intended enforcement, of any provision of this Act or of any other enactment relating to criminal conduct or the proceeds of such conduct.".

DEFINITIONS
"constable": s.102 of the CJA 1988.
"criminal conduct": s.93A(7) of the CJA 1988.

GENERAL NOTE
Section 93B of the CJA 1988 mirrors s.23A of the DTOA (as inserted by s.16(1) of the 1993 Act). Superficially, s.23A bears a resemblance to s.14(3) of the Criminal Justice (International Co-operation) Act 1990 but little is to be gained by comparing s.93B of the CJA 1988 with s.14(3) of the 1990 Act, other than to note differences in approach between the two provisions. Note that s.14(3) of the Criminal Justice (International Co-operation) Act 1990 is repealed by Sched. 6, Pt. I of the 1993 Act.

It is arguable that the word "acquires", as it appears in s.93B, is wide enough to embrace almost every dealing with property which passes through the hands of the defendant but, if that is the correct construction, then one might ask what purpose is served by specifically prohibiting the use or possession of that property? The answer may be that "acquires" denotes the acquisition of an interest in the property held by the defendant or held on more than a merely transitory or short-term basis. Presumably, the defendant (in order to be in possession) must known that he has it (see *Warner* v. *Metropolitan Police Commissioner* [1969] 2 A.C. 256) and this seems to be supported by s.93B(6) which appears to define possession in terms of "doing an act in relation to" the property. This may mean no more than a person exercising control over the property in question.

An essential exemption is given by s.93B(10) to persons who deal with the property in connection with the investigation, detection or judicial proceedings relating to drug trafficking matters by virtue of any enactment.

Section 93B is narrower than the old s.14(3) of the 1990 Act in terms of the *mens rea* required to be proved. Under s.14(3) it was enough if a defendant acquired property "knowing or having reasonable grounds to suspect" its drug trafficking origins. There is no objective element in s.93B and what is required is actual knowledge; suspicion is not enough.

S.93B(1) of the CJA 1988

What is required is proof of actual knowledge that the property represents the proceeds of another's "criminal conduct" but this phrase is defined by s.93A(7) to mean (in essence) an offence to which Pt. VI of the CJA 1988 applies and a drug trafficking offence is specifically excluded (see s.71(9)(c)(ii) of the CJA 1988). If s.93B(1) is construed to mean that the defendant must know of the nature, or type, of offence which was committed by another, then it would seem that the defendant should be acquitted if he believed that the property represented the proceeds of drug trafficking.

S.93B(2) of the CJA 1988

Under s.14(3) of the 1990 Act the burden was on the prosecution to prove that the defendant acquired the property for "no or inadequate consideration" but this last ingredient is omitted from s.93B of the CJA 1988. Instead, the burden is cast onto the defendant to prove that he provided "adequate consideration". Presumably, it will be for the jury to decide whether the consideration provided is in fact "adequate" for the purposes of s.93B(3) but it is likely that it will fall to the courts to decide what that phrase really means and to determine its parameters. Section 93B(3) provides two instances where consideration is "adequate" but is this section a closed category? If a person pays an excessive price for the property, is the consideration still to be regarded as being "adequate"? By s.102 of the CJA 1988 "property" includes money. If services are provided in consideration for a substantial sum of money which in fact represents the proceeds of an indictable offence, is it relevant to argue that the service was not worth what was claimed or charged? (see *Hansard*, H.C. Vol. 222, col. 907, Sir Ivan Lawrence, Q.C.). In the majority of cases, an issue as to value, is likely to be resolved with expert help.

It may seem a surprising result that it will be lawful to use property (*e.g.* a car) belonging to a person, when it is known that it represents the proceeds of an indictable offence providing that an adequate sum is paid for its use to the very person who has committed the criminal conduct complained of. It therefore seems that knowledge of the origins of the property will not taint the consideration nor will it negate the defence.

Section 93B(2) should be read in conjunction with s.93B(4).

S.93B(4) of the CJA 1988

This provision is designed to achieve the same result that s.14(5) of the 1990 Act formerly did. Section 14(5) is repealed by Sched. 6, Pt. I of the 1993 Act. The provisions of s.93B(4) are designed to exclude persons who provide goods or services to another so long as the goods or services supplied were not of "assistance to him in drug trafficking" (see s.23A(4) of the DTOA). If the goods or services are of assistance to him, then s.93B(4) creates a fiction, and deems the supply not to be adequate consideration. Section 93B(4) is intended to protect tradespeople who are paid for goods and services from the proceeds of drug trafficking (see Standing Committee B, col. 93, June 8, 1993). It is not clear whether the defendant must know or intend that the goods or services supplied "are of assistance to him in drug trafficking" for the purposes of s.93B(4).

S.93B(5), (7) and (8) of the CJA 1988

This follows the model provided by s.24(3) of the DTOA; and see Sched. 7 to the Prevention of Terrorism (Temporary Provisions) Act 1989. Section 93B(5) and (7) are designed to protect persons (particularly those employed in the financial sector) from any action for breach of contract, confidence or a duty arising out of their obligations to their clients.

Note that s.93B(5), (7) and (8) refers to the disclosure of "suspicions". Two reasons have been advanced as to why disclosure based on "suspicion" is said to be relevant. First, disclosure based on any higher standard (*e.g.* at least a belief) would confront individuals with a dilemma as to whether to make a disclosure or not based on what may be a finely balanced assessment of the facts. The disclosure of a mere suspicion removes that anxiety (*Hansard*, H.L. Vol. 3, col. 1114). Secondly, law enforcement agencies act on suspicion and accordingly a great deal of "intelligence" could be lost if all that could be disclosed were beliefs. It was clearly the Government's view that it should be "up to policemen, the professionals, (and) the investigators to decide whether or not [the suspicion] was true" (*per* Earl Ferrers, *Hansard*, H.L., Vol. 540, col. 753).

Concealing or transferring proceeds of criminal conduct

31. The following section shall be inserted in the Criminal Justice Act 1988, after section 93B—

> **"Concealing or transferring proceeds of criminal conduct**
> 93C.—(1) A person is guilty of an offence if he—
> (a) conceals or disguises any property which is, or in whole or in part directly or indirectly represents, his proceeds of criminal conduct; or
> (b) converts or transfers that property or removes it from the jurisdiction,
> for the purpose of avoiding prosecution for an offence to which this Part of this Act applies or the making or enforcement in his case of a confiscation order.
>
> (2) A person is guilty of an offence if, knowing or having reasonable grounds to suspect that any property is, or in whole or in part directly or indirectly represents, another person's proceeds of criminal conduct, he—
> (a) conceals or disguises that property; or
> (b) converts or transfers that property or removes it from the jurisdiction,
> for the purpose of assisting any person to avoid prosecution for an offence to which this Part of this Act applies or the making or enforcement in his case of a confiscation order.
>
> (3) In subsections (1) and (2) above, the references to concealing or disguising any property include references to concealing or disguising its nature, source, location, disposition, movement or ownership or any rights with respect to it.
>
> (4) A person guilty of an offence under this section is liable—
> (a) on summary conviction, to imprisonment for a term not exceeding six months or a fine not exceeding the statutory maximum or to both; or
> (b) on conviction on indictment, to imprisonment for a term not exceeding fourteen years or a fine or to both.".

DEFINITIONS
"criminal conduct": s.93A(7) of the CJA 1988.

GENERAL NOTE
Section 93C(1) and (2) seem to be modelled on s.14(1) and (2) of the Criminal Justice (International Co-operation) Act 1990. Section 93C(1) is directed against the offender who seeks to launder, or to hide, the proceeds of his own crime. It would seem that if his purpose was solely commercial in nature, *e.g.* to invest the proceeds or to save his gains, then he falls outside s.93C(1). His purpose must be to avoid prosecution for an offence to which Pt. VI of the 1988 Act applies (in practice that will be the offence which provided him with the proceeds), or where he sought to avoid the making or enforcement of a confiscation order.

For the purposes of s.93C(2) it is enough if the defendant had reasonable grounds to suspect the criminal origin of the proceeds.

Tipping-off

32. The following section shall be inserted in the Criminal Justice Act 1988, after section 93C—

"**Tipping-off**
93D.—(1) A person is guilty of an offence if—
(a) he knows or suspects that a constable is acting, or is proposing to act, in connection with an investigation which is being, or is about to be, conducted into money laundering; and
(b) he discloses to any other person information or any other matter which is likely to prejudice that investigation, or proposed investigation.
(2) A person is guilty of an offence if—
(a) he knows or suspects that a disclosure ("the disclosure") has been made to a constable under section 93A or 93B above; and
(b) he discloses to any other person information or any other matter which is likely to prejudice any investigation which might be conducted following the disclosure.
(3) A person is guilty of an offence if—
(a) he knows or suspects that a disclosure of a kind mentioned in section 93A(5) or 93B(8) above ("the disclosure") has been made; and
(b) he discloses to any person information or any other matter which is likely to prejudice any investigation which might be conducted following the disclosure.
(4) Nothing in subsections (1) to (3) above makes it an offence for a professional legal adviser to disclose any information or other matter—
(a) to, or to a representative of, a client of his in connection with the giving by the adviser of legal advice to the client; or
(b) to any person—
(i) in contemplation of, or in connection with, legal proceedings; and
(ii) for the purpose of those proceedings.
(5) Subsection (4) above does not apply in relation to any information or other matter which is disclosed with a view to furthering any criminal purpose.
(6) In proceedings against a person for an offence under subsection (1), (2) or (3) above, it is a defence to prove that he did not know or suspect that the disclosure was likely to be prejudicial in the way mentioned in that subsection.
(7) In this section "money laundering" means doing any act which constitutes an offence under section 93A, 93B or 93C above or, in the case of an act done otherwise than in England and Wales or Scotland, would constitute such an offence of done in England and Wales or (as the case may be) Scotland.
(8) For the purposes of subsection (7) above, having possession of any property shall be taken to be doing an act in relation to it.
(9) A person guilty of an offence under this section shall be liable—
(a) on summary conviction, to imprisonment for a term not exceeding six months or a fine not exceeding the statutory maximum or to both; or
(b) on conviction on indictment, to imprisonment for a term not exceeding five years or a fine or to both.
(10) No constable or other person shall be guilty of an offence under this section in respect of anything done by him in the course of

acting in connection with the enforcement, or intended enforcement, of any provision of this Act or of any other enactment relating to an offence to which this Part of this Act applies.".

DEFINITIONS
"constable": s.102 of the CJA 1988.
"disclosure": s.93D(2)(a) of the CJA 1988.
"money laundering": s.93D(7) of the CJA 1988.

GENERAL NOTE
Section 93D of the CJA 1988 creates three offences. First, it is an offence for a defendant who knows or suspects that an investigation into money laundering is being conducted (or is about to be) to divulge that fact, or other information, which is likely to prejudice such an investigation (s.93D(1)). Secondly, if a disclosure of a suspicion (or information) has been lawfully made to a constable (*e.g.* by a bank) under s.93A or s.93B, then it is an offence if that fact is disclosed to another and which is likely to prejudice an investigation which might be conducted on the basis of the original disclosure; (s.93D(2)). Third, the same offence as in s.93D(2), above, but where the original disclosure was made to an "appropriate person" (*e.g.* an employer); (s.93D(3)).
There is an exemption in the case of legal advisers (within the terms of s.93D(4) and (5)).
It is a defence to each of the three offences if the defendant proves that he did not know or suspect that the disclosure was likely to be prejudicial (s.93D(6)).

Application to Scotland of sections 93A to 93D of 1988 Act

33. The following section shall be inserted in the Criminal Justice Act 1988, after section 93D—

> ### "Application of sections 93A to 93D to Scotland
> 93E. In the application of sections 93A to 93D above to Scotland—
> "offence to which this Part of this Act applies" means an offence triable on indictment (whether or not such offence is also triable summarily) other than—
>> (a) an offence to which section 1 of the Criminal Justice (Scotland) Act 1987 (confiscation of proceeds of drug trafficking) relates; or
>> (b) an offence under Part III of the Prevention of Terrorism (Temporary Provisions) Act 1989; and
> "proceeds of criminal conduct" does not include—
>> (a) proceeds of drug trafficking ("drug trafficking" having the meaning assigned by section 1(6) of the said Act of 1987); or
>> (b) terrorist funds within the meaning of section 11 of the said Act of 1989.".

Enforcement of Northern Ireland orders: proceeds of criminal conduct

34.—(1) In section 94 of the Criminal Justice Act 1988 (enforcement of Northern Ireland orders), in subsection (1), for "89" there shall be substituted "88" and the following subsection shall be inserted after subsection (3)—

> "(3A) An Order in Council under this section may, in particular, provide for section 18 of the Civil Jurisdiction and Judgments Act 1982 (enforcement of United Kingdom judgments in other parts of the United Kingdom) not to apply in relation to such orders as may be prescribed by the Order.".

(2) In section 95 of the Act of 1988 (enforcement of Northern Ireland orders in Scotland), the following subsection shall be inserted after subsection (2)—

> "(2A) An Order in Council under this section may, in particular, provide for section 18 of the Civil Jurisdiction and Judgments Act 1982 (enforcement of United Kingdom judgments in other parts of the

United Kingdom) not to apply in relation to such orders as may be prescribed by the Order.".

Prosecution by order of the Commissioners of Customs and Excise

35. The following section shall be inserted in the Criminal Justice Act 1988, after section 93E—

> **"Prosecution by order of the Commissioners of Customs and Excise**
> 93F.—(1) Proceedings for an offence to which this section applies ("a specified offence") may be instituted by order of the Commissioners.
> (2) Any proceedings for a specified offence which are so instituted shall be commenced in the name of an officer.
> (3) In the case of the death, removal, discharge or absence of the officer in whose name any proceedings for a specified offence were commenced, those proceedings may be continued by another officer.
> (4) Where the Commissioners investigate, or propose to investigate, any matter with a view to determining—
>> (a) whether there are grounds for believing that a specified offence has been committed; or
>> (b) whether a person should be prosecuted for a specified offence;
> that matter shall be treated as an assigned matter within the meaning of the Customs and Excise Management Act 1979.
> (5) Nothing in this section shall be taken—
>> (a) to prevent any person (including any officer) who has power to arrest, detain or prosecute any person for a specified offence from doing so; or
>> (b) to prevent a court from proceeding to deal with a person brought before it following his arrest by an officer for a specified offence, even though the proceedings have not been instituted by an order made under subsection (1) above.
> (6) In this section—
>> "the Commissioners" means the Commissioners of Customs and Excise;
>> "officer" means a person commissioned by the Commissioners;
>> "proceedings", as respects Scotland, means summary proceedings; and
>> "specified offence" means—
>>> (a) any offence under sections 93A to 93D above;
>>> (b) attempting to commit, conspiracy to commit or incitement to commit any such offence; or
>>> (c) any other offence of a kind prescribed in regulations made by the Secretary of State for the purposes of this section.
> (7) The power to make regulations under subsection (6) above shall be exercisable by statutory instrument.
> (8) Any such instrument shall be subject to annulment in pursuance of a resolution of either House of Parliament.".

PART IV

FINANCING ETC. OF TERRORISM

GENERAL NOTE
Acts of terrorism are considered no less serious than drug trafficking and in respect of both

activities the circulation of monies and property has prompted draconian measures designed to prevent their use in further criminal enterprises. The Prevention of Terrorism (Temporary Provisions) Act 1989 (the "PTA") contains provisions which make it an offence to raise funds or to make contributions for terrorist purposes to terrorist organisations (see ss.9 and 10 of the PTA) or to assist in the retention or control of terrorist funds (s.11) and provides a defence where disclosures are made to law enforcement agencies of any suspicion or belief that the property is related to terrorist activities (s.12). Money or property related to offences committed under ss.9, 10 or 11 may be forfeited (s.13). However, the PTA falls far short of the type of provisions to be found in the DTOA. Accordingly, the Northern Ireland (Emergency Provisions) Act 1991 (the "EPA") was enacted to widen the courts' powers to confiscate the proceeds of terrorist related activities.

The reasoning behind the present legislation is, perhaps fully explained by the former Secretary of State for Northern Ireland (Peter Brooke) who said:

"The Government are convinced that an effective strategy for the eradication of terrorism in Northern Ireland must be one which includes effective measures for tackling terrorism at its financial roots. Finance is the life blood of terrorism. It is required not simply for the acquisition of weapons, explosive and other terrorist material, some of it very sophisticated and expensive—it also pays the so-called 'volunteers'—those who carry out acts of terrorism on behalf of their organisation. The provisions before us represent an important additional element in what we intend should be a comprehensive range of measures for curbing the financing of terrorism, itself an increasingly diversified activity. There is, I suggest, little doubt that such measures are necessary.

It is well known that terrorist organisations in Northern Ireland and those who handle money on their behalf are becoming ever more sophisticated in the means by which they raise and launder funds. Increasingly, persons of substance, including business men and accountants, are involved. It is a particularly worrying feature of the current scene that persons known to be involved with terrorist organisations are involved in the running of what may be regarded as legitimate businesses, with the principal objective of using those businesses to raise or launder funds intended to finance terrorism.

There is good reason to believe that some of these people have been involved in such terrorist-financing activity for several years and that they have derived substantial personal benefit from their involvement. There is in the Government's view—which is fully shared by the Royal Ulster Constabulary—a serious risk that unless effective action is taken soon, persons acting on behalf of terrorist organisations will succeed in establishing a commercial or business infrastructure capable of providing long-term support for terrorism. Perhaps just as much a matter for concern is the risk that, even after a cessation of political violence, such an infrastructure might remain in place, able to sustain a potential for more straightforwardly criminal racketeering. No one would wish to see a creation of a Mafia-style society anywhere in the U.K.

It was against this background, and with the concerns that I have just outlined, that the Government considered how they might use the opportunity created by this Bill to strengthen the law to allow more effective action against terrorist financiers. There were two principal outcomes of this consideration. The first was the new investigative powers for non-police officers, which were introduced by my Honorable friend the Minister of State in Committee, and which are now to be found in cl. 47 and Sched. 4 [see now s.57 and Sched. 5]. An ability to invoke these powers, and to secure the involvement in a financial investigation of persons with the special skills required for this task, should considerably ease the task of the R.U.C. in bringing to justice those involved in such activities.

The second main outcome of our consideration of possible new measures is the scheme for confiscation which is now before us. It addresses a gap in the existing law. As Lord Colville has pointed out in his recent report on the Prevention of Terrorism (Temporary Provisions) Act 1989, the present law, while providing some machinery for the confiscation of money or property, which it can be proved is intended for terrorist use, does not provide any means of depriving 'terrorist financiers' of the personal benefit which they derive from their involvement in such activity" (*Hansard*, H.C. Vol. 187, cols. 292–293).

The EPA therefore sought to address those deficiencies.

The 1993 Act introduces a considerable number of amendments to the PTA and the EPA, the effect of which is to broadly align the confiscation provisions, relating to the financing of terrorism, with the DTOA (as similarly amended by the 1993 Act, Pt. II). The fact that so many provisions are now to be found in an array of enactments and Statutory Instruments has, not surprisingly, prompted calls for the introduction of a single comprehensive model and a code which could be applied throughout Britain (or even overseas) (see the Standing Committee B, col. 114, June 8, 1993, *per* Mr. David Trimble). The call for codification has also been supported by Lord Colville who, in relation to the current legislation has said that:

"The [EPA] applies throughout the U.K.; the courts will have to be prepared to exercise powers under the Drug Trafficking Offences Act 1986, the Criminal Justice Act 1988, [PTE],

[EPA], and the Criminal Justice Act 1993. Not only do some of the powers overlap, but the codes are different in detail, as can be seen in Northern Ireland where the first two Acts mentioned above had their confiscation powers enacted by Order in Council. There is the additional dimension of the extension of these provisions to the Isle of Man, Jersey and Guernsey, which can be done to some, but not to a complete degree, by the U.K. government under [PTA], s.28(3) and [EPA] s.71(3). However it can also be done by legislation in Tynwald; at the moment the Isle of Man is ahead of the field in that their Prevention of Terrorism Act 1990 has valuable provisions for reciprocal enforcement. In the Channel Islands, negotiations are still proceeding as to the extent of legislation to be presented to the respective States. It cannot be easy for any of them to keep up with the flow of legislative changes on the financial front and it is particularly important that they should be up-to-date in light of the facilities which would otherwise be available to terrorists in these off-shore market places. A U.K. codification would give them the opportunity to legislate on the basis of a single, comprehensive model".

Broadly stated, the effect of Pt. IV is as follows:
Section 36 transfers to the Northern Ireland (Emergency Provisions) Act 1991 much of ss.7 and 8 of the 1993 Act. That is, it allows the court to make a confiscation order for a nominal amount in certain circumstances, clarifies that the civil standard of proof applies to confiscation proceedings and clarifies the procedure for postponing the confiscation hearing.
Section 37 contains the equivalent of new ss.5B and 5C of the DTOA, introduced by s.12 of the 1993 Act. It allows the court to make or revise an order at a later date if further evidence emerges of the defendant having benefited from terrorist related activities.
Section 38 matches the provision in s.10 of the 1993 Act in relation to the provision of relevant information to the court by the prosecution. Section 39 introduces similar provision to those in s.10, allowing the court to require the defendant to provide specified information to assist the court in considering confiscation.
Section 40 contains the equivalent of s.11 of the 1993 Act in allowing a receiver to apply for the downward variation of a confiscation order in certain circumstances. Section 41 makes equivalent changes to s.13 including, in relation to imprisonment and default of payment, the availability of restraint and charging orders on the conclusion of proceedings.
Section 42 introduces similar provisions to those in s.14 of the 1993 Act, allowing the court to make a confiscation order against a deceased or absconded defendant in certain circumstances. Finally, s.43 is the equivalent of s.15 of the 1993 Act and provides for the cancellation or variation of a confiscation order made against a person who absconds before conviction and for repayment of appropriate compensation.

Amendments of the 1991 Act

Confiscation orders

36.—(1) In section 47(7) of the Northern Ireland (Emergency Provisions) Act 1991 (confiscation orders), for "the amount that might then be so realised" there shall be substituted "—
(a) the amount that might then be so realised, or
(b) a nominal amount, where it appears to the court (on the information available to it at the time) that the amount that might then be so realised is nil".
(2) In section 47 of the Act of 1991, the following subsection shall be added at the end—
"(9) The standard of proof required to determine any question arising under this Part of this Act as to—
(a) whether a person has benefited from terrorist-related activities engaged in by him or another;
(b) the value of his proceeds of those activities;
(c) any matter of which the court must be satisfied under subsection (5) above; or
(d) the amount to be required to be paid under a confiscation order made in his case,
shall be that applicable in civil proceedings.".

(3) Section 48 of that Act (postponed confiscation orders etc.) shall be amended as follows.

(4) In subsection (2), for "a period not exceeding six months after the date of conviction" there shall be substituted "such period as it may specify".

(5) After subsection (2) there shall be inserted—

"(2A) More than one postponement may be made under subsection (2) above in relation to the same case.

(2B) Unless it is satisfied that there are exceptional circumstances, the court shall not specify a period under subsection (2) above which—

(a) by itself, or

(b) where there have been one or more previous postponements under subsection (2) above or (3) below, when taken together with the earlier specified period or periods,

exceeds six months beginning with the date on which the defendant was convicted.".

(6) In subsection (3) the words "during the period of postponement" shall cease to have effect and for the words from "on the application of the prosecution" to the end there shall be substituted—

"on that account—

(a) postpone making the confiscation order for such period as it may specify, or

(b) where it has already exercised its powers under this section to postpone, extend the specified period;

but, without prejudice to Article 11 of the Treatment of Offenders (Northern Ireland) Order 1989, the court may notwithstanding any postponement under this section proceed to sentence or otherwise deal with the defendant in respect of the conviction.".

(7) After subsection (3) there shall be inserted—

"(3A) A postponement or extension under subsection (2) or (3) above may be made—

(a) on application by the defendant or the prosecution, or

(b) by the court of its own motion.

(3B) Unless the court is satisfied that there are exceptional circumstances, any postponement or extension under subsection (3) above shall not exceed the period ending three months after the date of determination of the appeal.".

GENERAL NOTE

The EPA is concerned with the confiscation of the proceeds of terrorist related activities following the conviction of a "relevant offence" (defined by s.49) and which, by Sched. 1 to the EPA, covers a very wide range of non-drug trafficking offences. Before making an order the court must be satisfied that (i) the defendant has engaged in terrorist activities (see s.47(2)(a) of the EPA); (ii) he has benefited from such terrorist activities (see s.47(2)(b) of the EPA); (iii) the convicted person has had in his possession since the commission of the relevant offence "realisable property" exceeding £20,000 (see ss.47(5), and 50(1) and (2) (definition) of the EPA). Property which is subject to deprivation or forfeiture orders as specified in s.50(2) cannot be realisable property; (iv) in the period of six years ending when the present proceedings were instituted the convicted person has committed another relevant offence on a separate occasion and has been convicted of that offence in those same proceedings, or has been shown to have committed another such relevant offence (s.47(3) of the EPA). An offence taken into consideration will be regarded for the purposes of this part of the Act as a conviction (see s.47(4) of the EPA); and (v) the court must be satisfied that in making the order it is not acting in an unfair or oppressive manner (s.47(6) of the EPA).

If the court is satisfied that the amount that might be realised at the time of the making of a confiscation order is less than the value of the proceeds of terrorist related activity, the order shall require the convicted person to pay the amount that can actually be realised or a "nominal amount" where it appears to the court that "the amount that might be realised is nil" (see s.47(7) of the EPA as amended by s.36(1) of the 1993 Act). The inclusion of a "nominal amount" is to enable the court under Sched. 4, para. 11 to the 1991 Act, to vary the order if it subsequently emerges that the defendant has more realisable property than was at first believed. This can only be done under para. 11 if there is a confiscation order which is not a nil order.

Subs. (2)
This follows the amendment made to the DTOA by s.7(2) of the 1993 Act; see the commentary thereto.

Subs. (3) *to* (7)
These provisions broadly mirror subss. (2), (3), (5) and (6) of s.1A of the DTOA (the amendments being made by s.8 of the 1993 Act) but whereas the DTOA (as originally drafted) permitted no postponement, this was not the case under the provisions of the EPA, s.48 which by s.48(2) permitted specified periods of postponements either to enable further information to be obtained or when the defendant appealed against conviction. One effect of the amendments to s.48 is to give the court greater flexibility to postpone determinations for longer periods than was previously permissible having regard to the particular circumstances of the case.

Revised assessments

37. The following sections shall be inserted in the Northern Ireland (Emergency Provisions) Act 1991, after section 48—

> **"Re-assessment of whether defendant has benefited**
> 48A.—(1) This section applies where—
> (a) a court proceeding under section 47(1) above decided not to make a confiscation order ("the decision"); and
> (b) the statement made by the court under section 48(8) above was to the effect that the reason, or one of the reasons, for the decision was that the court was not satisfied that the defendant had benefited.
> (2) If the prosecution has evidence—
> (a) which was not considered by the court, but
> (b) which the prosecution believes would have led the court to decide that the defendant had benefited,
> the prosecution may apply to the Crown Court for it to consider that evidence.
> (3) If, having considered the evidence, the court considers that it would have been satisfied that the defendant had benefited if that evidence had been available to it, section 47 shall apply as if the court were convicting the defendant.
> (4) The court may take into account any money or other property obtained by the defendant on or after the date of the decision, but only if the prosecution shows that it was obtained by him as a direct or indirect result of terrorist-related activities carried on by the defendant or another on or before that date.
> (5) In considering any evidence under this section which relates to any money or other property to which subsection (4) above applies, the court shall not make the assumptions which would otherwise be required by section 51 below.
> (6) No application shall be entertained by the court under this section if it is made after the end of the period of six years beginning with the date on which the defendant was convicted.
> (7) Subsections (1) to (7) of section 48 above shall not apply where the court is proceeding under section 47 above by virtue of this section.
> (8) Where the court—
> (a) has, in dealing with the defendant in respect of the conviction or any of the convictions concerned, made an order for the payment of compensation under Article 3 of the Order of 1980, and

(b) makes a confiscation order by virtue of this section,
it shall, if it is of the opinion that the defendant will not have sufficient means to satisfy both orders in full, direct that so much of the compensation as will not in its opinion be recoverable because of the insufficiency of his means is to be paid out of any sums recovered under the confiscation order.

(9) Where the prosecution makes an application to the court under this section it shall, on making the application, give the court a statement under section 52 below.

(10) Where the High Court—

(a) has been asked to proceed under section 52B below in relation to a defendant who has absconded, but

(b) has decided not to make a confiscation order against him,

this section shall not apply at any time while he remains an absconder.

(11) In this section "benefited" means benefited from terrorist-related activities as mentioned in section 47(1) above.

Revised assessments

48B.—(1) This section applies where the court has made a confiscation order by reference to an amount assessed under section 47(1) above ("the current assessment").

(2) Where the prosecution is of the opinion that the real value of the defendant's proceeds of terrorist-related activities was greater than their assessed value, the prosecution may apply to the Crown Court for the evidence on which it has formed that opinion to be considered by the court.

(3) In subsection (2) above—

"assessed value" means the value of the defendant's proceeds of terrorist-related activities as assessed by the court under section 47(1) above; and

"real value" means the value of the defendant's proceeds of terrorist-related activities which took place—

(a) in the period by reference to which the current assessment was made; or

(b) in any earlier period.

(4) If, having considered the evidence, the court is satisfied that the real value of the defendant's proceeds of terrorist-related activities is greater than their assessed value (whether because the real value was higher at the time of the current assessment than was thought or because the value of the proceeds in question has subsequently increased), the court shall make a fresh determination of the amount to be required to be paid under section 47 above.

(5) In relation to any determination by virtue of this section, section 47(7) above shall have effect as it has effect in relation to the making of a confiscation order.

(6) For any determination by virtue of this section, section 47(8) above shall not apply in relation to any of the defendant's proceeds of terrorist-related activities taken into account in respect of the current assessment.

(7) Sections 50(4) and 52(4)(a) and (7) below shall have effect in relation to any such determination as is for "confiscation order" there were substituted "determination" and section 50(3) below shall so have effect as if for "a confiscation order is made" there were substituted "of the determination".

(8) The court may take into account any money or other property obtained by the defendant on or after the date of the current assessment, but only if the prosecution shows that it was obtained by him as

a direct or indirect result of terrorist-related activities carried on by the defendant or another on or before that date.

(9) In considering any evidence under this section which relates to any money or other property to which subsection (8) above applies, the court shall not make the assumptions which would otherwise be required by section 51 below.

(10) If, as a result of making the determination required by sub-section (4) above, the amount to be required to be paid exceeds the amount set in accordance with the current assessment, the court may substitute for the amount required to be paid under the confiscation order such greater amount as it thinks just in all the circumstances of the case.

(11) Where the court varies a confiscation order under subsection (10) above it shall substitute for the term of imprisonment or of detention fixed under section 35(1)(c) of the Criminal Justice Act (Northern Ireland) 1945 in respect of the amount required to be paid under the order a longer term determined in accordance with that section (as it has effect by virtue of paragraph 2 of Schedule 4 to this Act) in respect of the greater amount substituted under subsection (10) above.

(12) Subsection (11) above shall apply only if the effect of the substitution is to increase the maximum period applicable in relation to the order under paragraph 2(1)(b) of Schedule 4 to this Act.

(13) Where the prosecution makes an application to the court under this section—

(a) it shall, on making the application, give the court a statement under section 52 below; and

(b) section 52A shall apply.

(14) Where a confiscation order has been made in relation to any defendant by virtue of section 52B below, this section shall not apply at any time while he is an absconder.

(15) No application shall be entertained by the court under this section if it is made after the end of the period of six years beginning with the date on which the defendant was convicted.".

GENERAL NOTE

By s.48A of the EPA, the court appears to be required to form an opinion based on hindsight, *i.e.* that it "would have" determined that the defendant had benefited from terrorist related activities if the evidence which ultimately came to light had been available to it. Payments received by the defendant after the date on which the court originally concluded he received no benefit, may be taken into account but the prosecution will not be able to rely on the statutory assumptions (s.48A(5) of the EPA). Note that no application shall be entertained if it is made six years after the date on which the defendant was convicted (s.48A(6) of the EPA).

S.48B of the EPA

By s.48B, the court may reassess the value of the defendant's *proceeds* derived from terrorist related activities if new evidence comes to light. Prosecutors will be anxious to keep this figure under review because it represents the maximum that can be recovered under a confiscation order. Accordingly, where the prosecutor successfully applies to the High Court, and then to the Crown Court, for an increased confiscation order on the basis that there were more realisable assets in existence than at first known (*i.e.* under Sched. 4, para. 11 to the EPA) it follows that any increase in the amount to be paid cannot, in any event, exceed the amount originally determined to be the total value of the defendant's proceeds derived from terrorist related activities. Accordingly, if it is discovered (after a confiscation order was originally made) that the defendant's realisable assets actually far exceeded the sum assessed to represent his total proceeds, then the prosecutor will have to decide whether he can ask the court to reassess the latter figure.

There appears to be a difference of scope in the ambit of these provisions when s.48B(2) is read in contrast with s.48B(4). Section 48B(2) seems to look to the "real value" as defined by s.48B(3), *i.e.* that the value was higher at the time the assessment was originally made than was first thought, or because the value of the proceeds in question has subsequently increased. It appears that under s.48B(2), the prosecutor should form an opinion based on the "real value" of the proceeds, without reference to any subsequent increase in their value. The court therefore looks at the current value of the proceeds (which were ascertained by the date the confiscation order was originally made) (s.48B(4)) plus, any payments received by the defendant on, or after, that date which were the fruits of terrorist related activities carried on by the defendant or another before that moment (s.48B(8)). The prosecution cannot rely on the statutory assumptions (s.48B(9)). However, the "amount to be required to be paid", under a fresh confiscation order, is, prima facie, the "amount that might be realised" (s.47(7) of the EPA as amended). It follows that if the defendant's finances have improved by the date of the subsequent determination, it is the higher figure which is relevant. Given that the court is being asked to make a fresh confiscation order it follows that s.47(8) of the EPA must be disregarded and that is what s.48B(6) achieves. Even if, prima facie, the "amount required to be paid" (being the "amount that might be realised") is greater than it was originally assessed to be, nevertheless, the court need only order such greater amount as it thinks just in all the circumstances of the case (s.48B(11) of the EPA).

Statements, etc. relevant to making confiscation orders

38.—(1) Section 52 of the Northern Ireland (Emergency Provisions) Act 1991 shall be amended as follows.

(2) The following subsections shall be substituted for subsection (1)—

"(1) In this section, except in subsection (4) below, "a statement" means a statement in the case of a defendant as to any matters relevant—

(a) to determining whether he has benefited from terrorist-related activities,

(b) to assessing the value of his proceeds of those activities, or

(c) to determining whether the requirements of section 47(5) above are satisfied.

(1A) Where section 47(1) above applies—

(a) the court may require the prosecution to give it a statement within such period as it may direct; and

(b) the prosecution may at any time give a statement to the court.

(1B) Where the prosecution has given the court a statement—

(a) it may at any time give the court a further statement; and

(b) the court may at any time require it to give the court a further statement, within such period as the court may direct.

(1C) Where—

(a) a statement has been given to the court under this section, and

(b) the defendant accepts to any extent any allegation in the statement,

the court may treat his acceptance as conclusive of the matters to which it relates.".

(3) In subsection (2)—

(a) for "is tendered under subsection (1)(a) above" there shall be substituted "is given under this section"; and

(b) after first "indicate" there shall be inserted "within such period as the court may direct".

(4) The following subsection shall be inserted after subsection (2)—

"(2A) Where the court has given a direction under this section it may at any time vary it by giving a further direction.".

(5) In subsection (4), for "tendered" there shall be substituted "given".

(6) In subsection (5), for the words from "either" to the end there shall be substituted "in such manner as may be prescribed by rules of court or as the court may direct".

GENERAL NOTE
These provisions are similar to the amendments to the DTOA set out in s.10.

Provision of information

39. The following section shall be inserted in the Northern Ireland (Emergency Provisions) Act 1991, after section 52—

"**Provision of information by defendant**
52A.—(1) This section applies where the Crown Court is proceeding under section 47(1) above.
(2) For the purpose of obtaining information to assist it in carrying out its functions, the court may at any time order the defendant to give it such information as may be specified in the order.
(3) An order under subsection (2) above may require all, or any specified part, of the required information to be given to the court in such manner, and before such date, as may be specified in the order.
(4) Rules of court may make provision as to the maximum or minimum period that may be allowed under subsection (3) above.
(5) If the defendant fails, without reasonable excuse, to comply with any order under this section, the court may draw such inference from that failure as it considers appropriate.
(6) Where the prosecution accepts to any extent any allegation made by the defendant in giving to the court information required by an order under this section, the court may treat that acceptance as conclusive of the matters to which it relates.
(7) For the purposes of this section, an allegation may be accepted in such manner as may be prescribed by rules of court or as the court may direct.".

GENERAL NOTE
    These provisions follow, very closely, those set out in s.3A of the DTOA, as inserted by s.10 of the 1993 Act.

Variation of confiscation orders

40.—(1) Paragraph 15 (variation of confiscation orders) of Schedule 4 to the Northern Ireland (Emergency Provisions) Act 1991 shall be amended as follows.
(2) In sub-paragraph (1), after "defendant" there shall be inserted "or a receiver appointed under this Schedule, or in pursuance of a charging order, made".
(3) In sub-paragraph (3), for "defendant" there shall be substituted "person who applied for it".
(4) The following shall be added at the end—
    "(5) Rules of court may make provision—
    (a) for the giving of notice of any application under this paragraph; and
    (b) for any person appearing to the court to be likely to be affected by any exercise of its powers under this paragraph to be given an opportunity to make representations to the court.".

GENERAL NOTE
    See s.11 of the 1993 Act which introduces similar provisions into the DTOA.

Availability of powers and satisfaction of orders

41.—(1) Schedule 4 to the Northern Ireland (Emergency Provisions) Act 1991 (supplementary provisions about confiscation orders) shall be amended as follows.

(2) In paragraph 2 (application of procedure for enforcing fines), the following shall be added at the end—

"(6) Where the defendant serves a term of imprisonment or detention in default of paying any amount due under a confiscation order, his serving that term does not prevent the confiscation order from continuing to have effect, so far as any other method of enforcement is concerned.".

(3) In paragraph 4 (cases in which restraint orders and charging orders may be made), the following sub-paragraphs shall be substituted for sub-paragraphs (1) and (2)—

"(1) The powers conferred on the High Court by paragraphs 5(1) and 6(1) below are exercisable where—

(a) proceedings have been instituted in Northern Ireland against the defendant for a relevant offence or an application has been made by the prosecution in respect of the defendant under section 48A, 48B or 52B of this Act or paragraph 11 below,

(b) the proceedings have not, or the application has not, been concluded, and

(c) the court is satisfied that there is reasonable cause to believe—

(i) in the case of an application under section 48B of this Act or paragraph 11 below, that the court will be satisfied as mentioned in section 48B(4) of this Act or, as the case may be, paragraph 11(1)(b) below, or

(ii) in any other case, that the defendant has benefited from terrorist-related activities.

(2) Those powers are also exercisable where—

(a) the High Court is satisfied that, whether by the making of a complaint or otherwise, a person is to be charged with a relevant offence or that an application of a kind mentioned in sub-paragraph (1)(a) above is to be made in respect of the defendant, and

(b) it appears to the court that there is reasonable cause to believe—

(i) in the case of a proposed application under section 48B of this Act or paragraph 11 below, that the court will be satisfied as mentioned in section 48B(4) of this Act or, as the case may be, paragraph 11(1)(b) below, or

(ii) in any other case, that the defendant has benefited from terrorist-related activities.".

(4) The following sub-paragraphs shall be added at the end of paragraph 4—

"(5) Where the court has made an order under paragraph 5(1) or 6(1) below in relation to a proposed application, by virtue of sub-paragraph (2) above, the court shall discharge the order if the application is not made within such time as the court considers reasonable.

(6) The court shall not exercise powers under paragraph 5(1) or 6(1) below, by virtue of sub-paragraph (1) above, if it is satisfied that—

(a) there has been undue delay in continuing the proceedings or application in question; or

(b) the prosecution does not intend to proceed.".

(5) In paragraph 5 (restraint orders), the following sub-paragraph shall be substituted for sub-paragraph (6)—

"(6) A restraint order—

(a) may be discharged or varied in relation to any property, and

(b) shall be discharged on the conclusion of the proceedings or of the application in question.".

(6) In paragraph 6 (charging orders), the following sub-paragraph shall be substituted for sub-paragraph (6)—

"(6) In relation to a charging order the court—

(a) may make an order discharging or varying it, and

(b) shall make an order discharging it—
    (i) on the conclusion of the proceedings or of the application in question, or
    (ii) on payment into court of the amount payment of which is secured by the charge.".

(7) In paragraph 10 (realisation of property), the following sub-paragraph shall be substituted for sub-paragraph (1)—

"(1) Where a confiscation order—
(a) has been made under this Act,
(b) is not satisfied, and
(c) is not subject to appeal,

the High Court may, on an application by the prosecution, exercise the powers conferred by sub-paragraphs (2) to (6) below.".

(8) In paragraph 16 (bankruptcy of defendant), the following shall be substituted for paragraphs (a) and (b) of sub-paragraph (6)—

"(a) no order shall be made under Article 312 or 367 of the said Order of 1989 (avoidance of certain transactions) in respect of the making of the gift at any time when—
    (i) proceedings for a relevant offence have been instituted against him and have not been concluded;
    (ii) an application has been made in respect of the defendant under section 48A, 48B or 52B of this Act or paragraph 11 below and has not been concluded; or
    (iii) property of the person to whom the gift was made is subject to a restraint order or charging order; and
(b) any order made under either of those Articles after the conclusion of the proceedings or of the application shall take into account any realisation under this Schedule of property held by the person to whom the gift was made.".

(9) In paragraph 1 (interpretation), the following sub-paragraphs shall be substituted for sub-paragraph (3)—

"(3) Proceedings for a relevant offence are concluded—
(a) when the defendant is acquitted;
(b) if he is convicted, but the court decides not to make a confiscation order against him, when it makes that decision; or
(c) if a confiscation order is made against him in those proceedings, when the order is satisfied.

(3A) An application under section 48A or 52B of this Act is concluded—
(a) if the court decides not to make a confiscation order against the defendant, when it makes that decision; or
(b) if a confiscation order is made against him as a result of that application, when the order is satisfied.

(3B) An application under section 48B of this Act or paragraph 11 below is concluded—
(a) if the court decides not to vary the confiscation order in question, when it makes that decision; or
(b) if the court varies the confiscation order as a result of the application, when the order is satisfied.

(3C) For the purposes of this Schedule, a confiscation order is satisfied when no amount is due under it.

(3D) For the purposes of paragraph 16 below, a confiscation order is also satisfied when the defendant in respect of whom it was made has served a term of imprisonment or detention in default of payment of the amount due under the order.".

GENERAL NOTE
The broad approach is that the amount of a confiscation order shall be treated as if the

amount were a fine imposed by the Crown Court (see Sched. 4, para. 2 to the EPA). It follows that a term of imprisonment must be imposed in default of payment (*ibid.*)

Originally, the practical consequences flowing from the defendant's commitment to prison were three-fold. First, the period to be served in default relieved the defendant of the requirement to satisfy that proportion of the order which remained outstanding. The defendant therefore effectively "served" his way out of paying the order and so defeated the primary purpose of the Act. Secondly, a warrant (in England), once issued, cannot be withdrawn by the magistrates' court (*R.* v. *Newport Pagnell Justices*, ex p. *Smith* [1988] 152 J.P. 475). Thirdly, proceedings for the purposes of the EPA were "concluded" upon the defendant serving a term of imprisonment in default (Sched. 4, para. 1(3)(b)). This provision has now been substantially amended by s.41(9) of the 1993 Act. Powers conferred on the High Court in respect of the making of a restraint or charging order, or the realisation of property by the appointment of a receiver, are only exercisable where proceedings are not concluded (see Sched. 4, paras. 4 and 10 to the EPA).

By Sched. 4, para. 2(2) to the EPA, a term of imprisonment (or detention) ordered to be served in default of payment, shall run after the defendant has served any sentences of imprisonment which were imposed in respect of the offences for which he appeared at the Crown Court. Once a defendant has served a term of imprisonment in default, his property is not liable to confiscation wherever it is situated. The Home Office working Group (1991) therefore recommended that a term of imprisonment served in default should not expunge what ought to be regarded as a "debt" (para. 3.11). Accordingly, para. 2(6) was inserted into Sched. 4 to the EPA by s.41(2) of the 1993 Act.

The remaining provisions are primarily designed to bring the EPA into line with the DTOA following the changes which have been introduced by the other provisions of the 1993 Act. As originally drafted the circumstances in which proceedings for an offence under ss.9, 10 and 11 of the EPA were to be treated as "concluded" were relatively straightforward.

Not only will proceedings now not be concluded upon serving a sentence in default of payment (para. 2(6)) but the ability of the prosecution to seek a re-determination of issues under the EPA over a period of six years from the date of the relevant conviction of determination means that the machinery necessary to enforce the satisfaction of the order had to be redefined. Thus:

(a) the powers of the High Court, under Sched. 4, paras. 5 and 6, are extended to applications brought by the prosecutor under ss.48A, 47B and 52B (defendant who has died or absconded) of the EPA;

(b) the same powers exist even if any such applications are to be made subject to the safeguards set out in Sched. 4, para. 4(5) (added by s.41(4) of the Criminal Justice Act 1993);

(c) restraint orders, under Sched. 4, para. 5 to the EPA, may be varied, etc., under para. 5(6), as amended by s.41(5) of the Criminal Justice Act 1993;

(d) similarly, charging orders may be varied, etc., under Sched. 4, para. 6 as amended by s.41(6) of the Criminal Justice Act 1993;

(e) powers under Sched. 4, para. 10 of the EPA may be exercised where an order is not satisfied (see s.41(7) of the Criminal Justice Act 1993);

(f) rules relevant to bankruptcy appear under Sched. 4, para. 16 (see s.41(8) of the Criminal Justice Act 1993);

(g) the circumstances in respect of proceedings for "drug trafficking offences", which can be said to be "concluded", are redefined (Sched. 4, para. 1(3), as amended by s.41(9) of the Criminal Justice Act 1993).

Defendant who has died or absconded

42. The following section shall be inserted in the Northern Ireland (Emergency Provisions) Act 1991, after section 52A—

"Powers of High Court where defendant has died or absconded
52B.—(1) Subsection (2) below applies where a person has been convicted of a relevant offence.

(2) If the prosecution asks it to proceed under this section, the High Court may exercise the powers of the Crown Court under this Act to make a confiscation order against the defendant if satisfied that the defendant has died or absconded.

(3) Subsection (4) below applies where proceedings have been instituted against the defendant for one or more relevant offences but have not been concluded.

(4) If the prosecution asks it to proceed under this section, the High Court, if satisfied that the defendant has absconded, may exercise the powers of the Crown Court under this Act to make a confiscation order against the defendant as if the defendant had been convicted of the relevant offence or each of the relevant offences for which the proceedings had been instituted.

(5) The power conferred by subsection (4) above may not be exercised at any time before the end of the period of two years beginning with the date which is, in the opinion of the court, the date on which the defendant absconded.

(6) Where the prosecution makes an application to the court under this section it shall, on making the application, give the court a statement under section 52 above.

(7) In any proceedings on an application under this section—
(a) sections 51, 52(1C), (2) and (3) and 52A above shall not apply,
(b) the court shall not make a confiscation order against a person who has absconded unless it is satisfied that the prosecution has taken reasonable steps to contact him, and
(c) any person appearing to the court to be likely to be affected by the making of a confiscation order by the court shall be entitled to appear before the court and make representations.

(8) Where the High Court has made a confiscation order by virtue of this section, in a case where the defendant has been or is subsequently convicted of one or more of the offences concerned, sections 47 and 48(1) to (5) and (7) above shall not apply in respect of his conviction of that offence or those offences; but any court dealing with him in respect of that conviction or any of those convictions—
(a) shall take account of the order before—
(i) imposing any fine on him; or
(ii) making any order involving any payment by him, other than an order under Article 3 of the Criminal Justice (Northern Ireland) Order 1980 (compensation orders); or
(iii) making any order under Article 7 of that Order (deprivation orders),
but subject to that shall leave the order out of account in determining the appropriate sentence or other manner of dealing with him; and
(b) if it makes an order for the payment of compensation under Article 3 of the Order of 1980, and is of the opinion that the defendant will not have sufficient means to satisfy both that order and the confiscation order in full, shall direct that so much of the compensation as will not in its opinion be recoverable because of the insufficiency of his means is to be paid out of any sums recovered under the confiscation order.".

GENERAL NOTE

   As the law stood, where a defendant either died or absconded before a confiscation order was made, the court was powerless to make a confiscation order. An indication of the sort of problems that can arise where a defendant absconds were demonstrated in *R.* v. *Chrastny (No. 2)* [1991] 1 W.L.R. 1385, a case under the DTOA. In that case the court had to determine whether property held jointly between husband and wife (both of whom had been jointly charged with a drug trafficking offence) was "realisable" for the purposes of s.4(3) of the DTOA, in circumstances where the wife had been convicted but where the husband had absconded. The court answered the question affirmatively. If the husband were to be apprehended, tried and convicted then the court could not include in any confiscation order against him, property realised to satisfy the order payable by his wife because the property was no longer under his control (*per* Glidewell L.J. at 1394).

The Home Office Working Group on Confiscation identified three situations to which different considerations may apply but which originally fell outside the ambit of the DTOA, namely: (1) death after conviction but before a confiscation order is made; (2) the defendant absconds after conviction but before the order is made; and (3) the defendant either dies or absconds before conviction.

Death or absconding after conviction

The Working Group, in their Report on the Drug Trafficking Offences Act 1986 (1991), saw no reason to distinguish between the two cases (in principle) and found that it should be possible to make confiscation orders in each case (para. 5.6). The EPA (as amended by s.42 of the 1993 Act) follows that general approach. Section 52B(1) of the EPA requires a conviction of a relevant offence. However, only the High Court may make a confiscation order and accordingly the prosecutor must apply to that court upon evidence being adduced, to the satisfaction of the High Court, that the defendant has either died or absconded (s.52B(2) of the EPA). Section 52B(3), (4) and (5) does not apply if the defendant is deceased. The difference between s.52B(1) and s.52B(2) is that s.52B(1) is applicable where there is a conviction, whereas s.52B(3) applies even if there is no conviction but proceedings have been instituted. However, s.52B(3), (4) and (5) are linked and should therefore be read together. Those three provisions form a set, which apply only to absconders, whether or not they are convicted of an offence. The result is that a confiscation order may not be made until two years after the date on which the defendant (in the opinion of the court) absconded.

It is not clear what the position would be if a defendant inexplicably went "missing", *e.g.* after a boating trip in mysterious circumstances pending a certification enquiry. Would the court treat him as having "absconded" or must the court wait seven years until he could be presumed dead? Note the obligation imposed on the prosecution by s.52B(7). Note that the statutory assumptions do not apply under s.51 (see s.52B(7)(a)).

Note that the court is required to make a confiscation order before sentencing the absent defendant (s.52B(8) of the EPA).

Defendant dies or absconds before conviction

Note that subss. (3), (4) and (5) of s.52B linked to form a set of provisions (see above). Accordingly, only as against an absconder can the High Court exercise the powers of the Crown Court to make a confiscation order (subject to s.52B(7) of the EPA). Parliament clearly took the view that it would be too drastic a step to extend the provisions of s.52B to those who died and who could never answer the indictment which they faced.

Where an absconder is acquitted (whether in his absence or otherwise) the court by which the defendant was acquitted (*e.g.* the Crown Court) may cancel the confiscation order (s.20B of the EPA (inserted by s.43 of the 1993 Act)) and apply for compensation, if he has suffered loss, as is just in all the circumstances of the case (s.20A of the EPA (inserted by s.43 of the 1993 Act)).

Compensation

43. In Schedule 4 to the Northern Ireland (Emergency Provisions) Act 1991, the following paragraphs shall be inserted after paragraph 20—

"*Compensation etc. where absconder is acquitted*

20A.—(1) This paragraph applies where—
(a) the High Court has made a confiscation order by virtue of section 52B(4) of this Act, and
(b) the defendant is subsequently tried for the offence or offences concerned and acquitted on all counts.

(2) The court by which the defendant is acquitted shall cancel the confiscation order.

(3) The High Court may, on the application of a person who held property which was realisable property, order compensation to be paid to the applicant if it is satisfied that the applicant has suffered loss as a result of the making of the confiscation order.

(4) The amount of compensation to be paid under this paragraph shall be such as the court considers just in all the circumstances of the case.

(5) Rules of court may make provision—

(a) for the giving of notice of any application under this paragraph; and

(b) for any person appearing to the court to be likely to be affected by any exercise of its powers under this paragraph to be given an opportunity to make representations to the court.

(6) Any payment of compensation under this paragraph shall be made by the Lord Chancellor out of money provided by Parliament.

(7) Where the court cancels a confiscation order under this paragraph it may make such consequential or incidental order as it considers appropriate in connection with the cancellation.

Power to discharge confiscation order and order compensation where absconder returns

20B.—(1) This paragraph applies where—

(a) the High Court has made a confiscation order by virtue of section 52B(4) of this Act in relation to an absconder,

(b) the defendant has ceased to be an absconder, and

(c) paragraph 20A above does not apply.

(2) The High Court may, on the application of the defendant, cancel the confiscation order if it is satisfied that—

(a) there has been undue delay in continuing the proceedings in respect of which the power under section 52B(4) above was exercised; or

(b) the prosecution does not intend to proceed.

(3) Where the High Court cancels a confiscation order under this paragraph it may, on the application of a person who held property which was realisable property, order compensation to be paid to the applicant if it is satisfied that the applicant has suffered loss as a result of the making of the confiscation order.

(4) The amount of compensation to be paid under this paragraph shall be such as the court considers just in all the circumstances of the case.

(5) Rules of court may make provision—

(a) for the giving of notice of any application under this paragraph; and

(b) for any person appearing to the court to be likely to be affected by any exercise of its powers under this paragraph to be given an opportunity to make representations to the court.

(6) Any payment of compensation under this paragraph shall be made by the Lord Chancellor out of money provided by Parliament.

(7) Where the court cancels a confiscation order under this paragraph it may make such consequential or incidental order as it considers appropriate in connection with the cancellation.

Variation of confiscation orders made by virtue of section 52B

20C.—(1) This paragraph applies where—

(a) the High Court has made a confiscation order by virtue of section 52B(4) of this Act, and

(b) the defendant has ceased to be an absconder.

(2) If the defendant alleges that—

(a) the value of his proceeds of terrorist-related activities in the period by reference to which the assessment in question was made (the "original value"), or

(b) the amount that might have been realised at the time the confiscation order was made,

was less than the amount required to be paid under the confiscation order, he may apply to the High Court for it to consider his evidence.

(3) If, having considered that evidence, the court is satisfied that the defendant's allegation is correct it—

(a) shall proceed under section 47(1) of this Act to make a fresh assessment of the value of his proceeds of terrorist-related activities, and

(b) may, if it considers it just in all the circumstances, vary the amount required to be paid under the confiscation order.

(4) For any assessment under section 47 of this Act by virtue of this paragraph, section 47(8) shall not apply in relation to any of the defendant's proceeds of terrorist-related activities taken into account in assessing the original value.

(5) Where the court varies a confiscation order under this paragraph—

(a) it shall substitute for the term of imprisonment or detention fixed in respect of the order under subsection (1)(c) of section 35 of the Criminal Justice Act (Northern Ireland) 1945 (imprisonment in default of payment) a shorter term if the effect of the substitution under sub-paragraph (3) above is to reduce the maximum period applicable in relation to the order under subsection (2) of that section as it has effect by virtue of paragraph 2(1)(b) above; and

(b) on the application of a person who held property which was realisable property, it may order compensation to be paid to the applicant if—

(i) it is satisfied that the applicant has suffered loss as a result of the making of the confiscation order; and

(ii) having regard to all the circumstances of the case, the court considers it to be appropriate.

(6) The amount of compensation to be paid under this paragraph shall be such as the court considers just in all the circumstances of the case.

(7) Rules of court may make provision—

(a) for the giving of notice of any application under this paragraph; and

(b) for any person appearing to the court to be likely to be affected by any exercise of its powers under this paragraph to be given an opportunity to make representations to the court.

(8) Any payment of compensation under this paragraph shall be made by the Lord Chancellor out of money provided by Parliament.

(9) No application shall be entertained by the court under this paragraph if it is made after the end of the period of six years beginning with the date on which the confiscation order was made.".

GENERAL NOTE

See the commentary to s.42, above, and see also the commentary to s.15 of the 1993 Act.

Realisable property

44. In section 50 of the Northern Ireland (Emergency Provisions) Act 1991 (realisable property, value and gifts), in subsection (2), the following paragraphs shall be inserted after paragraph (c)—

"(d) section 43 of the Powers of Criminal Courts Act 1973; or

(e) section 223 or 436 of the Criminal Procedure (Scotland) Act 1975,".

Enforcement

45.—(1) Section 67 of the Northern Ireland (Emergency Provisions) Act 1991 (orders and regulations) shall be amended as follows.

(2) In subsection (5), after the words "paragraph 7(3)" there shall be inserted "or 19(1)(a)".

(3) Subsection (6) shall cease to have effect.

Enforcement of orders outside Northern Ireland

46. In paragraph 19 of Schedule 4 to the Northern Ireland (Emergency Provisions) Act 1991 (enforcement of orders outside Northern Ireland), the following sub-paragraphs shall be added at the end—

"(3) An Order under this paragraph may contain such incidental, consequential and transitional provisions as Her Majesty considers expedient.

(4) An Order under sub-paragraph (1)(a) above may, in particular, provide for section 18 of the Civil Jurisdiction and Judgments Act 1982 (enforcement of United Kingdom judgments in other parts of the United Kingdom) not to apply.".

Offences relating to proceeds of terrorist-related activities

47.—(1) In section 53 of the Northern Ireland (Emergency Provisions) Act 1991 (assisting another to retain proceeds of terrorist-related activities) the following subsection shall be inserted after subsection (3)—

"(3A) Where a person discloses to a constable a suspicion or belief that any funds or investments are derived from or used in connection with terrorist-related activities or any matter on which such a suspicion or belief is based, the disclosure shall not be treated as a breach of any restriction upon the disclosure of information imposed by statute or otherwise.".

(2) In section 53 of that Act the following subsection shall be inserted after subsection (4)—

"(4A) In the case of a person who was in employment at the relevant time, subsections (3), (3A) and (4)(c) above shall have effect in relation to disclosures, and intended disclosures, to the appropriate person in accordance with the procedure established by his employer for the making of such disclosures as they have effect in relation to disclosures, and intended disclosures, to a constable.".

(3) In subsection (3) of section 54 of that Act (concealing or transferring proceeds of terrorist-related activities), for the words from "that property" to the end of that subsection, there shall be substituted "or uses that property or has possession of it".

(4) In section 54 of that Act, the following subsection shall be inserted after subsection (3)—

"(3A) It is a defence to a charge of committing an offence under this section that the person charged acquired or used the property or had possession of it for adequate consideration.".

(5) For section 54(5) of that Act there shall be substituted—

"(5) For the purposes of subsection (3A) above—

(a) a person acquires property for inadequate consideration if the value of the consideration is significantly less than the value of the property;

(b) a person uses or has possession of any property for inadequate consideration if the value of the consideration is significantly less than the value of his possession or use of the property; and

(c) the provision for any person of services or goods which are of assistance to him in terrorist-related activities shall not be treated as consideration.

(5A) Where a person discloses to a constable a suspicion or belief that any property is, or in whole or in part directly or indirectly represents, another person's proceeds of terrorist-related activities or any matter on which such a suspicion or belief is based—
   (a) the disclosure shall not be treated as a breach of any restriction upon the disclosure of information imposed by statute or otherwise; and
   (b) if he does any act in contravention of subsection (3) above, he does not commit an offence under that subsection if—
      (i) the disclosure is made before he does the act concerned and that act is done with the consent of the constable; or
      (ii) the disclosure is made after he does the act but on his initiative and as soon as it is reasonable for him to make it.
(5B) For the purposes of this section, having possession of any property shall be taken to be doing an act in relation to it.
(5C) In proceedings against a person for an offence under subsection (3) above, it is a defence to prove that—
   (a) he intended to disclose to a constable such a suspicion, belief or matter as is mentioned in subsection (5A) above; but
   (b) there is reasonable excuse for his failure to make a disclosure in accordance with paragraph (b) of that subsection.
(5D) In the case of a person who was in employment at the relevant time, subsections (5A) and (5C) above shall have effect in relation to disclosures, and intended disclosures, to the appropriate person in accordance with the procedure established by his employer for the making of such disclosures as they have effect in relation to disclosures, and intended disclosures, to a constable.
(5E) No constable or other person shall be guilty of an offence under subsection (3) above in respect of anything done by him in the course of acting in connection with the enforcement, or intended enforcement, of any provision of this Act or of any other enactment relating to terrorism or the proceeds or resources of such terrorism.".

GENERAL NOTE
   This provision brings the EPA into line with corresponding provisions under the DTOA and the CJA 1988 (see the commentary to Pts. II and III). Section 47(1) inserts s.53(3A) into the EPA, so as to afford immunity in respect of disclosures made under s.53 of the EPA. Section 47(2) extends the category of person to whom a disclosure may be made, namely an "appropriate person".

Subs. (4)
   This amends s.54 of the EPA by adding subs. (3A). Under this provision the burden is cast onto the defendant to prove that he provided "adequate consideration". Presumably, it will be for the jury to decide whether the consideration provided is in fact "adequate" having regard to s.54(5) but it is likely that it will fall to the courts to decide what that phrase really means. Subsection (5) provides two instances where consideration is "inadequate" but is subs. (5) a closed category? If a person pays an excessive price for the property in question, is the consideration to be regarded as being "inadequate"? If services are provided in consideration for a substantial sum of money which represent the proceeds of a relevant offence, is it relevant to argue that the service was not worth what was claimed or charged? (see *Hansard*, H.C. Vol. 222, col. 907, Sir Ivan Lawrence, Q.C.). In the majority of cases any issue as to value may be resolved with the help of expert assistance.

Subs. (5)
   This inserts new subss. (5A), (5B), (5C), (5D)–(5E) into s.54 of the EPA. This follows the model provided by s.24(3) of the DTOA (and see Sched. 7 to the Prevention of Terrorism (Temporary Provisions) Act 1989). Section 54(5A)–(5E) is designed to protect persons (particularly those employed in the financial sector) from any action for breach of contract, confidence or a duty arising out of their obligations to their clients.
   These provisions include the disclosure of "suspicions". There would seem to be two reasons why disclosure based on "suspicion" is said to be relevant. First, disclosure based on any higher

standard (*e.g.* belief) would present individuals with a difficult issue of fact to resolve. How much information do they need to satisfy themselves before they could (or are required to) disclose a belief? (see *Hansard*, H.L. Vol. 474, col. 1114 in relation to the DTOA). Secondly, law enforcement agencies act on suspicion and accordingly a lot of intelligence could be lost if all that could be disclosed were beliefs. The Government consider that it is "up to the policemen, the professionals, the investigators to decide whether or not [the suspicion] was true" (*per* Earl Ferrers, *Hansard*, H.L. Vol. 540, col. 753).

Failure to disclose knowledge or suspicion relating to proceeds of terrorist-related activities

48. The following section shall be inserted in the Northern Ireland (Emergency Provisions) Act 1991, after section 54—

> **"Failure to disclose knowledge or suspicion of offences under sections 53 and 54**
>
> 54A.—(1) A person is guilty of an offence if—
> (a) he knows, or suspects, that another person is acting in the proscribed manner,
> (b) the information, or other matter, on which that knowledge or suspicion is based came to his attention in the course of his trade, profession, business or employment, and
> (c) he does not disclose the information or other matter to a constable as soon as is reasonably practicable after it comes to his attention.
>
> (2) Subsection (1) above does not make it an offence for a professional legal adviser to fail to disclose any information or other matter which has come to him in privileged circumstances.
>
> (3) It is a defence to a charge of committing an offence under this section that the person charged had a reasonable excuse for not disclosing the information or other matter in question.
>
> (4) Where a person discloses to a constable—
> (a) his suspicion or belief that another person is acting in the proscribed manner, or
> (b) any information or other matter on which that suspicion or belief is based,
> the disclosure shall not be treated as a breach of any restriction imposed by statute or otherwise.
>
> (5) Without prejudice to subsection (3) or (4) above, in the case of a person who was in employment at the relevant time, it is a defence to a charge of committing an offence under this section that he disclosed the information or other matter in question to the appropriate person in accordance with the procedure established by his employer for the making of such disclosures.
>
> (6) A disclosure to which subsection (5) above applies shall not be treated as a breach of any restriction imposed by statute or otherwise.
>
> (7) In this section "acting in the proscribed manner" means doing any act which constitutes an offence under section 53 or 54 above or, in the case of an act done otherwise than in the United Kingdom, which would constitute such an offence if done in the United Kingdom.
>
> (8) For the purposes of subsection (7) above, having possession of any property shall be taken to be doing an act in relation to it.
>
> (9) For the purposes of this section, any information or other matter comes to a professional legal adviser in privileged circumstances if it is communicated, or given, to him—
> (a) by, or by a representative of, a client of his in connection with the giving by the adviser of legal advice to the client;

(b) by, or by a representative of, a person seeking legal advice from the adviser; or

(c) by any person—
    (i) in contemplation of, or in connection with, legal proceedings; and
    (ii) for the purpose of those proceedings.

(10) No information or other matter shall be treated as coming to a professional legal adviser in privileged circumstances if it is communicated or given with a view to furthering any criminal purpose.

(11) A person guilty of an offence under this section shall be liable—

(a) on summary conviction, to imprisonment for a term not exceeding six months or a fine not exceeding the statutory maximum or to both, or

(b) on conviction on indictment, to imprisonment for a term not exceeding five years or a fine or to both.".

GENERAL NOTE

   This follows the model which appears in s.18 of the 1993 Act (inserting new s.26B into the DTOA). A full commentary appears in respect of that provision. Note also s.51 of the 1993 Act, which creates a similar offence under s.18 of the Prevention of Terrorism (Temporary Provisions) Act 1989.

Amendments of the 1989 Act

Financial assistance for terrorism

49.—(1) In section 9 of the Prevention of Terrorism (Temporary Provisions) Act 1989 (contributions towards acts of terrorism), the following shall be inserted at the end of subsection (1)(b)—
    "or
(c) uses or has possession of, whether for consideration or not, any money or other property,".

(2) In section 10 of that Act (contributions to the resources of proscribed organisations), in subsection (1)(b), after the words "or accepts" there shall be inserted "or uses or has possession of".

(3) In section 12 of that Act (disclosure of information about terrorist funds) for the word "contract", in subsection (1), there shall be substituted "statute or otherwise".

(4) In section 12 of that Act, the following subsection shall be inserted after subsection (2)—
    "(2A) For the purposes of subsection (2) above a person who uses or has possession of money or other property shall be taken to be concerned in a transaction or arrangement.".

(5) In section 12(3) of that Act, after "section 9(1)(b)" there shall be inserted "or (c)".

(6) The following subsections shall be added at the end of section 12 of that Act—
    "(4) In the case of a person who was in employment at the relevant time, subsections (1) to (3) above shall have effect in relation to disclosures, and intended disclosures, to the appropriate person in accordance with the procedure established by his employer for the making of such disclosures as they have effect in relation to disclosures, and intended disclosures, to a constable.

    (5) No constable or other person shall be guilty of an offence under section 9(1)(b) or (c) or (2) or 10(1)(b) or (c) above in respect of anything done by him in the course of acting in connection with the enforcement, or intended enforcement, of any provision of this Act or

of any other enactment relating to terrorism or the proceeds or resources of terrorism.

(6) For the purposes of subsection (5) above, having possession of any property shall be taken to be doing an act in relation to it.".

Investigation of terrorist activities

50.—(1) Section 17 (investigation of terrorist activities) of the Prevention of Terrorism (Temporary Provisions) Act 1989 shall be amended as follows.

(2) In subsection (1)(a)(ii)—

(a) for "or 11 above" there shall be substituted "11, 18 or 18A of this Act"; and

(b) for "or 28" there shall be substituted "28, 53, 54 or 54A".

(3) For subsection (2) there shall be substituted—

"(2) A person is guilty of an offence if, knowing or having reasonable cause to suspect that a constable is acting, or is proposing to act, in connection with a terrorist investigation which is being, or is about to be, conducted, he—

(a) discloses to any other person information or any other matter which is likely to prejudice the investigation or proposed investigation, or

(b) falsifies, conceals or destroys or otherwise disposes of, or causes or permits the falsification, concealment, destruction or disposal of, material which is or is likely to be relevant to the investigation, or proposed investigation.

(2A) A person is guilty of an offence if, knowing or having reasonable cause to suspect that a disclosure ("the disclosure") has been made to a constable under section 12, 18 or 18A of this Act or section 53, 54 or 54A of the Northern Ireland (Emergency Provisions) Act 1991, he—

(a) discloses to any other person information or any other matter which is likely to prejudice any investigation which might be conducted following the disclosure; or

(b) falsifies, conceals or destroys or otherwise disposes of, or causes or permits the falsification, concealment, destruction or disposal of, material which is or is likely to be relevant to any such investigation.

(2B) A person is guilty of an offence if, knowing or having reasonable cause to suspect that a disclosure ("the disclosure") of a kind mentioned in section 12(4) or 18A(5) of this Act or section 53(4A), 54(5D) or 54A(5) of the Act of 1991 has been made, he—

(a) discloses to any person information or any other matter which is likely to prejudice any investigation which might be conducted following the disclosure; or

(b) falsifies, conceals or destroys or otherwise disposes of, or causes or permits the falsification, concealment, destruction or disposal of, material which is or is likely to be relevant to any such investigation.

(2C) Nothing in subsections (2) to (2B) above makes it an offence for a professional legal adviser to disclose any information or other matter—

(a) to, or to a representative of, a client of his in connection with the giving by the adviser of legal advice to the client; or

(b) to any person—

(i) in contemplation of, or in connection with, legal proceedings; and

(ii) for the purpose of those proceedings.

(2D) Subsection (2C) above does not apply in relation to any information or other matter which is disclosed with a view to furthering any criminal purpose.

(2E) No constable or other person shall be guilty of an offence under this section in respect of anything done by him in the course of acting in connection with the enforcement, or intended enforcement, of any provision of this Act or of any other enactment relating to terrorism or the proceeds or resources of terrorism.".

(4) In subsection (3) (defence in respect of disclosure), after "investigation" there shall be inserted "or proposed investigation".

(5) The following shall be inserted after subsection (3)—

"(3A) In proceedings against a person for an offence under subsection (2A)(a) or (2B)(a) above it is a defence to prove—

(a) that he did not know and had no reasonable cause to suspect that his disclosure was likely to prejudice the investigation in question; or

(b) that he had lawful authority or reasonable excuse for making his disclosure.".

(6) In subsection (4) (defence in respect of falsifying material etc.), for the words from "the persons" to the end there shall be substituted "any person conducting, or likely to be conducting, the investigation or proposed investigation".

(7) The following shall be inserted after subsection (4)—

"(4A) In proceedings against a person for an offence under subsection (2A)(b) or (2B)(b) above, it is a defence to prove that he had no intention of concealing any information contained in the material in question from any person who might carry out the investigation in question.".

(8) In subsection (5) (penalties) after "(2)" there shall be inserted "(2A) or (2B)".

(9) The following subsection shall be added at the end—

"(6) For the purposes of subsection (1) above, as it applies in relation to any offence under section 18 or 18A below or section 54A of the Act of 1991, "act" includes omission.".

Failure to disclose knowledge or suspicion of financial assistance for terrorism

51. The following section shall be inserted in the Prevention of Terrorism (Temporary Provisions) Act 1989, after section 18—

"Failure to disclose knowledge or suspicion of offences under sections 9 to 11

18A.—(1) A person is guilty of an offence if—

(a) he knows, or suspects, that another person is providing financial assistance for terrorism;

(b) the information, or other matter, on which that knowledge or suspicion is based came to his attention in the course of his trade, profession, business or employment; and

(c) he does not disclose the information or other matter to a constable as soon as is reasonably practicable after it comes to his attention.

(2) Subsection (1) above does not make it an offence for a professional legal adviser to fail to disclose any information or other matter which has come to him in privileged circumstances.

(3) It is a defence to a charge of committing an offence under this section that the person charged had a reasonable excuse for not disclosing the information or other matter in question.

(4) Where a person discloses to a constable—

(a) his suspicion or belief that another person is providing financial assistance for terrorism; or

    (b) any information or other matter on which that suspicion or
        belief is based;
the disclosure shall not be treated as a breach of any restriction
imposed by statute or otherwise.

    (5) Without prejudice to subsection (3) or (4) above, in the case of
a person who was in employment at the relevant time, it is a defence
to a charge of committing an offence under this section that he
disclosed the information or other matter in question to the appropriate person in accordance with the procedure established by his
employer for the making of such disclosures.

    (6) A disclosure to which subsection (5) above applies shall not be
treated as a breach of any restriction imposed by statute or otherwise.

    (7) In this section "providing financial assistance for terrorism"
means doing any act which constitutes an offence under section 9, 10
or 11 above or, in the case of an act done otherwise than in the United
Kingdom, which would constitute such an offence if done in the
United Kingdom.

    (8) For the purposes of subsection (7) above, having possession of
any property shall be taken to be doing an act in relation to it.

    (9) For the purposes of this section, any information or other
matter comes to a professional legal adviser in privileged circumstances if it is communicated, or given, to him—

    (a) by, or by a representative of, a client of his in connection with
        the giving by the adviser of legal advice to the client;

    (b) by, or by a representative of, a person seeking legal advice
        from the adviser; or

    (c) by any person—
            (i) in contemplation of, or in connection with, legal pro-
        ceedings; and
            (ii) for the purpose of those proceedings.

    (10) No information or other matter shall be treated as coming to a
professional legal adviser in privileged circumstances if it is communicated or given with a view to furthering any criminal purpose.

    (11) A person guilty of an offence under this section shall be
liable—

    (a) on summary conviction, to imprisonment for a term not
        exceeding six months or a fine not exceeding the statutory
        maximum or to both; or

    (b) on conviction on indictment, to imprisonment for a term not
        exceeding five years or a fine or to both.".

GENERAL NOTE
    See the commentary to s.48 of the 1993 Act.

PART V

INSIDER DEALING

GENERAL NOTE
    Part V of the 1993 Act repeals, in its entirety, the Company Securities (Insider Dealing) Act
1985 and the Company Securities (Insider Dealing) (Northern Ireland) Order 1986. Part VI
substantially amends the law on insider dealing. Insider dealing was made an offence in this
country by ss.68–73 of the Companies Act 1980 (Pt. V), following much press and public
attention during the 1970's culminating in the publication of a White Paper, *The Conduct of the
Company Directors* (1977). Earlier attempts to make insider dealing an offence failed in the
Companies Bills of 1973 and 1978. The overall object of insider dealing laws is "... to protect
corporate confidences and to prevent insiders privy to such confidences from benefiting on an
unfair advantage when they deal in the market. When they do deal in those circumstances, they
abuse their position and the confidences imposed on them which, in turn, undermines the
integrity of the market" (*Public Prosecutor* v. *Allan Ng Poh Meng* [1990] 1 M.L.J. 5, *per* Senior
District Judge Foenander at p. 14). The Company Securities (Insider Dealing) Act 1985

re-enacted the previous law; it had been amended by the Financial Services Act 1986 and the Companies Act 1989.

Since 1980, 22 persons have been convicted of an insider dealing offence, 16 of whom have been convicted since 1987. However, on one view of those statistics the law should not be shown to be working "... only if it can be proved that enough people have broken it" (Standing Committee B, col. 140, June 10, 1993, *per* Mr. Jenkin). There is some force in the view (also expressed by Mr. Jenkin) that: "the purpose of insider dealing legislation is to set a moral climate and to create an atmosphere in which it is easy for professional institutions, professional advisers and companies to enforce the moral code of the City, which is that insider dealing is unacceptable" (*ibid.*, col. 140).

One of the primary purposes behind the enactment of Pt. V is to give effect to the European Council Directive 89/592/EEC which was agreed on November 18, 1989. By Art. 14, Member States were required to take measures necessary to comply with this Directive before June 1, 1992, but lack of Parliamentary time precluded compliance with Art. 14 (until Pt. V of the 1993 Act comes into force). Devising a framework to give effect to the Directive has clearly proved to be a very difficult task and this Part of the Act was heavily amended during its passage through both Houses of Parliament.

The European Community regard the secondary market, in transferable securities, as playing an important role in the financing of economic agents and that the smooth running of that market depends on the confidence of investors who must be protected against the "improper use" of insider dealing. Defining the circumstances in which insider dealing is "improper" is a vexed question and the courts will be required to determine the parameters of what is a legal or illegal use of insider information. Article 1 defines inside information to mean information which has not been made public of a "precise nature relating to one or several issuers of transferable securities or to one or several transferable securities, which, if it were made public, would be likely to have a significant effect on the price of the transferable security of securities in question".

The use of the word "precise" in Art. 1 is of significance because it suggests that the information is narrowly focused, and not of a merely general nature, which is less likely to be of value and thus less likely to have a destabilising effect on the secondary market. It will be seen that, by contrast, the definition of inside information in s.56 closely follows Art. 1, but whereas Art. 1 refers to information of a "precise nature", s.56(1)(b) adds the word "specific" as an alternative. This is discussed more fully below but one criticism of the word "specific" is that it is broader in scope and may catch disclosures which are general in content. Thus for an employee to say that "business is down on last year" is "specific" but in the absence of any statistical data it is not precise. Nevertheless, by s.56(1), all four ingredients must be satisfied and, arguably, the most significant element is s.56(1)(d). Each case will therefore turn very much on its own facts having regard to the economic climate (and other considerations) prevailing at the relevant time.

Again, it is plain from Art. 1 that only a limited range of "securities" should form the subject matter of protection, *i.e.* "transferable securities" and these are defined in Art. 1(2) of the Directive. Accordingly, s.54(1) of and Sched. 2 to the 1993 Act give effect to Art. 1(2) especially those securities which form that subject matter of Pt. V. The 1993 Act prefers the term "price-affected-securities" (s.56(2)). Article 2 of the Directive specifies three categories of persons who possess inside information but shall not take improper advantage of it. It also embraces those who deal in what the 1993 Act calls "price-affected-securities". Put shortly, persons falling within any of those categories are not to deal in "prime-affected-securities" (or to encourage others to do so) where dealing (either by acquisition or disposal (s.52(3))) occurs on a "regulated market", whether or not such dealing is achieved through a professional intermediary, Art. 2(3), and that the dealing was in consequence of (*i.e.* "in relation to") the information held by that person; see s.52(1) and (2).

The categories of person described in Art. 2 are roughly based on s.57 which provides a comprehensive definition of "insiders". Traditionally, there has been a distinction drawn between "insiders" and "tippees". However, this terminology whilst incurring a certain degree of amusement also incurred displeasure in Parliament and thus such terminology, although featured in the early drafts of the Bill, has been dropped from the 1993 Act. Accordingly, s.57 (which follows from a recasting of the offence of insider dealing) defines someone as having information as an insider if the information is, and the person knows it is, inside information and he has it, and knows he has it, from an inside source whether through being a director, employee or shareholder of an issuer of securities, or through having access to the information by virtue of employment, profession or office or, directly or indirectly, from a source which falls within either of those groups. To this extent the 1993 Act differs from the previous legislation which required a connection between the individual insider and the "company" which enabled him to come into possession of the information in question.

By Art. 3 of the Directive, Member States are required to prohibit an insider from disclosing inside information to any third party unless such disclosure is made in the normal course of the exercise of his employment, profession or duties. This provision is mirrored in s.52(2)(b) of the 1993 Act.

It will be seen from s.56(1)(c) that inside information means information which, *inter alia*, has not been made public. This is obviously an important aspect which goes to the heart of the mischief which the legislation seeks to prevent. However, defining the circumstances in which it can properly be said that information is in the public domain, is not a straightforward exercise. The fact that observation of factory premises would show that the factory gates are often closed (and therefore suggest a discontented workforce or a downward trend in the factory's fortunes) could, without statutory or judicial definition be argued to be sufficient material in the public domain. The problem is assessing to what degree information must be at least available to the general public before it can be safely said that information is in the public domain. Section 58 of the 1993 Act gives statutory guidance by setting out a number of instances in which information is to be regarded as having been made public (see s.58(2)) and those categories where information "may be treated as made public" even though steps may have to be taken by individuals or sections of the public in order to obtain the information in question (see s.58(3)). These categories are not exhaustive (see s.58(1)). Accordingly, it will be for the courts to determine the parameters of s.58.

Part V of the 1993 Act has been drafted in such a way that definitions are grouped together in order to make the legislation clearer while giving effect to the European Directive. Thus s.52 defines the three offences of insider trading (acquiring and disposing of securities; and encouraging another to deal in securities; and disclosing inside information) in one section. Similarly, defences are grouped under s.53 with reference to Sched. 1 where "special defences" may apply.

The offence of insider dealing

The offence

52.—(1) An individual who has information as an insider is guilty of insider dealing if, in the circumstances mentioned in subsection (3), he deals in securities that are price-affected securities in relation to the information.

(2) An individual who has information as an insider is also guilty of insider dealing if—

(a) he encourages another person to deal in securities that are (whether or not that other knows it) price-affected securities in relation to the information, knowing or having reasonable cause to believe that the dealing would take place in the circumstances mentioned in subsection (3); or

(b) he discloses the information, otherwise than in the proper performance of the functions of his employment, office or profession, to another person.

(3) The circumstances referred to above are that the acquisition or disposal in question occurs on a regulated market, or that the person dealing relies on a professional intermediary or is himself acting as a professional intermediary.

(4) This section has effect subject to section 53.

GENERAL NOTE

Three offences are grouped under s.52 namely (i) the acquisition and disposal of securities; (ii) encouraging another to deal in securities; and (iii) the disclosure of inside information. As to the first category, an individual must be proved to have information as an insider and secondly, that the individual concerned deals in securities which are "price-affected-securities" in relation to the information in circumstances which are set out in s.52. Those circumstances include that he either deals on a regulated market or that he is, or operates through, a "professional intermediary" (see s.59). The second and third categories of the offence are "anti-avoidance" measures designed to prohibit the encouragement, for example, of the illegal use of inside information in circumstances where the insider knows or had reasonable cause to believe that dealing would take place in the circumstances mentioned in s.52(3) of the 1993 Act. Not all disclosure which takes place during the course of employment is permissible; thus it would be improper to disclose confidential information even if the disclosure was made for the employer's financial benefit to a person whom the defendant did not intend should benefit personally.

Defences

53.—(1) An individual is not guilty of insider dealing by virtue of dealing in securities if he shows—

(a) that he did not at the time expect the dealing to result in a profit attributable to the fact that the information in question was price-sensitive information in relation to the securities, or

(b) that at the time he believed on reasonable grounds that the information had been disclosed widely enough to ensure that none of those taking part in the dealing would be prejudiced by not having the information, or

(c) that he would have done what he did even if he had not had the information.

(2) An individual is not guilty of insider dealing by virtue of encouraging another person to deal in securities if he shows—

(a) that he did not at the time expect the dealing to result in a profit attributable to the fact that the information in question was price-sensitive information in relation to the securities, or

(b) that at the time he believed on reasonable grounds that the information had been or would be disclosed widely enough to ensure that none of those taking part in the dealing would be prejudiced by not having the information, or

(c) that he would have done what he did even if he had not had the information.

(3) An individual is not guilty of insider dealing by virtue of a disclosure of information if he shows—

(a) that he did not at the time expect any person, because of the disclosure, to deal in securities in the circumstances mentioned in subsection (3) of section 52; or

(b) that, although he had such an expectation at the time, he did not expect the dealing to result in a profit attributable to the fact that the information was price-sensitive information in relation to the securities.

(4) Schedule 1 (special defences) shall have effect.

(5) The Treasury may by order amend Schedule 1.

(6) In this section references to a profit include references to the avoidance of a loss.

GENERAL NOTE

The defences set out in this section are largely self-explanatory. The terms of the section were explained by the Economic Secretary to the Treasury (Mr. Anthony Nelson) who said:

"The new section provides that there is no offence for dealing in three particular circumstances. The first is that the person dealing did not expect to make a profit attributable to the fact that he possessed information that was price sensitive to the securities in question. That defence might apply when, for example, someone sold shares while in possession of information [that] he expected to receive a favourable reaction from the market.

The second defence applies when someone believed on reasonable grounds that the information had been disclosed widely enough to ensure that none of those taking part in the dealing would be prejudiced by not having the information. That defence can come into play when the parties to a transaction are in contact with each other and they both possess information that can or cannot yet be made public. That is of particular importance in ensuring that the legislation does not impinge on properly conducted corporate finance transaction such as underwriting offers of listed securities and such like. The third defence applies when someone can show that he would have done what he did even if he had not had the information; for example, it allows a trustee who possesses insider information to deal in price-affected securities on the basis of independent investment advice. Analogous defences are also provided for the encouraging offence.

The position for disclosure is slightly different because the offence itself excludes disclosure in the proper performance of someone's employment and because the second defence applicable to dealing and encouraging is not applicable, as the defence itself requires both parties to possess the same information. Accordingly, the disclosure defences are provided when no dealing was expected or the dealing was not expected to lead to someone making a profit attributable to the fact that the securities involved were price affected in relation to the information in question.

The new clause provides also that the defences in the new schedule, which we shall discuss soon, will take effect and allow amendment to those defences by order". (Standing Committee B, col. 175, June 10, 1993).

Special defences are provided by Sched. 1. These defences are largely self explanatory and apply to a limited category of cases although the Treasury may, by order, amend Sched. 1.

Interpretation

Securities to which Part V applies

54.—(1) This Part applies to any security which—
(a) falls within any paragraph of Schedule 2; and
(b) satisfies any conditions applying to it under an order made by the Treasury for the purposes of this subsection;
and in the provisions of this Part (other than that Schedule) any reference to a security is a reference to a security to which this Part applies.

(2) The Treasury may by order amend Schedule 2.

GENERAL NOTE
This section merely defines those securities to which Pt. V of the 1993 Act apply and which are specified in Sched. 2 to the Act. Note that the Treasury may by order amend Sched. 2.

"Dealing" in securities

55.—(1) For the purposes of this Part, a person deals in securities if—
(a) he acquires or disposes of the securities (whether as principal or agent); or
(b) he procures, directly or indirectly, an acquisition or disposal of the securities by any other person.

(2) For the purposes of this Part, "acquire", in relation to a security, includes—
(a) agreeing to acquire the security; and
(b) entering into a contract which creates the security.

(3) For the purposes of this Part, "dispose", in relation to a security, includes—
(a) agreeing to dispose of the security; and
(b) bringing to an end a contract which created the security.

(4) For the purposes of subsection (1), a person procures an acquisition or disposal of a security if the security is acquired or disposed of by a person who is—
(a) his agent,
(b) his nominee, or
(c) a person who is acting at his direction,
in relation to the acquisition or disposal.

(5) Subsection (4) is not exhaustive as to the circumstances in which one person may be regarded as procuring an acquisition or disposal of securities by another.

GENERAL NOTE
This section provides a number of definitions which appear in this Part of the Act. They are largely self explanatory.

"Inside information", etc.

56.—(1) For the purposes of this section and section 57, "inside information" means information which—
(a) relates to particular securities or to a particular issuer of securities or to particular issuers of securities and not to securities generally or to issuers of securities generally;

(b) is specific or precise;
(c) has not been made public; and
(d) if it were made public would be likely to have a significant effect on the price of any securities.

(2) For the purposes of this Part, securities are "price-affected securities" in relation to inside information, and inside information is "price-sensitive information" in relation to securities, if and only if the information would, if made public, be likely to have a significant effect on the price of the securities.

(3) For the purposes of this section "price" includes value.

GENERAL NOTE
Section 56(1) defines the meaning of inside information. Reference to this provision has already been made in the introduction to Pt. V. This provision is central to Pt. V. Note that s.56(1)(b) uses the phrase "specific" or "precise", whereas Art. 1.1 of Directive 89/592/EEC merely refers to information "of a precise nature" which has not been made public. The purpose of s.56(1)(b) appears to be to ensure that inside information does not include rumour. It was clearly the Government's view that the word "specific" is somewhat wider than the word "precise". The significance of this provision was again explained by the Economic Secretary to the Treasury when he said:
"I suggest that if somebody were to say during such a lunch as has been mentioned, 'Our results will be much better than the market expects or knows', that would not be precise. The person would not have disclosed what the results of the company were to be. However, it would certainly be specific because he would be saying something about the company's results, and making it pretty obvious that the information had not been made public. In such circumstances it should not have been disclosed. It would be insider information because it would be specific.
If precise information is disclosed, for example, if the person were to say, 'Our profits will be at a certain level, and the market does not know that', without stating whether they would be significantly better or worse than the market expected, it would be up to the recipient of the information to judge whether he had been given information that was not available to the market and was likely to be price sensitive—to move the price of the shares. We have attempted to catch both of them.
We have added not only the words of the Directive but the words of existing legislation. To go wider would run the serious risk of improperly, unduly and unreasonably inhibiting the analytical relationships and assessment of companies that are as much in the interest of investors in the financial markets as they are in the companies that want to encourage such relationships". (Standing Committee B, col. 175, June 10, 1993).

"Insiders"

57.—(1) For the purposes of this Part, a person has information as an insider if and only if—
(a) it is, and he knows that it is, inside information, and
(b) he has it, and knows that he has it, from an inside source.
(2) For the purposes of subsection (1), a person has information from an inside source if and only if—
(a) he has it through—
(i) being a director, employee or shareholder of an issuer of securities; or
(ii) having access to the information by virtue of his employment, office or profession; or
(b) the direct or indirect source of his information is a person within paragraph (a).

Information "made public"

58.—(1) For the purposes of section 56, "made public", in relation to information, shall be construed in accordance with the following provisions of this section; but those provisions are not exhaustive as to the meaning of that expression.
(2) Information is made public if—

(a) it is published in accordance with the rules of a regulated market for the purpose of informing investors and their professional advisers;
(b) it is contained in records which by virtue of any enactment are open to inspection by the public;
(c) it can be readily acquired by those likely to deal in any securities—
    (i) to which the information relates, or
    (ii) of an issuer to which the information relates; or
(d) it is derived from information which has been made public.
(3) Information may be treated as made public even though—
(a) it can be acquired only by persons exercising diligence or expertise;
(b) it is communicated to a section of the public and not to the public at large;
(c) it can be acquired only by observation;
(d) it is communicated only on payment of a fee; or
(e) it is published only outside the United Kingdom.

GENERAL NOTE
The effect of this provision has already been explained in the introduction to Pt. V of the Act.

"Professional intermediary"

59.—(1) For the purposes of this Part, a "professional intermediary" is a person—
(a) who carries on a business consisting of an activity mentioned in subsection (2) and who holds himself out to the public or any section of the public (including a section of the public constituted by persons such as himself) as willing to engage in any such business; or
(b) who is employed by a person falling within paragraph (a) to carry out any such activity.
(2) The activities referred to in subsection (1) are—
(a) acquiring or disposing of securities (whether as principal or agent); or
(b) acting as an intermediary between persons taking part in any dealing in securities.
(3) A person is not to be treated as carrying on a business consisting of an activity mentioned in subsection (2)—
(a) if the activity in question is merely incidental to some other activity not falling within subsection (2); or
(b) merely because he occasionally conducts one of those activities.
(4) For the purposes of section 52, a person dealing in securities relies on a professional intermediary if and only if a person who is acting as a professional intermediary carries out an activity mentioned in subsection (2) in relation to that dealing.

Other interpretation provisions

60.—(1) For the purposes of this Part, "regulated market" means any market, however operated, which, by an order made by the Treasury, is identified (whether by name or by reference to criteria prescribed by the order) as a regulated market for the purposes of this Part.
(2) For the purposes of this Part an "issuer", in relation to any securities, means any company, public sector body or individual by which or by whom the securities have been or are to be issued.
(3) For the purposes of this Part—
(a) "company" means any body (whether or not incorporated and wherever incorporated or constituted) which is not a public sector body; and
(b) "public sector body" means—
    (i) the government of the United Kingdom, of Northern Ireland or of any country or territory outside the United Kingdom;
    (ii) a local authority in the United Kingdom or elsewhere;

(iii) any international organisation the members of which include the United Kingdom or another member state;

(iv) the Bank of England; or

(v) the central bank of any sovereign State.

(4) For the purposes of this Part, information shall be treated as relating to an issuer of securities which is a company not only where it is about the company but also where it may affect the company's business prospects.

Miscellaneous

Penalties and prosecution

61.—(1) An individual guilty of insider dealing shall be liable—

(a) on summary conviction, to a fine not exceeding the statutory maximum or imprisonment for a term not exceeding six months or to both; or

(b) on conviction on indictment, to a fine or imprisonment for a term not exceeding seven years or to both.

(2) Proceedings for offences under this Part shall not be instituted in England and Wales except by or with the consent of—

(a) the Secretary of State; or

(b) the Director of Public Prosecutions.

(3) In relation to proceedings in Northern Ireland for offences under this Part, subsection (2) shall have effect as if the reference to the Director of Public Prosecutions were a reference to the Director of Public Prosecutions for Northern Ireland.

Territorial scope of offence of insider dealing

62.—(1) An individual is not guilty of an offence falling within subsection (2) of section 52 unless—

(a) he was within the United Kingdom at the time when he is alleged to have done any act constituting or forming part of the alleged dealing;

(b) the regulated market on which the dealing is alleged to have occurred is one which, by an order made by the Treasury, is identified (whether by name or by reference to criteria prescribed by the order) as being, for the purposes of this Part, regulated in the United Kingdom; or

(c) the professional intermediary was within the United Kingdom at the time when he is alleged to have done anything by means of which the offence is alleged to have been committed.

(2) An individual is not guilty of an offence falling within subsection (2) of section 52 unless—

(a) he was within the United Kingdom at the time when he is alleged to have disclosed the information or encouraged the dealing; or

(b) the alleged recipient of the information or encouragement was within the United Kingdom at the time when he is alleged to have received the information or encouragement.

Limits on section 52

63.—(1) Section 52 does not apply to anything done by an individual acting on behalf of a public sector body in pursuit of monetary policies or policies with respect to exchange rates or the management of public debt or foreign exchange reserves.

(2) No contract shall be void or unenforceable by reason only of section 52.

Orders

64.—(1) Any power under this Part to make an order shall be exercisable by statutory instrument.

(2) No order shall be made under this Part unless a draft of it has been laid before and approved by a resolution of each House of Parliament.

(3) An order under this Part—

(a) may make different provision for different cases; and

(b) may contain such incidental, supplemental and transitional provisions as the Treasury consider expedient.

PART VI

MISCELLANEOUS

GENERAL NOTE

Many of the provisions which feature in Pt. VI are the result of recent public and judicial disquiet concerning the administration of the criminal justice system and the operation of certain aspects of the Criminal Justice Act 1991. The Minister of State for the Home Office, when the 1993 Act was being examined in Committee, acknowledged that various provisions of the 1991 Act "... were not having the desired effect on the sentencing powers of the courts ... [and] ... were not working as they were intended to" (Standing Committee B, col. 239, June 17, 1993). The system of unit fines resulted in a number of well publicised cases which challenged the validity of such a system but, more importantly s.29 of the 1991 Act, which restricted the courts' ability to have regard to a defendant's previous convictions for the purposes of sentencing, also attracted much criticism in the press, and from commentators and the judiciary. Put shortly, s.29 in its old form has gone. Part I of the 1991 Act has been remodelled so that sentencing practice (as it existed before October 1, 1992) has largely been restored.

On one view, the 1993 Act is not the appropriate vehicle for rectifying deficiencies and shortcomings in the 1991 Act. This is because Pts. I to V of the 1993 Act were principally designed to reform and amend particular areas of criminal law which have an international impact as well as being domestically important. However, the clamour of opinion in favour of swift and decisive action, to remedy failings and shortcomings in the administration of justice, resulted in Parliament adding provisions to what is now Pt. VI.

Abolition of Unit Fines

The system of "unit fines" has been abolished (s.65), in favour of a flexible approach which has regard to the circumstances of the case including the financial circumstances of the offender. This may sound obvious until it is remembered that traditionally fines would be set to match the gravity of the offence but that sum could be reduced having regard to the means of the offender. What is enacted (or at least so Parliament thinks) is that the court will have power to fix a fine at a higher or lower rate than is strictly commensurate with the seriousness of the offence so that the effect of the fine will be "felt" by the offender—whatever his wealth. Parliament clearly hopes that this principle will not be taken so far that the amount of the fine looks totally disproportionate to the nature of the offence. It is significant that the unit fine system was introduced as a way of ensuring that the amount of the fine was not only commensurate with the seriousness of the offence, but also with the disposable wealth of the offender, so that the "impact" of the punishment would "feel" the same—irrespective of wealth. In the event, a system which had been created in the interests of fairness, perished because it proved (or was perceived) to be unfair. Cases where defendants were fined, say £1,000 for dropping litter, were criticised not in the context of an omission on the part of the defendant to provide a statement of means (as was generally the case) but as a criticism of the court not keeping the seriousness of the offence in perspective.

The unit fine system was controversial at the time it was being considered by Parliament in 1991, but it had also been the subject of various pilot studies, the results of which sufficiently encouraged the Legislature to incorporate the system into the 1991 Act. A variety of explanations have been given as to why similar results were not repeated under the 1991 Act. There were key differences between the pilot schemes and the statutory schemes brought about by "severe changes" in the courts' powers to raise (as well as lower) fines to reflect different levels of income (see Standing Committee B, cols. 241–242, June 17, 1993). This topic is dealt with more fully below (see s.65).

Seriousness of the Offence—relevance of other offences

The sentencer has now been given greater freedom to determine the appropriate sentence which is commensurate with the seriousness of the offence, having regard to the circumstances of the case. Section 1(2)(a) of the 1991 Act is amended so that the sentencer may have regard to all offences committed by a defendant for the purposes of determining (a) whether imprisonment or a community sentence is justified (s.66(1) and (4) of the 1993 Act); and (b) the length of imprisonment (or the type of sentence) for any sentence to be imposed (see s.66(2) and (5) of the 1993 Act amending ss.2 and 7 of the 1991 Act).

For the above purposes, the court is now empowered to take into account information about the circumstances of all offences, "associated" with the offence to be sentenced (see s.66(3) of the 1993 Act, amending s.3(3)(a) of the 1991 Act) and similar provision is made in connection with restrictions on the imposition of "community sentences" (see s.66(4) and (5) of the 1993 Act, amending ss.6 and 7 of the 1991 Act).

Seriousness of the Offence—previous convictions and sentences (s.29 of the 1991 Act)

In considering the seriousness of any offence, the court may take into account any previous convictions of the offender or any failure to respond to previous sentences (see s.66(6) of the 1993 Act, amending s.29 of the 1991 Act). This represents a major shift by Parliament in its sentencing policy. A significant theme of Pt. I of the 1991 Act was (and arguably still is) that the court must focus on the seriousness of the offence before it and not to sentence offenders on their criminal past (see *Hansard*, H.L. Vol. 528, cols. 1480–1504). Accordingly, by s.29 of the 1991 Act (as originally drafted), an offence was not to be regarded as more serious by reason of any previous convictions of an offender or any failure of his to respond to previous sentences. When s.29(1) and (2) of the 1991 Act were read in conjunction with ss.1, 2 and 31(2) of that Act, their effect was to force the court to look to the inherent seriousness of the specific offence for which the defendant was to be sentenced.

Although this policy ensured that a person was not punished on his record (and recognised that every offence had a "gravity value") it was a policy which was ill-equipped to deal with the case of multiple offences in which each offence (viewed in isolation) could be described as "minor" but, when viewed together, amounted to offending on a substantial scale. These problems were certainly not unforeseen and they were well aired particularly in the House of Lords. On the one hand the view of the Government was clearly spelt out by the Secretary of State when he said that: "our view is that people who commit minor offences, even if committed in considerable numbers, should not necessarily be sent to prison ... as a general rule the sentence for each offence should be that which is commensurate with the seriousness of the offence and not based on the offender's previous response to sentencing" (*Hansard*, H.L. Vol. 259, cols. 582 and 583). These aims were attacked (principally by Lord Ackner) as imposing upon the courts a "blinkered approach to sentencing" (*Hansard*, H.L. Vol. 527, col. 1621) and he gave the example of the thief who steals £100 per week from his employers and thereby acquires £10,000. In isolation, each act of theft was minor compared with the end result. The approach, prior to 1991, of regarding an offence as more serious because it repeated previous offending, was forbidden under the 1991 Act. All a court could do, was to look at the offence (or the offence and one other associated with it) and enquire whether the circumstances of either offence disclosed any aggravating features (see *R. v. Bexley* [1993] 2 All E.R. 23).

Section 66(6) radically amends s.29 of the 1991 Act. Neither s.29(1) or (2) have survived; their place has been taken by four new subsections. Under new s.29(1) the court may now take into account "any" previous convictions of the offender or "any failure of his to respond to previous sentences".

Consequential Amendments

The amendments made by s.66 of the 1993 Act take effect even if the defendant was convicted (but not sentenced) before this section came into force.

The totality of offending is also relevant for the purposes of s.12D of the Children and Young Persons Act 1969 and s.38 of the Magistrates' Courts Act 1980.

Penalty for Causing Death by Dangerous or Careless Driving

Causing death by dangerous driving (s.1 of the Road Traffic Act 1988 (as amended)) or causing death by careless driving while under the influence of drink or drugs (s.3A of the CJA 1988) now attracts a sentence of 10 years imprisonment. The penalty was formerly five years imprisonment.

Fixing of fines

65.—(1) The following section shall be substituted for section 18 of the Criminal Justice Act 1991 (fixing of certain fines by reference to units)—

"Fixing of fines

18.—(1) Before fixing the amount of any fine, a court shall inquire into the financial circumstances of the offender.

(2) The amount of any fine fixed by a court shall be such as, in the opinion of the court, reflects the seriousness of the offence.

(3) In fixing the amount of any fine, a court shall take into account the circumstances of the case including, among other things, the financial circumstances of the offender so far as they are known, or appear, to the court.

(4) Where—

(a) an offender has been convicted in his absence in pursuance of section 11 or 12 of the Magistrates' Courts Act 1980 (non-appearance of accused),

(b) an offender—

    (i) has failed to comply with an order under section 20(1) below; or

    (ii) has otherwise failed to co-operate with the court in its inquiry into his financial circumstances, or

(c) the parent or guardian of an offender who is a child or young person—

    (i) has failed to comply with an order under section 20(1B) below; or

    (ii) has otherwise failed to co-operate with the court in its inquiry into his financial circumstances,

and the court considers that it has insufficient information to make a proper determination of the financial circumstances of the offender, it may make such determination as it thinks fit.

(5) Subsection (3) above applies whether taking into account the financial circumstances of the offender has the effect of increasing or reducing the amount of the fine.".

(2) Section 19 of the Act of 1991 (fixing of fines in cases to which the unit fines system did not apply) shall cease to have effect.

(3) The further amendments made by Schedule 3 shall have effect.

(4) The amendments made by this section and that Schedule shall apply in relation to offenders convicted (but not sentenced) before the date on which this section comes into force as they apply in relation to offenders convicted after that date.

GENERAL NOTE

The Government in their White Paper "*Crime, Justice and Protecting the Public*" (Cmnd. 965) expressed their belief that "there are substantial benefits to be gained from maximising the effectiveness of fines" (para. 5.1). However, financial penalties have the drawback that (a) they are not regarded as suitable for very serious offences; (b) the offender must have financial resources to pay a fine; and (c) the level of the fine can seem derisory where the offender is wealthy (see para. 5.1). Nevertheless, substantial fines have been imposed upon offenders convicted of serious fraud, *e.g.* in the "*Guinness*" fraud case. Indeed there is often no limit on the fine which may be imposed where the offender is convicted in the Crown Court. In determining the amount of the fine, the court assesses a figure which is commensurate with the seriousness of the offence and then adjusts that figure in accordance with the means of the offender. Prior to the 1991 Act, the practice was to reduce the amount of the fine where the offender's means are inadequate but not to increase the amount of the fine where the offender is well off (*R.* v. *Messana* (1981) 3 Cr.App.R.(S.) 186).

Sections 18, 19, 21 and 22 of the 1991 Act (as originally drafted) endeavoured to change that practice as far as certain magistrates' court cases were concerned, so that the gravity of the offence was marked by reference to the "number of units" assessed as being commensurate with the offence and which was then used as a multiplier to the value of the defendant's disposable weekly income. The maximum number of units corresponded to the appropriate scale of financial penalties which the offence in question attracted by statute. It was up to the court to ensure that it had sufficient information, as to the defendant's means, and the defendant could be asked to provide a statement of means. When defendants declined to do so or where they failed to fully co-operate with the court in providing that information, the court (under what was s.18(8)(b) of the 1991 Act) could make such determinations as it saw fit.

The reason for the abolition of the unit fine system was explained (on behalf of the Government) by the Minister of State for the Home Office on the basis that there was:

"widespread dissatisfaction with its operation among sentencers and the general public. We are concerned about the anomalous results that have been produced in several cases . . . with the benefit of experience of the scheme's operation, we believe it to have been over-mechanistic and over-complicated. It interfered unnecessarily with the magistrates' discretion to impose appropriate fines in individual cases" (Standing Committee B, col. 240, June 17, 1993).

The principle of unit fines was not new to this country or other jurisdictions; they have been applied in varying forms in Finland since 1921, in Sweden since 1931, in Denmark since 1939 and in five other European countries including France and West Germany (see *Hansard*, H.C. Vol. 227, col. 908).

To what extent the unit fine system operated unfairly or unsatisfactorily is difficult to gauge. There have, of course, been well publicised cases but even at May 1993, a Minister of State was heard to say that "statistical information about fines imposed since October 1, 1992 is still being collected. It will be published in due course in the usual way". (*Hansard*, H.C. Vol. 225, col. 343).

What is clear is that the abolition of the unit fine system followed considerable consultation with the public, the judiciary and interested bodies.

Consideration had been given by Parliament, to the introduction of a banding scheme, involving the creation of five or more bands of income so that fines would be assessed with reference to the relevant income band. This scheme failed to win support in Parliament on the grounds that the scheme would create more scope for misunderstanding, and disproportionate results would inevitably occur (given that the division between two bands was bound to be separated by a slim margin of income). An alternative scheme (which also faltered) was that the courts would be required to decide a weekly amount that an offender could afford to pay and then multiply that sum by the number of weeks that was determined to be commensurate with the seriousness of the offence (see *Hansard*, H.C. Vol. 227, col. 915). One difficulty with that scheme is that it could be perceived as punishing offenders excessively in relation to the actual seriousness of the offence (*e.g.* a £2,000 fine for dropping litter notwithstanding that the offender's income was high).

How the new provisions are intended to operate in practice

The way the Government intend s.18 of the 1991 Act (as amended) to now operate was explained by the Minister of State for the Home Office, thus:

"First, we are placing on the courts a new duty to inquire into the financial circumstances of the offender. . . . The new provisions leave it to the courts to determine how, and in what depth, that inquiry should be made in each case. It is not intended that there should be a prescribed statutory form for inquiring into financial circumstances. The more sensible approach is to allow courts to develop locally those arrangements which they find most useful . . . we do not want to fetter the discretion of the courts. . . . Secondly, [s.18] . . . places certain duties on a court in considering how much an offender should be fined. Under [s.18(2)] the fine must reflect the court's opinion of the seriousness of the offence . . . under [s.18(3)] a court must take into account the circumstances of the case, including the offender's financial circumstances . . ." (Standing Committee B, col. 244, June 17, 1993).

When considering the offender's financial circumstances, regard must be had to the provisions of Sched. 3, para. 2 to the 1993 Act. Section 20 of that Act is now replaced by new provisions set out in para. 2, which provide for the obtaining of statements as to an offender's financial circumstances. Parliament considered whether the Legal Aid form would not be sufficient but this idea was rejected partly on the basis that a change in the law would be required to remove the need for the offender to give his consent to the form being used for this purpose and that such a change could act as a disincentive to defendants applying for legal aid.

Note that the terminology has also changed from "a statement of means" to a "statement of financial circumstances"; see Sched. 3, para. 2 to the 1993 Act. The reason for that change has probably nothing to do with avoiding the criticism of "means testing" but is intended to make it plain that the "circumstances of the case", which are to be considered when assessing the amount of the fine, include the "financial circumstances" of the offender. Thus, the Minister of State added that:

"in fixing a fine that reflects the seriousness of the offence, the court should take the offender's financial circumstances into account and *raise or lower the fine accordingly*" [emphasis added] (Standing Committee B, col. 244, June 17, 1993).

However, the Minister warned that the process of raising or lowering the level of the fine "cannot be carried out *ad absurdum*". The fine should therefore bear a "reasonable relationship to the offence committed" (Standing Committee B, col. 244, June 17, 1993).

Note that amendments have also been made to the way in which fines may be "remitted" (*i.e.* a downward variation). Fines may be remitted under s.21 of the 1991 Act, in cases where an offender (i) has been convicted in his absence; or (ii) he has failed to furnish a statement as to his financial circumstances under s.20(1) (as amended by Sched. 3, para. 2 to the 1993 Act); or (iii) has otherwise failed to co-operate with the court in its enquiry into his financial circumstances. In those cases, a court is entitled to make a determination as to his financial position as "it thinks fit". The court may simply try to make a realistic determination from the limited information available to it, or (and there seems to be nothing wrong in principle with this approach), it may assume that an offender is well able to pay any fine the court may impose unless and until the offender establishes the contrary. If he later complains that he cannot pay the fine or that he now wishes to co-operate with the court, then s.21(2) (as amended by Sched. 3, para. 3) provides that the court may remit the whole, or any part, of the fine providing that the court completed a further determination of the offender's financial circumstances and the results would (originally) have persuaded the court to impose a smaller fine on the offender, or not to have fined him at all.

These provisions similarly apply in the case of the parent or guardian who has responsibility for a child or young person (see Sched. 3, para. 5 to the 1993 Act; and see s.18(4)(c) of the 1991 Act as amended by s.65 of the 1993 Act).

Powers of courts to deal with offenders

66.—(1) In section 1 of the Criminal Justice Act 1991 (restrictions on imposing custodial sentences), the following shall be substituted for subsection (2)(a)—

"(a) that the offence, or the combination of the offence and one or more offences associated with it, was so serious that only such a sentence can be justified for the offence; or".

(2) In section 2 of the Act of 1991 (length of custodial sentences), in subsections (2)(a) and (3), for the word "other" there shall be substituted "one or more".

(3) In section 3 of the Act of 1991 (procedural requirements for custodial sentences), in subsection (3)(a), the words "or (as the case may be) of the offence and the offence or offences associated with it," shall be inserted after the word "offence".

(4) In section 6 of the Act of 1991 (restrictions on imposing community sentences)—

(a) in subsection (1), for the words "other offence" there shall be substituted "or more offences"; and

(b) in subsection (2)(b), for the word "other" there shall be substituted "one or more".

(5) In section 7 of the Act of 1991 (procedural requirements for community sentences), in subsection (1), the words "or (as the case may be) of the offence and the offence or offences associated with it," shall be inserted after the word "offence".

(6) For section 29 of the Act of 1991 (effect of previous convictions) there shall be substituted—

"Effect of previous convictions and of offending while on bail

29.—(1) In considering the seriousness of any offence, the court may take into account any previous convictions of the offender or any failure of his to respond to previous sentences.

(2) In considering the seriousness of any offence committed while the offender was on bail, the court shall treat the fact that it was committed in those circumstances as an aggravating factor.

(3) A probation order or conditional discharge order made before 1st October 1992 (which, by virtue of section 2 or 7 of the Powers of Criminal Courts Act 1973, would otherwise not be a sentence for the purposes of this section) is to be treated as a sentence for those purposes.

(4) A conviction in respect of which a probation order or conditional discharge order was made before that date (which, by virtue of section 13 of that Act, would otherwise not be a conviction for those purposes) is to be treated as a conviction for those purposes.".

(7) In subsection (1) of section 12D of the Children and Young Persons Act 1969 (duty of court to state in certain cases that requirement is in place of custodial sentence), in paragraph (ii)(a) for the words "other offence" there shall be substituted "or more offences".

(8) In section 38 of the Magistrates' Courts Act 1980 (committal for sentence on summary trial of offence triable either way), in subsection (2)(a), for the word "other" there shall be substituted "one or more".

(9) The amendments made by this section shall apply in relation to offenders convicted (but not sentenced) before the date on which this section comes into force as they apply in relation to offenders convicted after that date.

GENERAL NOTE

The Minister of State for the Home Office explained that the purpose of this section was to answer the criticisms that Pt. I of the 1991 Act "unnecessarily fettered the hand of the courts and imposed a strait-jacket on their ability to sentence justly individual cases . . . and places discretion back in the hands of the court" (Standing Committee B, col. 281, June 17, 1993). There can be no question other than that changes made to Pt. I of the 1991 Act represent a major shift in sentencing policy. The Government's White Paper, *Crime, Justice and Protecting the Public* (Cmnd. 965), coupled with the speeches in both Houses of Parliament, and the very wording of Pt. I, make it plain that the philosophy of Pt. I was to give legislative force to the principle that the court had to focus on the inherent seriousness of the offence for the purposes of sentencing. The reason given by the Government, in 1991, for the inclusion of the words "and one other offence associated with it" was explained by Earl Ferrers when he said:

"there are bound to be borderline cases. That is what the reference to 'one other offence' is meant to address . . . the two offences concerned would have to be relatively serious individually before, taken together, they would justify a custodial sentence . . . The provision therefore allows a second offence to tip the balance between a custodial sentence and a community penalty in a borderline case" (*Hansard*, H.L. Vol. 528, col. 1504).

The justification for concentrating on one offence, was tied in with the "just desserts" principle which, when translated into statutory language, meant that the sentence had to be "commensurate with the seriousness of the offence". This remains the general idea. However, a hint of a rather different reason (justifying the restrictive provisions appearing in Pt. I) was given when the 1993 Act was examined as a Bill in committee, namely that:

"there will be bad judges and magistrates who get things wrong, and it is madness to try to frame statute law to deal with those cases . . . When it is believed that a judge or a magistrate has paid too much attention to previous convictions in imposing a sentence, it is a matter for the Court of Appeal. Judges receive better training than ever before . . . and better training and education is the way to tackle the problem. We should not attempt a mechanistic framework in statutory law to guard against the odd case" (Standing Committee B, cols. 281–282, June 17, 1993).

With respect, this explanation for the former restrictive provisions of Pt. I, does not bear critical examination. However, there can be no doubt that one of the aims of Pt. I of the 1991 Act was to achieve consistency in sentencing, but sound progress was being made in this difficult area before the 1991 Act was passed. The so-called "guide-line cases" give one example of that development (*e.g. R. v. Bibi* [1980] 1 W.L.R. 1193; *R. v. Aramah* (1982) 4 Cr.App.R.(S.) 407; *R. v. Barrick* (1985) 81 Cr.App.R. 78.

The effect of the amendments made to the 1991 Act is that the pre-existing sentencing practice has been reinstated in part *but* the court must still look at the seriousness of the offence (and see D.A. Thomas, Custodial Sentences, Archbold News, September 14, 1993). Thus, the courts have been given increased discretion to deal with offenders, by amending s.1(2)(a) of the 1991 Act, so that the sentencer may have regard to *all* offences committed by the defendant for the purposes of determining (a) whether a prison sentence is justified (s.66(1)); and (b) the length of any sentence to be imposed (see s.66(2) amending s.2 of the 1991 Act). The court may, therefore, take into account information about the circumstances of all offences "associated" with the offence to be sentenced (see s.66(3), amending s.3(3)(a) of the 1991 Act). Similar provision is made in connection with restrictions on the imposition of "community sentences" (see s.66(4) and (5), amending ss.6 and 7 of the 1991 Act).

Section 66(6) radically amends s.29 of the 1991 Act. Neither s.29(1) nor (2) has survived; their place has been taken by four new subsections. Under s.29(1) the court may now take into account "any" previous convictions of the offender or "any failure of his to respond to previous sentences".

Even as originally drafted, s.29 did not prevent a court from treating as an aggravating factor the commission of an offence whilst on bail. This was because bail is not a sentence (see *R. v. Bexley, ibid.*). However, the commission of an offence by the defendant, in breach of a suspended sentence of imprisonment or a probation order, could not be taken into account because a probation order (by virtue of the 1991 Act) and a suspended term of imprisonment, were "sentences" for the purposes of the 1991 Act and were therefore subject to the embargo imposed by s.29. This anomaly has now disappeared by virtue of s.29(1). Parliament has gone further. It imposes a mandatory obligation on the sentencer, to treat the fact that the offence was committed whilst on bail, as an aggravating factor (s.29(2)).

Section 29(1) now permits the court to take into account any failure by the offender to respond to "previous sentences". Not every order a court can make is a "sentence" or a "conviction" for the purposes of the 1991 Act (even as amended). Before the 1991 Act came into force (October 1, 1992), neither a probation order, nor a conditional discharge, was to be regarded as a "conviction" (and therefore neither could be regarded as resulting in a "sentence") (see ss.2 and 7 of the Powers of the Criminal Courts Act 1974). Both ss.2 and 7 of the PCCA 1974 were repealed by the 1991 Act but that still means that pre-1991 Act probation orders and conditional discharges were not convictions or sentences. Accordingly, an offence committed during the operational period of an "old" probation order or a conditional discharge, could not, without further provision, be taken into account under s.29 (as amended), because the offence could not be seen as a failure to respond to a "previous sentence" (see the wording of s.29(1) of the 1991 Act as amended).

To get round this problem, s.29(3) treats pre-1991 Act probation orders or conditional discharges as "sentences". Similarly, such orders may be treated as if they were "convictions".

Schedule 3, para. 6, lists a large number of statutes which are all amended to include a provision which reads "... a fine imposed under [the relevant provision of the Act in question] shall be deemed, for the purposes of any enactment, to be a sum adjudged to be paid by a conviction". One effect of this provision is to treat the punished act as a conviction (and no doubt, therefore, to treat the fine as a "sentence") for the purposes of the 1991 Act (as it is now amended).

Penalty for causing death by dangerous driving or by careless driving

67.—(1) In Part I of Schedule 2 to the Road Traffic Offenders Act 1988 (prosecution and punishment of offences), in the entries relating to section 1 of the Road Traffic Act 1988 (causing death by dangerous driving) and section 3A of that Act (causing death by careless driving while under influence of drink or drugs), in column 4, for "5 years" there shall be substituted "10 years".

(2) In section 53(2) of the Children and Young Persons Act 1933 (punishment of certain serious crimes), the following shall be inserted after the word "law" in paragraph (a)—

"(aa) a young person is convicted of—
    (i) an offence under section 1 of the Road Traffic Act 1988 (causing death by dangerous driving); or
    (ii) an offence under section 3A of that Act (causing death by careless driving while under influence of drink or drugs);".

GENERAL NOTE
See the General Note to Pt. VI of the 1993 Act.

Appeals in Scotland against lenient disposals, etc.

68.—(1) In section 228(1) of the Criminal Procedure (Scotland) Act 1975 (right of appeal of person convicted on indictment)—
  (a) after paragraph (b) (and before the word "or") insert—
    "(bb) against his absolute discharge or admonition;
    (bc) against any probation order or any community service order under the Community Service by Offenders (Scotland) Act 1978;
    (bd) against any order deferring sentence;"; and
  (b) in paragraph (c), after "sentence" add "or disposal or order".

(2) In section 228A of that Act (appeal by Lord Advocate against sentence in solemn proceedings etc.)—
  (a) after "conviction" insert "or against any probation order or any community service order under the Community Service by Offenders

(Scotland) Act 1978 or against the person's absolute discharge or admonition or against any order deferring sentence"; and
(b) for paragraph (a) substitute—
    "(a) if it appears to the Lord Advocate that, as the case may be—
        (i) the sentence is unduly lenient;
        (ii) the making of the probation order or community service order is unduly lenient or its terms are unduly lenient;
        (iii) to dismiss with an admonition or to discharge absolutely is unduly lenient; or
        (iv) the deferment of sentence is inappropriate or on unduly lenient conditions,".

(3) In section 442(1) of that Act (rights of appeal in summary proceedings)—
  (a) in paragraph (a)—
    (i) after "person convicted" insert ", or found to have committed an offence,";
    (ii) in sub-paragraph (i), after "conviction" insert "or finding";
    (iii) after sub-paragraph (ii) (and before the word "or") insert—
      "(iia) against his absolute discharge or admonition or any probation order or any community service order under the Community Service by Offenders (Scotland) Act 1978 or any order deferring sentence,"; and
    (iv) in sub-paragraph (iii), after "sentence" add "or disposal or order"; and
  (b) in paragraph (c)—
    (i) after "conviction" insert "or, whether the person has been convicted or not, against any probation order or any community service order under the Community Service by Offenders (Scotland) Act 1978 or against the person's absolute discharge or admonition or against any order deferring sentence";
    (ii) for "the sentence is unduly lenient'; substitute—
  ", as the case may be—
      (i) the sentence is unduly lenient;
      (ii) the making of the probation order or community service order is unduly lenient or its terms are unduly lenient;
      (iii) to dismiss with an admonition or to discharge absolutely is unduly lenient; or
      (iv) the deferment of sentence is inappropriate or on unduly lenient conditions;".

Supervised release of certain young offenders in Scotland

69. In section 212A of the Criminal Procedure (Scotland) Act 1975 (which makes provision for the supervised release of short-term prisoners in Scotland) at the end add—
    "(7) The foregoing provisions of this section apply to a person sentenced under section 207 or 415 of this Act as the provisions apply to a person sentenced to a period of imprisonment.".

Penalties under implementation regulations

70.—(1) Paragraphs 8(3), 9(2) and 10(3) of Schedule 8 to the Banking Co-ordination (Second Council Directive) Regulations 1992 shall cease to have effect.
(2) Regulations under section 2(2) of the European Communities Act 1972 for the purpose of implementing—
  (a) Article 15 of the Second Banking Co-ordination Directive (which requires the United Kingdom to make provision for the exercise in

the United Kingdom by supervisory authorities of other member States of information and inspection powers in relation to institutions authorised by them), or

(b) Articles 3, 6 and 7 of the Supervision of Credit Institutions Directive (which make similar provision in relation to the consolidated supervision of credit institutions),

may, notwithstanding paragraph 1(1)(d) of Schedule 2 to that Act, create offences punishable in the same way as offences under sections 39, 40 and 41 of the Banking Act 1987.

(3) In this section—

"the Second Banking Co-ordination Directive" means the Community Council Directive No. 89/646/EEC on the co-ordination of laws, regulations and administrative provisions relating to the taking up and pursuit of the business of credit institutions and amending Directive 77/780/EEC; and

"the Supervision of Credit Institutions Directive" means the Community Council Directive No. 92/30/EEC on the supervision of credit institutions on a consolidated basis.

(4) Subsection (1) shall not affect the punishment for an offence committed before that subsection comes into force.

GENERAL NOTE

This section implements two major European Council Directives concerning the operation, regulation and administration of "credit institutions". The Second Banking Co-ordination Directive (the "SBCD") (89/646/EEC) will permit credit institutions such as banks to offer services and to establish branches throughout the European Community on the basis of one licence ("authorisation") and to be supervised on a consolidated basis by the regulator of at least one Member State (see the European Council Directive (92/30/EEC) which is also known as the "second consolidated supervision directive" (the "Supervision Directive")). Both of these Directives will be implemented by secondary legislation under the European Communities Act 1972. Both of the Directives (plus those dealing with "own funding" and "solvency ratios") are important in preventing difficulties which have manifested themselves in the collapse of BCCI.

Under Art. 15 of the SBCD, the U.K. is required to make provision to enable "supervisory authorities" abroad to have access to information, and to have powers of inspection, in respect of branches of credit institutions which are operating in the U.K. under a licence granted abroad. These powers are obviously important to effective supervision of credit institutions and thus similar powers are required by the "Supervision Directive" (see Art. 3, para. 4, Art. 6 and Art. 7, para. 1).

One difficulty which previously existed under U.K. law, was in respect of enforcement of these obligations. Under s.2(2) of the European Communities Act 1972, offences may be created by Regulation, but such Regulations carry only a maximum sentence of three months' imprisonment. Accordingly, if offences are created by Regulation to enforce the obligations, referred to above, the maximum term permissible would be three months and this would be inconsistent with comparable offences as they exist under ss.39, 40 and 41 of the Banking Act 1987 and which carry a maximum sentence of six months' imprisonment. Thus, what s.70 of the 1993 Act does is to make it lawful for the Regulations to provide a maximum term of six months' imprisonment.

Both Directives play a crucial part in liberalising movement of services (including financial services) within the internal market while permitting competition from countries outside the European Community. Previously, one of the greatest barriers which prevented U.K. credit institutions to operate branches abroad, was the maximum capital requirement and the maintenance (by each branch) of endowment capital (*i.e.* having their own funds) so that each branch was, in effect, a separate bank. This involved a waste of resources as large amounts of capital would be tied up to fund branches. The SBCD seeks to abolish the minimum endowment capital requirement in so far as it related to each branch. However, the proper and adequate funding of credit institutions is obviously important and, to this end, two other Directives are relevant, namely, the Council Directive (86/635/EEC) and the Council Directive on Solvency Ratios for credit institutions (89/647/EEC).

Offences in connection with taxation etc. in the EC

   71.—(1) A person who, in the United Kingdom, assists in or induces any

conduct outside the United Kingdom which involves the commission of a
serious offence against the law of another member State is guilty of an
offence under this section if—
  (a) the offence involved is one consisting in or including the contraven-
      tion of provisions of the law of that member State which relate to any
      of the matters specified in subsection (2);
  (b) the offence involved is one consisting in or including the contraven-
      tion of other provisions of that law so far as they have effect in relation
      to any of those matters; or
  (c) the conduct is such as to be calculated to have an effect in that
      member State in relation to any of those matters.
(2) The matters mentioned in subsection (1) are—
  (a) the determination, discharge or enforcement of any liability for a
      Community duty or tax;
  (b) the operation of arrangements under which reliefs or exemptions
      from any such duty or tax are provided or sums in respect of any such
      duty or tax are repaid or refunded;
  (c) the making of payments in pursuance of Community arrangements
      made in connection with the regulation of the market for agricultural
      products and the enforcement of the conditions of any such
      payments;
  (d) the movement into or out of any member State of anything in relation
      to the movement of which any Community instrument imposes, or
      requires the imposition of, any prohibition or restriction; and
  (e) such other matters in relation to which provision is made by any
      Community instrument as the Secretary of State may by order
      specify.
(3) For the purposes of this section—
  (a) an offence against the law of a member State is a serious offence if
      provision is in force in that member State authorising the sentencing,
      in some or all cases, of a person convicted of that offence to imprison-
      ment for a maximum term of 12 months or more; and
  (b) the question whether any conduct involves the commission of such an
      offence shall be determined according to the law in force in the
      member State in question at the time of the assistance or inducement.
(4) In any proceedings against any person for an offence under this section
it shall be a defence for that person to show—
  (a) that the conduct in question would not have involved the commission
      of an offence against the law of the member State in question but for
      circumstances of which he had no knowledge; and
  (b) that he did not suspect or anticipate the existence of those circum-
      stances and did not have reasonable grounds for doing so.
(5) For the purposes of any proceedings for an offence under this section,
a certificate purporting to be issued by or on behalf of the government of
another member State which contains a statement, in relation to such times
as may be specified in the certificate—
  (a) that a specified offence existed against the law of that member State,
  (b) that an offence against the law of that member State was a serious
      offence within the meaning of this section,
  (c) that such an offence consists in or includes the contravention of
      particular provisions of the law of that member State,
  (d) that specified provisions of the law of that member State relate to, or
      are capable of having an effect in relation to, particular matters,
  (e) that specified conduct involved the commission of a particular offence
      against the law of that member State, or
  (f) that a particular effect in that member State in relation to any matter
      would result from specified conduct,

shall, in the case of a statement falling within paragraphs (a) to (d), be conclusive of the matters stated and, in the other cases, be evidence, and in Scotland sufficient evidence, of the matters stated.

(6) A person guilty of an offence under this section shall be liable—

(a) on summary conviction, to a penalty of the statutory maximum or to imprisonment for a term not exceeding six months or to both; or

(b) on conviction on indictment, to a penalty of any amount or to imprisonment for a term not exceeding seven years or to both.

(7) Sections 145 to 152 and 154 of the Customs and Excise Management Act 1979 (general provisions as to legal proceedings) shall apply as if this section were contained in that Act; and that an offence under this section shall be treated for all purposes as an offence for which a person is liable to be arrested under the customs and excise Acts.

(8) The power of the Secretary of State to make an order under subsection (2)(e) shall be exercisable by statutory instrument; and no such order shall be made unless a draft of the order has been laid before, and approved by a resolution of, each House of Parliament.

(9) In this section—

"another member State" means a member State other than the United Kingdom;

"Community duty or tax" means any of the following, that is to say—

(a) any Community customs duty;

(b) an agricultural levy of the Economic Community;

(c) value added tax under the law of another member State;

(d) any duty or tax on tobacco products, alcoholic liquors or hydrocarbon oils which, in another member State, corresponds to any excise duty;

(e) any duty, tax or other charge not falling within paragraphs (a) to (d) of this definition which is imposed by or in pursuance of any Community instrument on the movement of goods into or out of any member State;

"conduct" includes acts, omissions and statements;

"contravention" includes a failure to comply; and

"the customs and excise Acts" has the same meaning as in the Customs and Excise Management Act 1979.

(10) References in this section, in relation to a Community instrument, to the movement of anything into or out of a member State include references to the movement of anything between member States and to the doing of anything which falls to be treated for the purposes of that instrument as involving the entry into, or departure from, the territory of the Community of any goods (within the meaning of that Act of 1979).

GENERAL NOTE

This section is designed to enable the U.K. to take action against fraud which is perpetrated against the European Community. The section bears a superficial resemblance to the type of offence to be found in s.20 of the Misuse of Drugs Act 1971 which creates a substantive offence, triable in this country, if a person assists in (or induces) the commission of an offence which contravenes a "corresponding law" abroad. Accordingly, s.71 of the 1993 Act makes it an offence to assist in or induce any conduct outside the U.K. which involves the commission of a "serious offence" against the law of another Member State (subs. (1)). A "serious offence" is one which (by the laws of the foreign state) carries a maximum sentence of at least 12 months' imprisonment (s.71(3)). The serious offence which is relevant here must relate to conduct specified in s.71(2) (*i.e.* taxation, payment of duties, agricultural spending, and, significantly, prohibitions and restrictions provided for by or under a Community instrument or Regulation). "Conduct" includes acts, omissions and statements (s.71(9)).

In certain cases the prosecution will also be required to prove that the conduct complained of was "calculated to have an effect in that Member State in relation to any of [the matters specified in s.71(2)]". This ingredient (if relevant) seems to require proof of, at least, foresight as to consequences, although it may be that the precise *mens rea* required to be proved, will vary depending on the category of conduct (as described in s.71(2)) in question.

Statutory defences are provided by s.71(4) and, once again, the burden of proving any of these defences falls upon the accused.

Backing of warrants: safeguards

72.—(1) The Backing of Warrants (Republic of Ireland) Act 1965 shall be amended as follows.

(2) In section 2 (proceedings before magistrates' courts), the following subsection shall be added at the end—

"(5) The Secretary of State may by order provide that an order may not be made under subsection (1) of this section if it is shown to the satisfaction of the court that no provision is made in the law of the Republic, in respect of a person delivered up to the Republic by the United Kingdom, corresponding to the provision made by or under sections 6A and 6B of this Act in respect of a person delivered up to the United Kingdom by the Republic.".

(3) The following sections shall be inserted after section 6—

"Persons delivered up by the Republic: the rule of speciality

6A.—(1) The Secretary of State may by order provide that, except in such cases as may be specified in the order, no person delivered up to the United Kingdom under corresponding arrangements in force in the Republic ("the defendant") may be dealt with for, or in respect of, any offence committed before his surrender, other than the offence for which he was delivered up.

(2) In subsection (1) of this section, "corresponding" means corresponding to provisions contained in this Act.

(3) Any order under this section may, in particular, specify the following cases for the purposes of subsection (1) of this section—

(a) where consent is given by a Minister of the Republic;

(b) where the defendant, having had an opportunity to leave the United Kingdom, has not done so within 45 days of his final discharge in respect of the offence for which he was delivered up;

(c) where the defendant has, after being returned to the United Kingdom, left the United Kingdom and subsequently returned to it;

(d) where the description of the offence charged in the United Kingdom is altered in the course of proceedings but the offence under its new description is shown by its constituent elements to be an offence for which the defendant could have been delivered up under the corresponding legislation.

Extradition to third country

6B.—(1) The Secretary of State may by order provide that, except in such cases as may be specified in the order, no person delivered up to the United Kingdom under corresponding arrangements in force in the Republic ("the defendant") may be delivered up to a territory other than the Republic to be dealt with for, or in respect of, any offence committed before his surrender to the United Kingdom.

(2) In subsection (1) of this section "corresponding" means corresponding to provisions contained in this Act.

(3) Any order under this section may, in particular, specify the following cases for the purposes of subsection (1) of this section—

(a) where consent is given by a Minister of the Republic;

(b) where the defendant, having had an opportunity to leave the United Kingdom, has not done so within 45 days of his final discharge in respect of the offence for which he was delivered up;

(c) where the defendant has, after being returned to the United Kingdom, left the United Kingdom and subsequently returned to it.

Provisions supplementing sections 2(5), 6A and 6B

6C.—(1) The power to make an order under section 2(5), 6A or 6B of this Act shall be exercisable by statutory instrument.

(2) Any such order shall be subject to annulment in pursuance of a resolution of either House of Parliament.

(3) Any such order may—

(a) make different provision for different cases; and

(b) make such incidental or supplemental provision as the Secretary of State considers appropriate.

(4) Any incidental or supplemental provision may, in particular, include—

(a) in the case of an order under section 2(5) of this Act, provision as to the circumstances in which, and the presumptions which may be applied in considering whether, provision made by the law to the Republic is to be treated as corresponding to provision made by or under section 6A or 6B of this Act;

(b) in the case of an order under section 6A or 6B of this Act—

(i) provision as to the notification of any consent;

(ii) provision as to the drawing up of any document to support a request for consent.

(5) Where any consent is notified in accordance with the provisions of an order under section 6A or 6B of this Act—

(a) judicial notice shall be taken of that consent; and

(b) a certificate of the Secretary of State to the effect that that consent was given in accordance with those provisions shall be evidence without further proof (or in Scotland sufficient evidence).".

Power of Secretary of State to make grants in relation to combating drug misuse

73.—(1) The Secretary of State may, with the consent of the Treasury, pay such grants, to such persons, as he considers appropriate in connection with measures intended—

(a) to combat or deal with drug trafficking or the misuse of drugs; or

(b) to deal with consequences of the misuse of drugs.

(2) Any such grant may be made subject to such conditions as the Secretary of State may, with the agreement of the Treasury, see fit to impose.

(3) Payments under this section shall be made out of money provided by Parliament.

Persons not eligible for early release

74.—(1) Part II of Schedule 1 to the Criminal Justice Act 1982 (persons convicted of offences under certain enactments not eligible for early release) shall be amended as follows.

(2) In the entry relating to the Drug Trafficking Offences Act 1986, the following paragraph shall be inserted before paragraph 26—

"25A. Section 23A (acquisition, possession or use of proceeds of drug trafficking).".

(3) In the entry relating to the Criminal Justice Act 1988, the following paragraphs shall be inserted before paragraph 30—

"29A. Section 93A (assisting another to retain the benefit of criminal conduct).

29B. Section 93B (acquisition, possession or use of the proceeds of criminal conduct).

29C. Section 93C (concealing or transferring proceeds of criminal conduct).".

Compassionate release of certain children and other persons in Scotland

75.—(1) In section 7(5) of the Prisoners and Criminal Proceedings (Scotland) Act 1993 (which applies provisions of that Act to certain children), for "Sections", where it first occurs, substitute "Without prejudice to section 6(1)(b)(ii) of this Act, sections 3,".

(2) In paragraph 2(2) of Schedule 6 to that Act (which makes transitional provision as respects release on licence on compassionate grounds) after "Act" insert ", and sections 12 and 17 of this Act in so far as relating to a licence granted, or person released, by virtue of this sub-paragraph,".

Life prisoners transferred to Scotland

76.—(1) The Prisoners and Criminal Proceedings (Scotland) Act 1993 shall be amended as follows.

(2) In section 10 (life prisoners transferred to Scotland)—

(a) in subsection (1), the words "(whether before or after the commencement of this section)" shall cease to have effect;

(b) in subsection (2), after "life prisoner" insert ", except such case as is mentioned in paragraph 7 of Schedule 6 to this Act,"; and

(c) in subsection (4)—

(i) in paragraph (a), after "has" insert "(whether before or after the commencement of this section)"; and

(ii) in paragraph (b), after "Scotland" insert "(whether before or after that commencement)".

(3) In Schedule 6 (transitional provisions and savings)—

(a) in paragraph 1, in the definition of "existing life prisoner", after "person" insert "(other than a transferred life prisoner)";

(b) in paragraph 2(1), for "paragraph 7 below" substitute "to section 10(4) of this Act"; and

(c) for paragraph 7 substitute—

"7. In the case of a transferred life prisoner who is a discretionary life prisoner for the purposes of Part II of the Criminal Justice Act 1991 by virtue of section 48 of or paragraph 9 of Schedule 12 to that Act, subsection (3) of section 10 of this Act applies and the certificate mentioned in paragraph (b) of that subsection is the certificate under the said section 48 or paragraph 9.".

Power to extend certain offences to Crown servants and to exempt regulators etc.

77. Schedule 4, which confers power to the Secretary of State to make regulations extending certain provisions to Crown servants and to make regulations exempting persons from certain offences, shall have effect.

PART VII

SUPPLEMENTARY

Commencement etc.

78.—(1) Sections 70 and 71 shall come into force at the end of the period of two months beginning with the day on which this Act is passed.

(2) Sections 68, 69, 75, 76 and 79(1) to (12), paragraph 2 of Schedule 5 and, in so far as relating to the Criminal Procedure (Scotland) Act 1975 and the Prisoners and Criminal Proceedings (Scotland) Act 1993, Schedule 6, shall come into force on the passing of this Act.

(3) The other provisions of this Act shall come into force on such day as may be appointed by the Secretary of State by an order made by statutory instrument.

(4) Different days may be appointed under subsection (3) for different provisions and different purposes.

(5) Nothing in any provision in Part I applies to any act, omission or other event occurring before the coming into force of that provision.

(6) Where a person is charged with a relevant offence which was committed before the coming into force of a provision of Part II, Part III, or (as the case may be) Part IV, that provision shall not affect the question whether or not that person is guilty of the offence or the powers of the court in the event of his being convicted of that offence.

(7) Section 4A(3) and (4) of the Drug Trafficking Offences Act 1986 (inserted by section 14) shall not apply to any proceedings—
   (a) for an offence committed before the commencement of section 14; or
   (b) for one or more offences, any one of which was so committed.

(8) Section 52B(3) and (4) of the Northern Ireland (Emergency Provisions) Act 1991 (inserted by section 42) shall not apply to any proceedings—
   (a) for an offence committed before the commencement of section 42; or
   (b) for one or more offences, any one of which was so committed.

(9) In subsection (6) "relevant offence" means an offence in relation to which provision is made by Part II, Part III or Part IV, other than an offence created by that Part.

(10) An order under subsection (3) may contain such transitional provisions and savings as the Secretary of State considers appropriate.

(11) For the purposes of section 27 of the Prevention of Terrorism (Temporary Provisions) Act 1989 (temporary provisions), any amendment made in that Act by a provision of Part IV of, or paragraph 15 of Schedule 5 to, this Act shall be treated, as from the time when that provision comes into force, as having been continued in force by the order under subsection (6) of that section which has effect at that time.

(12) For the purpose of section 69 of the Northern Ireland (Emergency Provisions) Act 1991 (temporary provisions), any amendment made in that Act by a provision of Part IV of, or paragraphs 17(1), (2), (5), (6) and (7) of Schedule 5 to, this Act (other than sections 43 and 45) shall be treated, as from the time when that provision comes into force, as having been continued in force by the order under section 69(3) of the Act of 1991 which has effect at that time.

Short title, extent etc.

79.—(1) This Act may be cited as the Criminal Justice Act 1993.

(2) The following provisions of this Act extend to the United Kingdom—
   Part V;
   sections 21(1) and (3)(h), 23, 24, 45 to 51, 70 to 72, 77, 78 and this section;
   Schedules 1 and 2; and
   paragraphs 4, 5 and 6 of Schedule 4.

(3) The following provisions of this Act extend only to Great Britain—
   sections 13(9) to (11), 21(3)(e), 24(2), (3) and (7) to (10), 29 to 32, 34(1), 35, 67(1) and 73; and
   paragraph 3 of Schedule 4.

(4) The following provisions of this Act extend only to Scotland—
   sections 17, 19, 20(2), 21(3)(c) and (d), 22(2), 24(12) to (15), 26(2), 33, 68, 69, 75 and 76; and
   paragraph 2 of Schedule 4.

(5) Sections 21(3)(f) and 34(2) extend to Scotland and Northern Ireland only.

(6) Sections 36 to 44 extend only to Northern Ireland.

(7) Section 72 also extends to the Channel Islands and the Isle of Man.

(8) The provisions of Schedules 5 and 6 have the same extent as the provisions on which they operate.

(9) Otherwise, this Act extends to England and Wales only.

(10) Her Majesty may by Order in Council direct that such provisions of this Act as may be specified in the Order shall extend, with such exceptions and modifications as appear to Her Majesty to be appropriate, to any colony.

(11) Subject to any Order made after the passing of this Act by virtue of subsection (1)(a) of section 3 of the Northern Ireland Constitution Act 1973, the regulations of insider dealing shall not be a transferred matter for the purposes of that Act but shall for the purposes of subsection (2) of that section be treated as specified in Schedule 3 to that Act.

(12) An Order in Council under paragraph 1(1)(b) of Schedule 1 to the Northern Ireland Act 1974 (legislation for Northern Ireland in the interim period) which contains a statement that it is made only for purposes corresponding to purposes of any of sections 16, 18 and 29 to 32—

(a) shall not be subject to paragraph 1(4) and (5) of that Schedule (affirmative resolution of both Houses of Parliament); but

(b) shall be subject to annulment in pursuance of a resolution of either House of Parliament.

(13) Schedule 5 (consequential amendments) shall have effect.

(14) The repeals and revocations set out in Schedule 6 (which include the repeal of two enactments which are spent) shall have effect.

SCHEDULES

Section 53(4)   SCHEDULE 1

SPECIAL DEFENCES

Market makers

1.—(1) An individual is not guilty of insider dealing by virtue of dealing in securities or encouraging another person to deal if he shows that he acted in good faith in the course of—

(a) his business as a market maker, or

(b) his employment in the business of a market maker.

(2) A market maker is a person who—

(a) holds himself out at all normal times in compliance with the rules of a regulated market or an approved organisation as willing to acquire or dispose of securities; and

(b) is recognised as doing so under those rules.

(3) In this paragraph "approved organisation" means an international securities self-regulating organisation approved under paragraph 25B of Schedule 1 to the Financial Services Act 1986.

Market information

2.—(1) An individual is not guilty of insider dealing by virtue of dealing in securities or encouraging another person to deal if he shows that—

(a) the information which he had as an insider was market information; and

(b) it was reasonable for an individual in his position to have acted as he did despite having that information as an insider at the time.

(2) In determining whether it is reasonable for an individual to do any act despite having market information at the time, there shall, in particular, be taken into account—

(a) the content of the information;

(b) the circumstances in which he first had the information and in what capacity; and

(c) the capacity in which he now acts.

3. An individual is not guilty of insider dealing by virtue of dealing in securities or encouraging another person to deal if he shows—

(a) that he acted—

(i) in connection with an acquisition or disposal which was under consideration or the subject of negotiation, or in the course of a series of such acquisitions or disposals; and

(ii) with a view to facilitating the accomplishment of the acquisition or disposal or the series of acquisitions or disposals; and

(b) that the information which he had as an insider was market information arising directly out of his involvement in the acquisition or disposal or series of acquisitions or disposals.

4. For the purposes of paragraphs 2 and 3 market information is information consisting of one or more of the following facts—

(a) that securities of a particular kind have been or are to be acquired or disposed of, or that their acquisition or disposal is under consideration or the subject of negotiation;

(b) that securities of a particular kind have not been or are not to be acquired or disposed of;

(c) the number of securities acquired or disposed of or to be acquired or disposed of or whose acquisition or disposal is under consideration or the subject of negotiation;

(d) the price (or range of prices) at which securities have been or are to be acquired or disposed of or the price (or range of prices) at which securities whose acquisition or disposal is under consideration or the subject of negotiation may be acquired or disposed of;

(e) the identity of the persons involved or likely to be involved in any capacity in an acquisition or disposal.

Price stabilisation

5.—(1) An individual is not guilty of insider dealing by virtue of dealing in securities or encouraging another person to deal if he shows that he acted in conformity with the price stabilisation rules.

(2) In this paragraph "the price stabilisation rules" means rules which—

(a) are made under section 48 of the Financial Services Act 1986 (conduct of business rules); and

(b) make provision of a description mentioned in paragraph (i) of subsection (2) of that section (price stabilisation rules).

Section 54   SCHEDULE 2

SECURITIES

Shares

1. Shares and stock in the share capital of a company ("shares").

Debt securities

2. Any instrument creating or acknowledging indebtedness which is issued by a company or public sector body, including, in particular, debentures, debenture stock, loan stock, bonds and certificates of deposit ("debt securities").

Warrants

3. Any right (whether conferred by warrant or otherwise) to subscribe for shares or debt securities ("warrants").

Depositary receipts

4.—(1) The rights under any depositary receipt.

(2) For the purposes of sub-paragraph (1) a "depositary receipt" means a certificate or other record (whether or not in the form of a document)—

(a) which is issued by or on behalf of a person who holds any relevant securities of a particular issuer; and

(b) which acknowledges that another person is entitled to rights in relation to the relevant securities or relevant securities of the same kind.

(3) In sub-paragraph (2) "relevant securities" means shares, debt securities and warrants.

Options

5. Any option to acquire or dispose of any security falling within any other paragraph of this Schedule.

Futures

6.—(1) Rights under a contract for the acquisition or disposal of relevant securities under which delivery is to be made at a future date and at a price agreed when the contract is made.

(2) In sub-paragraph (1)—

(a) the references to a future date and to a price agreed when the contract is made include references to a date and a price determined in accordance with terms of the contract; and

(b) "relevant securities" means any security falling within any other paragraph of this Schedule.

Contracts for differences

7.—(1) Rights under a contract which does not provide for the delivery of securities but whose purpose or pretended purpose is to secure a profit or avoid a loss by reference to fluctuations in—

(a) a share index or other similar factor connected with relevant securities;

(b) the price of particular relevant securities; or

(c) the interest rate offered on money placed on deposit.

(2) In sub-paragraph (1) "relevant securities" means any security falling within any other paragraph of this Schedule.

Section 65(3)   SCHEDULE 3

Financial penalties

Increases in certain maximum fines

1.—(1) In section 17 of the Criminal Justice Act 1991 (increases in certain maximum fines), subsection (3)(e) shall cease to have effect.

(2) In Schedule 4 to that Act (increase of certain maxima) Part V shall cease to have effect.

Statements as to offenders' financial circumstances

2.—(1) In section 20 of the Act of 1991 (statements as to offenders' means) the following shall be substituted for subsection (1)—

"(1) Where a person has been convicted of an offence, the court may, before sentencing him, make a financial circumstances order with respect to him.

(1A) Where a magistrates' court has been notified in accordance with section 12(2) of the Magistrates' Courts Act 1980 that a person desires to plead guilty without appearing before the court, the court may make a financial circumstances order with respect to him.

(1B) Before exercising its powers under section 55 of the Children and Young Persons Act 1933 against the parent or guardian of any person who has been convicted of an offence, the court may make a financial circumstances order with respect to the parent or (as the case may be) guardian.

(1C) In this section "a financial circumstances order" means, in relation to any person, an order requiring him to give to the court, within such periods as may be specified in the order, such a statement of his financial circumstances as the court may require.".

(2) In subsection (2) and (3) of section 20 of the Act of 1991, for the words "an order under subsection (1) above" there shall be substituted "a financial circumstances order".

(3) Section 20(5) of the Act of 1991 shall cease to have effect.

Remission of fines

3. The following section shall be substituted for section 21 of the Act of 1991 (remission of fines)—

"**Remission of fines**

21.—(1) This section applies where a court has, in fixing the amount of a fine, determined the offender's financial circumstances under section 18(4) above.

(2) If, on subsequently inquiring into the offender's financial circumstances, the court is satisfied that had it had the results of that inquiry when sentencing the offender it would—

(a) have fixed a smaller amount; or

(b) not have fined him,

it may remit the whole or any part of the fine.

(3) Where under this section the court remits the whole or part of a fine after a term of imprisonment has been fixed under section 82(5) of the Magistrates' Courts Act 1980 (issue of warrant of commitment for default) or section 31 of the Powers of Criminal Courts Act 1973 (powers of Crown Court in relation to fines), it shall reduce the term by the corresponding proportion.

(4) In calculating any reduction required by subsection (3) above, any fraction of a day shall be ignored.".

Default in paying unit fines

4. Section 22 of the Act of 1991 (default in paying fines fixed under section 18 of that Act) shall cease to have effect.

Responsibility of parents and guardians

5. In section 57 of the Act of 1991 (responsibility of parent or guardian for financial penalties), the following shall be substituted for subsections (3) and (4)—
"(3) For the purposes of any order under that section made against the parent or guardian of a child or young person—
(a) sections 18 and 21 above; and
(b) section 35(4)(a) of the 1973 Act (fixing amount of compensation order),
shall have effect (so far as applicable) as if any reference to the financial circumstances of the offender, or (as the case may be) to the means of the person against whom the compensation order is made, were a reference to the financial circumstances of the parent or guardian.
(4) For the purposes of any such order made against a local authority (as defined for the purposes of the Children Act 1989)—
(a) section 18(1) above, and section 35(4)(a) of the 1973 Act, shall not apply, and
(b) section 18(3) above shall apply as if the words from "including" to the end were omitted.".

Other amendments

6.—(1) In section 15 of the Children and Young Persons Act 1969 (variation and discharge of supervision orders), the following subsection shall be substituted for subsection (7)—
"(7) A fine imposed under subsection (3) or (4) above shall be deemed, for the purposes of any enactment, to be a sum adjudged to be paid by a conviction.".
(2) In section 27 of the Powers of Criminal Courts Act 1973 (breach of requirement of suspended sentence supervision order), the following subsection shall be substituted for subsection (4)—
"(4) A fine imposed under subsection (3) above shall be deemed, for the purposes of any enactment, to be a sum adjudged to be paid by a conviction.".
(3) In section 97 of the Magistrates' Courts Act 1980 (maximum fine for refusal to give evidence), the following subsection shall be substituted for subsection (5)—
"(5) A fine imposed under subsection (4) above shall be deemed, for the purposes of any enactment, to be a sum adjudged to be paid by a conviction.".
(4) In section 12 of the Contempt of Court Act 1981 (maximum fine for contempt in face of magistrates' court), the following subsection shall be substituted for subsection (2A)—
"(2A) A fine imposed under subsection (2) above shall be deemed, for the purposes of any enactment, to be a sum adjudged to be paid by a conviction.".
(5) In section 14 of that Act (maximum fine for contempt in an inferior court), the following subsection shall be substituted for the subsection (2A) inserted by the Criminal Justice Act 1991—
"(2A) A fine imposed under subsection (2) above shall be deemed, for the purposes of any enactment, to be a sum adjudged to be paid by a conviction.".
(6) In section 58 of the Criminal Justice Act 1991 (binding over of parent or guardian), the following subsection shall be substituted for subsection (4)—
"(4) A fine imposed under subsection (2)(b) above shall be deemed, for the purposes of any enactment, to be a sum adjudged to be paid by a conviction.".
(7) In paragraph 6 of Schedule 2 to the Criminal Justice Act 1991 (miscellaneous supplemental provisions), the following sub-paragraph shall be substituted for sub-paragraph (2)—
"(2) A fine imposed under paragraph 3(1)(a) or 4(1)(a) above shall be deemed, for the purposes of any enactment, to be a sum adjudged to be paid by a conviction.".

Section 77   SCHEDULE 4

EXTENSIONS AND EXEMPTIONS

The Drug Trafficking Offences Act 1986 (c. 32)

1. The following section shall be inserted in the Drug Trafficking Offences Act 1986, after section 36A—

"**Extension of certain offences to Crown servants and exemptions for regulators etc.**

36B.—(1) The Secretary of State may by regulations provide that, in such circumstances as may be prescribed, sections 23A, 24, 26B, 26C and 31 of this Act shall apply to such persons in the public service of the Crown, or such categories of person in that service, as may be prescribed.

(2) Section 26B of this Act shall not apply to—

(a) any person designated by regulation made by the Secretary of State for the purpose of this paragraph; or

(b) in such circumstances as may be prescribed, any person who falls within such category of person as may be prescribed for the purpose of this paragraph.

(3) The Secretary of State may designate, for the purpose of paragraph (a) of subsection (2) above, any person appearing to him to be performing regulatory, supervisory, investigative or registration functions.

(4) The categories of person prescribed by the Secretary of State, for the purpose of paragraph (b) of subsection (2) above, shall be such categories of person connected with the performance by any designated person of regulatory, supervisory, investigative or registration functions as he considers it appropriate to prescribe.

(5) In this section—

"the Crown" includes the Crown in right of Her Majesty's Government in Northern Ireland; and

"prescribed" means prescribed by regulations made by the Secretary of State.

(6) The power to make regulations under this section shall be exercisable by statutory instrument.

(7) Any such instrument shall be subject to annulment in pursuance of a resolution of either House of Parliament.".

The Criminal Justice (Scotland) Act 1987 (c.41)

2. The same section as is inserted in the Act of 1986 by paragraph 1 shall be inserted in the Criminal Justice (Scotland) Act 1987, after section 46, as section 46A, but with the substitution—

(a) in subsection (1), of "sections 42 to 43B of this Act" for "sections 23A, 24, 26B, 26C and 31 of this Act"; and

(b) in subsection (2), of "43A" for "26B".

The Criminal Justice Act 1988 (c.33)

3. The same section as is inserted in the Act of 1986 by paragraph 1 shall be inserted in the Criminal Justice Act 1988, after section 93F, as section 93G, but with—

(a) the substitution in subsection (1), of "sections 93A, 93B, 93C(2) and 93D above" for "sections 23A, 24, 26B, 26C and 31 of this Act"; and

(b) the omission of subsections (2) to (4).

The Prevention of Terrorism (Temporary Provisions) Act 1989 (c.4)

4. The same section as is inserted in the Act of 1986 by paragraph 1 shall be inserted in the Prevention of Terrorism (Temporary Provisions) Act 1989, immediately after section 19, as section 19A, but with the substitution—

(a) in subsection (1), of "sections 9 to 11, 17 and 18A above" for "sections 23A, 24, 26B, 26C and 31 of this Act"; and

(b) in subsection (2), of "18A" for "26B".

The Criminal Justice (International Co-operation) Act 1990 (c.5)

5. The same section as is inserted in the Act of 1986 by paragraph 1 shall be inserted in the Criminal Justice (International Co-operation) Act 1990, after section 23, as section 23A, but with—

(a) the substitution in subsection (1), of "section 14(2) above" for "sections 23A, 24, 26B, 26C and 31 of this Act"; and

(b) the omission of subsections (2) to (4).

The Northern Ireland (Emergency Provisions) Act 1991 (c.24)

6. The same section as is inserted in the Act of 1986 by paragraph 1 shall be inserted in the Northern Ireland (Emergency Provisions) Act 1991, after section 55, as section 55A, but with the substitution—

(a) in subsection (1), of "sections 53, 54(2) to (6) and 54A above" for "sections 23A, 24, 26B, 26C and 31 of this Act"; and

(b) in subsection (2), of "54A" for "26B".

SCHEDULE 5

CONSEQUENTIAL AMENDMENTS

PART I

ENACTMENTS

The Criminal Appeal Act 1968 (c. 19)

1. In section 50 of the Criminal Appeal Act 1968 (meaning of "sentence"), the following shall be substituted for subsection (1)—

"(1) In this Act "sentence", in relation to an offence, includes any order made by a court when dealing with an offender including, in particular—

(a) a hospital order under Part III of the Mental Health Act 1983, with or without a restriction order;

(b) an interim hospital order under that Part;

(c) a recommendation for deportation;

(d) a confiscation order under the Drug Trafficking Offences Act 1986 other than one made by the High Court;

(e) a confiscation order under Part VI of the Criminal Justice Act 1988;

(f) an order varying a confiscation order of a kind which is included by virtue of paragraph (d) or (e) above;

(g) an order made by the Crown Court varying a confiscation order which was made by the High Court by virtue of section 4A of the Act of 1986; and

(h) a declaration of relevance under the Football Spectators Act 1989.".

The Criminal Procedure (Scotland) Act 1975 (c.21)

2.—(1) The Criminal Procedure (Scotland) Act 1975 shall be amended as follows.

(2) In each of sections 181 and 382 (admonition in, respectively, solemn and summary proceedings), for "found guilty" substitute "convicted".

(3) In section 191 (effects of probation and absolute discharge; solemn proceedings), for paragraph (a) of subsection (3) substitute—

"(a) any right to appeal;".

(4) In section 233 (note of appeal)—

(a) in subsection (1)—

(i) in paragraph (a), for "against sentence alone" substitute "under section 228(1)(b), (bb), (bc) or (bd) of this Act" and after "sentence", where it occurs for the second time, insert "(or as the case may be, of the making of the order disposing of the case or deferring sentence)"; and

(ii) in paragraph (b), after "sentence" insert "(or as the case may be, of the making of the order disposing of the case or deferring sentence)"; and

(b) in subsection (4), for "against sentence alone" substitute "under section 228(1)(b), (bb), (bc) or (bd)".

(5) In section 238(1) (admission to bail), for paragraph (b) substitute—

"(b) any relevant appeal by the Lord Advocate under section 228A of this Act.".

(6) In section 244(2) (abandonment of appeal), after "sentence"—

(a) where it first occurs, insert "(or as the case may be against both conviction and disposal or order)"; and

(b) where it occurs for the second time, insert "(or disposal or order)".

(7) In section 254 (disposal of appeals in solemn proceedings)—

(a) in subsection (2)—

(i) after "appellant" insert "(or as the case may be any disposal or order made)";

(ii) in each of paragraphs (a) and (b), after "sentence" insert "(or disposal or order)";

(iii) after "sentence", where it occurs for the fourth time, insert "or make another (but not more severe) disposal or order"; and

(iv) after "sentence", where it occurs for the fifth time, insert ", disposal or order";

(b) in subsection (4), after "appellant" insert "(or disposal or order made)"; and

(c) after subsection (4) insert—

"(4A) In subsection (3) above, "appeal against sentence" shall, without prejudice to the generality of the expression, be construed as including an appeal under section 228(1)(bb), (bc) or (bd), and any appeal under section 228A, of this Act; and other references to sentence in that subsection shall be construed accordingly.".

(8) In section 268 (reckoning of time spent in custody pending appeal), in each of subsections (1) and (2), for "appeal by the Lord Advocate against the sentence passed on conviction" substitute "relevant appeal by the Lord Advocate under section 228A of this Act".

(9) In section 392 (effects of probation and absolute discharge: summary proceedings) for paragraph (a) of subsection (3) substitute—

"(a) any right to appeal;"

(10) In section 442B (method of appeal against sentence alone in summary proceedings)—

(a) after "person" insert ", or as the case may be a person found to have committed an offence,";

(b) the words "against sentence alone" shall cease to have effect; and

(c) after "442(1)(a)(ii)" insert "or (iia)".

(11) In section 443A (suspension of disqualification, forfeiture, etc.), in each of subsections (1) and (2), at the end add "(or disposal or order)".

(12) In section 444(1)(b) (contents of application for stated case), after "sentence" insert "or disposal or order".

(13) In section 452A (disposal of stated case)—

(a) in subsection (2), after "sentence", where it first occurs, insert "("sentence" being construed in this subsection and in subsection (3) below as including disposal or order)"; and

(b) after subsection (4) insert—

"(4A) Any reference in subsection (4) above to convicting and sentencing shall be construed as including a reference to convicting and making some other disposal or convicting and deferring sentence."

(14) In section 453B (appeals against sentence only in summary proceedings)—

(a) in each of subsections (1), (2), (7) and (8), after "442(1)(a)(ii)" insert "or (iia)";

(b) in subsection (2)—

(i) in paragraph (a), after "sentence" insert "(or as the case may be of the making of the order disposing of the case or deferring sentence)"; and

(ii) in paragraph (b), at the end add "(or making)";

(c) in subsection (3)(b), at the end add "(or as the case may be who disposed of the case or deferred sentence)"; and

(d) in subsection (4), after "sentence" add "(or within two weeks of the disposal or order)".

(15) In section 453C (disposal in summary proceedings of appeal by note of appeal)—

(a) in subsection (3), after "442(1)(a)(ii)" insert "or (iia)"; and

(b) at the end add—

"(4) In subsection (1) above, "appeal against sentence" shall, without prejudice to the generality of the expression, be construed as including an appeal under section 442(1)(a)(iia), and any appeal under section 442(1)(c), of this Act; and without prejudice to subsection (5) below, other references to sentence in that subsection and in subsection (3) above shall be construed accordingly.

(5) In disposing of any appeal in the case where the accused has not been convicted, the High Court may proceed to convict him; and where it does, the reference in subsection (3) above to the conviction in respect of which the sentence appealed against was imposed shall be construed as a reference to the disposal or order appealed against.".

The Criminal Appeal (Northern Ireland) Act 1980 (c.47)

3. The provisions of section 30 of the Criminal Appeal (Northern Ireland) Act 1980 (interpretation of Part I) shall become subsection (1) of that section and the following subsection shall be added—

"(2) In this Part of this Act "sentence" also includes—

(a) a confiscation order made by the Crown Court under the Northern Ireland (Emergency Provisions) Act 1991;

(b) an order varying such an order; and

(c) an order made by the Crown Court varying a confiscation order made by the High Court by virtue of section 52B of the Act of 1991.".

The Companies Act 1985 (c.6)

4.—(1) In section 744 of the Companies Act 1985 (interpretation), for the definition of "the Insider Dealing Act", there shall be substituted—

" "the insider dealing legislation" means Part V of the Criminal Justice Act 1993 (insider dealing)."

(2) In the 1985 Act for "Insider Dealing Act", wherever it occurs, there shall be substituted "insider dealing legislation".

The Drug Trafficking Offences Act 1986 (c.32)

5. In section 3(3) of the Drug Trafficking Offences Act 1986 (statements relating to drug trafficking) for "(2)" there shall be substituted "(1D)".

6. In section 38(1) of the 1986 Act (interpretation), the following definitions shall be inserted at the appropriate places—

" "confiscation order" means an order under section 1 of this Act and includes, in particular, an order under that section which is made by virtue of section 4A, 5A or 5B;"

" "defendant" means a person against whom proceedings have been instituted for a drug trafficking offence (whether or not he has been convicted);".

The Financial Services Act 1986 (c.60)

7. The Financial Services Act 1986 shall be amended as follows.

8. In section 128C(3)(b) (enforcement in support of overseas regulatory authority) for "the Company Securities (Insider Dealing) Act 1985" there shall be substituted "Part V of the Criminal Justice Act 1993 (insider dealing)".

9.—(1) In section 177 (investigations into insider dealing), in subsection (1)—
(a) for the words "there may have been a contravention of section 1, 2, 4 or 5 of the Company Securities (Insider Dealing) Act 1985" there shall be substituted "an offence under Part V of the Criminal Justice Act 1993 (insider dealing) may have been committed"; and
(b) for the words "contravention has occurred" there shall be substituted "offence has been committed".

(2) In subsection (3) of that section—
(a) for the word "contravention" there shall be substituted "offence"; and
(b) in paragraph (a) for the words from "relating to" to the end there shall be substituted "which appear to them to be relevant to the investigation".

(3) In subsection (4) of that section for the word "contravention" there shall be substituted "offence".

10.—(1) In section 178 (penalties for failure to co-operate with s.177 investigations), in subsection (1) for the words "contravention has occurred" there shall be substituted "offence has been committed".

(2) In subsection (6) of that section for the words "contravention or suspected contravention" there shall be substituted "offence or suspected offence".

11. In subsection (1) of section 189 (restriction of Rehabilitation of Offenders Act 1974), in paragraph (b) "(including insider dealing)" shall be omitted and at the end there shall be inserted "or insider dealing".

12.—(1) In section 199 (powers of entry), in subsection (1) for paragraph (b) there shall be substituted—

"(b) under Part V of the Criminal Justice Act 1993 (insider dealing).".

(2) After subsection (8) of that section there shall be inserted—

"(8A) In the application of this section to Northern Ireland for the references to information on oath substitute references to complain on oath.".

The Banking Act 1987 (c.22)

13. In section 84(6)(b) of the Banking Act 1987 (disclosure for facilitating discharge of functions by other supervisory authorities) for "the Company Securities (Insider Dealing) Act 1985" there shall be substituted "Part V of the Criminal Justice Act 1993 (insider dealing)".

The Criminal Justice Act 1988 (c.33)

14.—(1) Section 98 of the Criminal Justice Act 1988 (disclosure of information subject to contractual restriction on disclosure) shall cease to have effect.

(2) In section 172 of the 1988 Act (extent)—
(a) in subsection (2), after "84 to 88" there shall be inserted "sections 93A to 93D; sections 93F and 93G"; and
(b) in subsection (4), after "sections 90 to 93" there shall be inserted "section 93E".

The Prevention of Terrorism (Temporary Provisions) Act 1989 (c.4)

15. In section 19(1) of the Prevention of Terrorism (Temporary Provisions) Act 1989 (institution of proceedings) for the words "or 18" in both places where they occur there shall be substituted ", 18 or 18A".

The Companies Act 1989 (c.40)

16. In section 82(2)(b) of the Companies Act 1989 (request for assistance by overseas

regulatory authority) for "the Company Securities (Insider Dealing) Act 1985" there shall be substituted "Part V of the Criminal Justice Act 1993 (insider dealing)".

The Northern Ireland (Emergency Provisions) Act 1991 (c.24)

17.—(1) In section 49(1)(a) of the Northern Ireland (Emergency Provisions) Act 1991 (relevant offences)—
(a) after "(c)" there shall be inserted ", (dd)"; and
(b) after "(k)" there shall be inserted ", (kk);".
(2) In section 56(1) of the 1991 Act (interpretation of confiscation provisions), at the end of the definition of "confiscation order", there shall be added "and includes, in particular, an order under that section which is made by virtue of section 48A or 52B above".
(3) In section 69(2)(c) of the 1991 Act, for "paragraph 20" there shall be substituted "paragraphs 20 to 20C".
(4) In section 71(2) of the 1991 Act (extent), for "54" there shall be substituted "to 54A, 55A".
(5) In Part I of Schedule 1 (scheduled offences) to the 1991 Act—
(a) after paragraph 20(d) there shall be inserted—
  "(dd) section 18A (failure to disclose knowledge or suspicion of financial assistance for terrorism);" and
(b) after paragraph 22(k) there shall be inserted—
  "(kk) section 54A;".
(6) In paragraph 2(5) of Schedule 4 to the 1991 Act (application of procedure for enforcing fines), after "made by", where those words first occur, there shall be inserted "the High Court, by virtue of section 52B of this Act, or by".
(7) The following sub-paragraph shall be added at the end of paragraph 2 of Schedule 4 to the 1991 Act—
  "(7) Where the High Court makes a confiscation order by virtue of section 52B of this Act in relation to a defendant who has died, subparagraph (1) above shall be read as referring only to sections 35(1)(a), (b) and (d) and 35(4)(a) and (b) of the Act of 1945.".

PART II

ORDERS IN COUNCIL UNDER THE NORTHERN IRELAND ACT 1974

The Companies (Northern Ireland) Order 1986 (S.I. 1986/1032 (N.I. 6))

18.—(1) In Article 2(3) of the Companies (Northern Ireland) Order 1986 (interpretation), for the definition of "the Insider Dealing Order" there shall be substituted—
  " "the insider dealing legislation" means Part V of the Criminal Justice Act 1993 (insider dealing)";
(2) In the 1986 Order, for "Insider Dealing Order", wherever it occurs, there shall be substituted "insider dealing legislation".
19.—(1) In Article 442 of that Order (provision for security for information obtained), in paragraph (1), in sub-paragraph (c) for "Article 16A of the Insider Dealing Order or section 94" there shall be substituted "section 94 or 177".
(2) In paragraph (3) of that Article, in sub-paragraph (b) for "Article 16A of the Insider Dealing Order or section 94" there shall be substituted "section 94 or 177".
20. In paragraph (3) of Article 444A of that Order (disclosure of information by Department or inspector) in sub-paragraph (a) for "Article 16A of the Insider Dealing Order or section 94" there shall be substituted "section 94 or 177".

The Companies (Northern Ireland) Order 1989 (S.I. 1989/2404 (N.I. 18))

21. In Article 3(1) of the Companies (Northern Ireland) Order 1989 (interpretation), in the definition of "the companies legislation", for "the Insider Dealing Order" there shall be substituted "Part V of the Criminal Justice Act 1993 (insider dealing)".

The Insolvency (Northern Ireland) Order 1989 (S.I. 1989/2405 (N.I. 19))

22. In Article 104A(1)(c) of the Insolvency (Northern Ireland) Order 1989 (petition for winding-up on grounds of public interest) after "94" there shall be inserted "or 177".

SCHEDULE 6

REPEALS AND REVOCATIONS

PART I

REPEALS

Chapter	Short title	Extent of repeal
1975 c. 21.	The Criminal Procedure (Scotland) Act 1975.	In section 442B, the words "against sentence alone".
1980 c. 43.	The Magistrates' Courts Act 1980.	In section 12(1)(a) the words "and section 18 of the Criminal Justice Act 1991 (unit fines)".
1985 c. 8.	The Company Securities (Insider Dealing) Act 1985.	The whole Act.
1986 c. 32.	The Drug Trafficking Offences Act 1986.	In section 1, in subsection (5)(b)(iii), the words from "section 39" to "bankruptcy orders)" and subsection (8). In section 5(3), the words "sections 3 and 4 of". In section 26A(3), the words from "or by" to the end. In section 27(5), the words "or, as the case may be, the sheriff". In section 38(2), the entries relating to a confiscation order and a defendant.
1986 c. 60.	The Financial Services Act 1986.	Sections 173 to 176. In section 189(1)(b), the words "(including insider dealing)". In Schedule 16, paragraphs 28 and 43.
1987 c. 22.	The Banking Act 1987.	In section 84(1), in the Table, in the entry beginning "An inspector appointed under Part XV of the Companies (Northern Ireland) Order" in the left-hand column the words "or under Article 16A of the Company Securities (Insider Dealing) (Northern Ireland) Order 1986" and in the right-hand column the words "or that Article".
1987 c. 38.	The Criminal Justice Act 1987.	In section 3(6)(i), the words "or any corresponding enactment having effect in Northern Ireland".
1988 c. 33.	The Criminal Justice Act 1988.	Section 48. Section 98.
1989 c. 4.	The Prevention of Terrorism (Temporary Provisions) Act 1989.	In section 9(1), the word "or" immediately before paragraph (b).
1989 c. 40.	The Companies Act 1989.	Section 209.
1990 c. 5.	The Criminal Justice (International Cooperation) Act 1990.	Section 14(3) and (5).
1991 c. 24.	The Northern Ireland (Emergency Provisions) Act 1991.	In section 48(3), the words "during the period of postponement". In section 50(2), the word "or" immediately before paragraph (c). Section 51(3). Section 67(6).
1991 c. 53.	The Criminal Justice Act 1991.	Section 17(3)(e). Section 19. Section 20(5). Section 22.

Chapter	Short title	Extent of repeal
1993 c. 9.	The Prisoners and Criminal Proceedings (Scotland) Act 1993.	Section 28(3). In section 30(1), the words "or the Lord Chancellor". In Schedule 4, Part V. In Schedule 11, paragraph 24. In section 10(1), the words "(whether before or after the commencement of this section)".

PART II

REVOCATIONS

Number	Title	Extent of revocation
S.I. 1986/1034 (N.I. 8).	The Company Securities (Insider Dealing) (Northern Ireland) Order 1986.	The whole Order.
S.I. 1989/2404 (N.I. 18).	The Companies (Northern Ireland) Order 1989.	In Article 2(2), the definition of "the Insider Dealing Order". In Article 11(1), the words "or Article 16A of the Insider Dealing Order". Articles 27 to 34. Article 35(2) and (3).
S.I. 1989/2405 (N.I. 19).	The Insolvency (Northern Ireland) Order 1989.	Article 104A(1)(b).
S.I. 1990/1504 (N.I. 10).	The Companies (No. 2) (Northern Ireland) Order 1990.	In Article 2(2), the definition of "the Insider Dealing Order". Articles 21 to 23.
S.I. 1992/3218.	The Banking Coordination (Second Council Directive) Regulations 1992.	In Schedule 8, paragraphs 8(3), 9(2) and 10(3). In Schedule 10, paragraphs 17 and 25.

INDEX

36–144

NORTHERN IRELAND,
confiscation orders,
absconded defendant, return of, 43
acquittal of defendant, compensation in
case of, 43
dead or absconded defendant, powers in
relation to, 42
information, provision of, 39
powers, availability of, 41
realisable property, 44
revised assessments, 37
satisfaction of, 41
statements relevant to, 38
terrorist-related activities, proceeds of,
36
variation of, 40
drug trafficking orders, enforcement of, 22
enforcement of orders outside, 46
financing of terrorism, application of provisions on, Pt. IV, Intro
orders, enforcement of, 34, 45
regulations, enforcement of, 45

OFFENCES,
Crown servants, extension to, 77, Sched.4
drug trafficking. *See* DRUG TRAFFICKING
exemption from, regulations as to, 77,
Sched. 4
Group A,
attempt to commit, 3
conspiracy to commit, 3
jurisdiction, 2
list of, 1
omission, acts of, 2
relevant events, 2
Group B, list of, 1
insider dealing, 52
seriousness,
factors in, Pt. VI, Intro
sentences, procedural requirements for,
66
terrorism. *See* TERRORISM

PRICE,
meaning, 56
PRICE-AFFECTED SECURITIES,
meaning, 56
PROCEEDS OF CRIME. *See* CRIMINAL CONDUCT;
DRUG TRAFFICKING; MONEY LAUNDERING;
TERRORISM

REPUBLIC OF IRELAND,
warrants, backing of, 72

SCOTLAND,
compassionate release on licence, 75
drug trafficking offences. *See* DRUG
TRAFFICKING
lenient disposals, appeals against, 68
life prisoners transferred to, 76
money laundering provisions, application
of, 33
Northern Ireland orders, enforcement of,
34
young offenders, supervised release of, 69

SECURITIES,
insider dealing. *See* INSIDER DEALING
SENTENCES,
causing death by dangerous or careless
driving, for, 67
persons not eligible for early release, 74
powers of courts, 66
previous convictions, effect of, 66
Scotland,
lenient disposals, appeals against, 68
young offenders, supervised release of,
69

TAXATION,
European Community, offences in, 71
TERRORISM,
confiscation orders,
absconded defendant, return of, 43
acquittal of defendant, compensation in
case of, 43
dead or absconded defendant, powers in
relation to, 42
information, provision of, 39
powers, availability of, 41
realisable property, 44
revised assessments, 37
satisfaction of, 41
statements relevant to, 38
terrorist-related activities, proceeds of,
36
variation of, 40
financial assistance for,
amendment of provisions, 49
knowledge or suspicion, failure to disclose, 51
investigation of activities, 50
Northern Ireland, provisions applied to,
Pt. IV, Intro
proceeds of terrorist-related activities,
knowledge or suspicion, failure to disclose, 48
offences relating to, 47

UNIT FINES,
abolition, Pt. VI, Intro
default in paying, Sched. 3

WARRANTS,
backing, safeguards, 72
WORDS AND PHRASES,
another Member State, 71
assessed value, 37
Community duty or tax, 71
company, 60
date of conviction, 28
dealing in securities, 55
drug money laundering, 18
information made public, 58
inside information, 56
insider, 57
money laundering, 32
price, 56
price-affected securities, 56